# Away from It All

# Away from It All

## Sloan Wilson

G. P. PUTNAM'S SONS

NEW YORK

## Author's Note

This book is factual, except that when I say I don't like somebody or make him look like a fool, I change his name and other details in order to prevent hurt feelings and law suits. Fortunately or unfortunately, I can't fake the names of my family and have to trust their kindness.

# A Note from Robert H. Stephens
## Concerning the Account of Him in This Book

My son-in-law has just showed me this manuscript to a book he is calling *Away from It All,* and I see to my astonishment that he bandies my name about with the greatest abandon. One thing I've always said of my son-in-law is that he's a fine lad when it comes to handling a boat, and also, when it comes to making up a story out of whole cloth. At first I worried what my friends in Ireland would think when they read this tale of my behaving so freely in the United States, but then I remembered that my son-in-law is quite well known in Dublin, where they understand writers as a whole remarkably well. Everybody in Ireland knows that writers are fine fellows, but they are not to be trusted when the truth gets between them and the chance to spin a good yarn. If my son-in-law can actually make enough money to live on a yacht with my beautiful daughter by telling lies about me, I think I should be the last to object, but the thought that my sins, real or fanciful, could turn out so profitably for the family will be a terrible temptation to me the next time I visit the United States.

Anyway, I have signed a paper saying I will not sue him for this book, and in return he has promised me that if he gets a

bigger boat and comes back to Ireland, I can have a private
stateroom. My hope is eventually to write a book myself, telling
the plain truth about all of us, and then he's the lad who better
watch out.

# Away from It All

# 1

About two years ago I decided to buy a boat and run away to sea. In many ways it appeared to be a ridiculous decision. I was not a young man, footloose and fancy-free. On the contrary, I was forty-six years old, had two daughters in college, a son in his last year of preparatory school, and a two-year-old daughter who was not only the apple of my eye but a whole beribboned basket of fruit. I also had a young wife who was intrepid on Broadway but who had never been to sea in anything smaller than a Cunard liner and who professed a great fear of thunder and rain, never mind real storms. To compound the difficulties, I had failed to save much money and could not even dream of retiring aboard a yacht, however small.

There were five main reasons I decided to go anyway. The first concerned the ages of my children. The three older ones really did not need to have me around all the time anymore, and the littlest, Jessica, would not have to be in school for another three years. While she was still so young, we had a magical interval during which we did not have to be tied down anywhere.

The second reason was my wife. She knew I had always dreamed of living aboard a boat and said that regardless of her fears, we ought to try it, instead of just sitting around talking about it endlessly.

The third reason was that my profession allowed it. God knows there are many disadvantages to being a writer, such as a completely unpredictable income and the lack of a retirement plan, but one advantage is that in theory, at least, one can work anywhere and at almost any age.

The fourth reason was that I liked to consider myself as an old sailor and thought I had the necessary skills for taking care of my family safely and comfortably on the water. As a boy I had been brought up largely in Florida and had loved sailing in the way so many youngsters love baseball. When I was eighteen I was able, through a variety of odd circumstances, to run an 87-foot schooner in the charter business, and during World War II I had commanded three small Coast Guard ships in Greenland waters and the South Pacific. Since the end of the war I had been working too hard and had been too tied down by budgets and the schedules of children to do more than a little hasty boating on weekends. As a matter of fact, there hadn't even been much of that, because my first wife and my older children had conceived an early distaste for everything nautical. Still, the feeling persisted that I was somehow more competent at sea than I was on land, if I could only get a proper vessel under me.

The fifth and perhaps the most compelling reason was my growing dissatisfaction with the various ways I had tried to live, which is perhaps only another way of saying that I was growing almighty sick of myself and wanted to make some big changes. In the suburbs I had, one after the other, owned seven houses and had somehow contrived to be miserable in all of them. In New York City we had a handsome apartment overlooking Central Park, but despite a happy marriage, I was growing unbearably restless. When I wasn't working, I never knew quite what to do with myself, and there were long stretches when I, like many writers, couldn't think of any work to do. Much to my alarm, I was growing fat, which is a terrible thing to happen to a man who also has to carry more than the normal load of vanity. After all, to be vain is ridiculous and to be fat is absurd, but to be both is intolerable. One reason I was fat, I figured, was that I never got any exercise. Full of determination, I had bought a gym suit and tried jogging around the park. This I hated even more than being fat. Athletic clubs, horseback riding and bicycles—I had tried them all with equal revulsion. What I needed, I felt, was a more active life of a kind I really liked. On a boat I would have to hop around a lot, especially if I were to be captain of a good-sized yacht with only a baby and a woman as crew.

Although I didn't really admit it, I hoped that a boat would have other curative powers. One reason I was getting fat, I realized sometimes in the middle of the night, was that I was both eating and drinking too much. Like most of my friends, many of whom were successful lawyers, good doctors and prosperous businessmen, I had taken to sitting around an awful lot with a glass in my hand.

"What's wrong with a couple of martinis?" was a question often heard in my group. The best reply I ever heard was Lauren Bacall's: "Someday I am going to meet a man who is able to leave it at that."

The remark stayed with me. A short time later, when I suggested a famous actor I had always admired for a part in a film, my publisher said, "I'm afraid he's out of the question. The poor fellow hasn't sobered up in about three years."

Suddenly it seemed to me that almost everyone I knew, including myself, was drinking too much and was just kidding himself when he pretended he wasn't. And the trouble was, as those do-good television commercials put on by some committee kept saying, "Alcoholism is a progressive disease. . . ."

Of course I knew it was naïve to buy a boat to try to run away from myself. If one felt that he was drinking too much, the thing to do was to quit, no matter where he happened to be living, and if he couldn't, then it was time to go to A.A. or a psychiatrist, not some yacht broker. Anyone could tell you that, including many of my friends who had more or less successfully solved their liquor problems. The trouble was that lecture myself as I tried, I hated the idea of going to an A.A. meeting. After all, I wasn't that much of a drunk, and even if I was in danger of beginning to be, it was bad enough to be a drunk without having to seek out a bunch of reformed drunks for company. And as for psychiatrists, I had tried them several times for long periods when I was troubled, and I was getting tired of exploring myself. What do you do when all your inner conflicts turn out to be a bloody bore, and worse than that, the kind of bore which doesn't allow itself to be talked to death? Buy a boat, I decided. At least that would be, for me, a new approach.

Sometimes when I was brooding about all this, it seemed to me that I was just pussyfooting around, afraid to admit even to myself what I really thought. The fact was that with increasing speed not only I but the world seemed to be going mad, and I wanted to get the hell out of it as far as possible. Partly because I had a son approaching military age, the war in Viet Nam infuriated me. Because divorce is expensive and because, despite the fact that I had followed the advice of highly paid lawyers, my most prosperous years had left me with tax debts, I was constantly in financial trouble, no matter how much money I made, and every year the expense of educating my three older children and living with my new wife and daughter in New York soared higher. Somehow I had got involved with a group of friends who seemed even more backbiting, joyless and hysterically critical of each other than is usual for a literary set. My work was going badly because all I really had to pound into a typewriter was a kind of blind fury at everything or dreams of a better life which didn't seem realistic even to me. I was beginning to hate my profession, for how can a man write novels which make any sense when everything around him seems senseless? Perhaps it was a sign of my own neurosis, but almost everything I saw outside of my immediate family circle seemed without kindness, reason or morality, and any talk about working to help improve the world simply served to increase my own sense of complete helplessness and futility.

Why, when I had a movable office, was I keeping my wife and

daughter in such a combustible city as New York anyway? In my youth I had never thought of myself as either a commuter or a city man. Crowds make me hate people. I don't like pacing up and down an apartment or going to parties where everyone is trying to impress everyone else with his own importance or trying to sell something. I also don't like killing time by slumping in a chair in front of a television set with a can of beer or a highball in my hand. Underneath the fat, I felt my body was still strong and should be used for something which gave the illusion, at least, of being useful. For better or for worse, I had been born restless, and no view, even the spectacular one of downtown Manhattan which our apartment offered, was beautiful to me if I had to look at it too long. In my youth I had loved seeing strange islands climb out of the sea over the bow of my ship, sailing into a new port and dropping anchor in the reflected lights of a new city. Maybe if I could enjoy all that again, I could use some of the tension in my arms and back for hard work instead of trying to kill it with booze. That was a forlorn hope, perhaps, but one which would at least be fun to try. All my life I had had little respect for dogma and generalities, and when people told me it was always absurd to try to change myself by changing my surroundings, I found myself replying with unusual conviction, "Not necessarily! Not *always!*"

Whether the decision to run away to sea was wise or not, it had the immediate effect of making me feel happy and carefree.

"I hear that's the way some people feel when they decide to commit suicide," a morose friend said.

I laughed. It was late August in New York, and the trees in Central Park were already beginning to turn red.

"Before the snow hits, we should be in the Bahamas," I said to my wife, and I imagined the curve of a white sail against the jade sea.

"What will we do with the furniture?" she asked.

"Store it."

"That would be terribly expensive. How much is this boat going to cost? What will the upkeep be?"

"I don't know. I've sort of lost track of boat prices lately. We'll have to talk to a broker and look at some of the magazines."

Even worries about money didn't kill my euphoria. Dimly I realized that I was still treating the boat as a dream, not as a new reality with all kinds of difficult problems.

The friends I told about our new plans treated me indulgently. After all, New York is full of people who talk a lot about getting away from it all on a boat, and such chatter is rarely taken seriously. I got out a stack of old boating magazines I had collected over the years and started calling brokers to inquire about prices. The news I got came as a shock. In my head was a good deal of knowledge about what yachts used to sell for in the thirties, and for some reason I was astonished to discover that the cost of boats, like that of everything else, had gone up dramatically.

"Never mind," I said to Betty, my wife. "If we keep looking long enough, we'll find something."

My euphoria lasted only a few days. It ended with the familiar slap of mail being tossed at our front door. One long envelope was from our landlord.

"It's a new lease," Betty said in a small voice when she opened it. "We have to sign it now or give up the apartment within a month. And he's raised the rent fifty dollars."

"Of course we won't sign it," I said. "We're lucky the lease is up. At least we won't have to worry about subletting."

"Yes," she said and paused. "I guess we better get busy and find a boat."

The sudden imposition of a deadline sobered me beyond anything I had expected. The dreamboat I had carried in my mind for so long, a white island schooner about 80 feet long, suddenly seemed to telescope, to shrink before the hard winds of reality, ending up, perhaps, an ugly little plastic sloop which would drain all our money without offering even a comfortable place to sleep, never mind work. For the first time I began to wonder whether the whole scheme was just as crazy as some of my friends had warned.

"I'll call a broker and see what kind of a boat we can actually get," I said and telephoned a large firm on Madison Avenue which specialized in all kinds of yachts.

The young man I was referred to did not seem much impressed when I said I planned to live aboard a boat with my wife and two-year-old, but his interest obviously quickened when I said I had to find such a craft within a month because the lease on my apartment had expired.

"Let's meet for lunch," he said enthusiastically. "I'll bring some spec sheets along."

I arranged to meet him at one o'clock at the Harvard Club. Feeling as anxious as though I were applying for a new job, I showed up twenty minutes early. The boat was supposed to become a sobering influence in my life, but something about getting right down to buying it made me head straight for the bar. There I found several of the friends I had lunched with, off and on, for the past twenty years, ever since I first came to New York looking for a job.

"Found your boat yet?" an account executive asked with amusement. I had forgotten how much I had talked of my dream.

"I'm having lunch with a yacht broker in a few minutes. We've given up the lease on our apartment."

"So you're actually going to do it! Hey, fellows, this calls for a drink!"

A group gathered around me. They all wanted to know what kind of boat I expected to buy, where we wanted to go, and how long we expected to be away. Quite a few people I had never even met before inquired about the details of my plans. The look of tolerant amusement which had greeted me when I had just been dreaming was no longer evident, and many men said with obvious sincerity that they envied me, that some day they hoped to do the same.

There was only one question nobody asked me, and that was

the very question I had spent the most time brooding about myself: Why? *Why* was I fleeing New York to live aboard a boat with a woman and a small child? What makes a man run away to sea at the age of forty-six?

Apparently the men at the Harvard Club bar had been around New York long enough to feel that was a question which didn't even have to be asked. They knew that answer, and all they wanted to find out was: How?

# 2

⚓

The conviviality of my friends was such that I had to leave the bar quickly—certainly it would not be propitious to tank up on martinis before making decisions about buying a boat. In the vast reading room of the Harvard Club I sank into an overstuffed armchair and tried to focus my thoughts.

What was my top price for a boat? Certainly that would be one of the first questions the broker would ask. Twenty thousand dollars. What with taxes, college bills and all the rest of it, I would be lucky to raise that. To me it sounded like a lot of money for a boat, but after all, this was going to be our home, and that would not be considered excessive for a house. If I paid more than that I wouldn't have much left for operating expenses and would have to spend the first year tied up somewhere while I desperately tried to think of something to write.

What would the upkeep of a boat amount to nowadays, anyway? What did the marinas—a word which hadn't even existed when I had done most of my sailing—charge for an overnight visit? Had the prices for work at boatyards gone up as much as everything else?

Obviously I should investigate these things before I signed my name to any contract. As usual, the thought of money depressed me. If I were actually to live out this dream, I would probably have to pay whatever was necessary for an adequate craft and invent some way of meeting the costs. The age-old fear which I believe most authors face, the dread of discovering that I couldn't write anymore, or that no one would like what I did write, welled up in me, a familiar panic the years had not taught me how to handle very well. My mouth felt dry, and it was a relief to hear my name being paged.

The yacht broker was standing near the entrance to the club. He was impeccably dressed in a conservative gray suit, and he carried a polished brown attaché case. He was surprisingly young, not more than twenty-four or twenty-five. One of the curious aspects of middle age was the discovery that the people I met seemed to grow younger every year. Somehow I had expected a yacht broker to be rather a fatherly type like the man who had sold me my schooner long ago, but this boy looked a little like my son.

"It's good to meet you," he said with a shy smile when I introduced myself. "I've read some of your books and enjoyed them very much."

He was, after all, a salesman, and there was no reason to expect vituperative literary criticism from such a person, but I found myself ridiculously pleased by his approval.

"Do you want a drink before lunch?" I asked.

"That would be good."

We went to the room outside the bar and rang for the waiter. Putting his attaché case on the table, the broker said, "I went through our files, and I believe I have four boats you will find ideal for living aboard. One, the *Lady Luck,* is a real beauty, especially designed for the Bahamas. I sailed aboard her last winter and can't recommend her too highly. Her owner died recently, and the estate is anxious to sell."

"Do you have a picture of her?" I asked eagerly.

In reply he snapped open his attaché case and handed me a piece of onionskin paper on which the specifications of the boat had been typed. Clipped to the upper right corner was a photograph of a 60-foot ketch, so beautiful that for a moment she almost stopped my breath.

"How much is she?" I asked.

"They're asking a hundred thousand, but I believe you could get her for less. I don't think they'd be hurt if you tried eighty."

"Did you ring?" a waiter asked.

"I want a martini," I said. "What will you have?"

"The same," the broker said. "She's only two years old, and she cost more than two hundred thousand dollars to build."

"How come they dropped the price so much?"

"She's not rigged for racing, and without modifications she wouldn't be much good for the charter business. The owner had her designed to give the utmost comfort to his wife, himself and two guests."

"I could never handle such a big boat by myself. My wife hasn't had much experience. . . ."

"The past owner was elderly, but he got by quite well with a captain and one paid hand."

"She's much too expensive for me," I said, wondering why it was so hard to blurt that sentence out.

"How much are you prepared to pay?"

Somehow I could not bring myself to name what now seemed to be the wretched sum of $20,000.

"Naturally, I want to pay as little as possible for an adequate craft. The main thing is to get something small enough for me to handle myself."

"Without a crew?"

"A paid crew always seems to me to destroy the privacy which is one of a boat's greatest charms."

"How big a boat do you think you can handle by yourself?"

"When I was eighteen," I said nostalgically, "I once took an eighty-seven-foot schooner from Boston to New York single-handed. I just used the foresail, the staysail and the engine. I'm no longer that reckless or that active, of course."

The waiter arrived with our drinks, and the young man sipped his, apparently glad that he didn't have to make an immediate comment.

"I doubt if any man can handle anything much more than

thirty-five or forty feet safely by himself," I finished lamely and took a gulp of my drink.

"That puts us in a whole new category," he said and started rummaging through his attaché case.

Somewhere in the back of the Harvard Club a man gave a loud derisive laugh. There was a long wait while the broker explored the very bottom of his portable files.

"Here's a good buy," he said finally. "Another estate sale."

"What happens to all these yacht owners?"

"That's one of the tragedies of the business," he said with a slight smile. "A lot of men save all their lives to buy a boat. When they finally get it, they don't have much time to enjoy it. I keep telling my prospective customers not to wait too long. It's always later than we think."

On this jolly note he handed me a specification sheet with a picture of a handsome small motor sailer named the *Bad Penny*.

"How much are they asking for her?" I asked.

"She was recently appraised at fifty thousand dollars. I have the papers in my office."

"That's still too much for me. I have three children in school, and you know how taxes are."

"She was appraised before the owner died. He wanted a bigger boat and was going to give her to some nonprofit corporation for a tax write-off. In such cases they make the appraisal high. I believe the estate will take a more realistic view of her value."

"Like what?"

"You could try thirty thousand dollars. Maybe even twenty-five. The heirs are anxious to sell before she incurs any more bills."

"Sounds interesting," I said. "Where can we see her?"

"She's in Connecticut. We could take a run out this afternoon."

"I'll call my wife and see if she can go."

"This isn't what you'd call a woman's boat, but she's real

salty. The past owner took her to Bermuda and the Bahamas twice."

"Sounds great," I said and looked at the photograph again. The *Bad Penny* was something of a comedown after the *Lady Luck,* but she did have sweet lines, and a kind of jaunty, self-confident look. Carrying my drink with me, I went to the telephone.

"Want to go out to Connecticut and look at a boat this afternoon?" I asked when I got my wife on the wire.

"Sure," she said and filled that one word with all kinds of excitement.

"She's a forty-footer called the *Bad Penny*. Real salty. Her owner sailed her to Bermuda and the Bahamas twice."

"Why is he selling her?"

"He's dead."

"Of exhaustion? How much is she?"

"She's been appraised for fifty thousand dollars, but the broker thinks we might get her for about half that."

"Why?"

"We can go into that later. Let's take a look first."

"Can I wear a dress, or do I have to put on blue jeans?"

Probably blue jeans would be best for inspecting a boat, but Betty hated them because she knew I don't like them on women. We hadn't talked much about life on a boat, but I guessed that if it meant putting away all her pretty dresses, she would be disappointed. It might be important to get off to a festive start, not a grubby one.

"Wear anything you want," I said. "After we see the boat, we can stop somewhere nice and have a good dinner."

"Should I bring Jessie or get a sitter?"

"We might as well start this adventure together. She's going to have to get used to boats sooner or later."

"Pick us up in an hour," she said, sounding breathless, and hung up.

After finishing our drinks, the broker and I went into the dining room. He was a good salesman, for he obviously loved boats and perhaps had chosen his curious profession mostly in order to be near them.

"I plan to buy a boat someday and live aboard," he said. "I'd do it now, but around here it's a little tough in the winter. In the spring and fall I manage to spend a lot of time afloat, though. My wife and I deliver yachts. We're heading south with a big cruiser in a few weeks."

"How is the inland route these days?"

"Beautiful! We enjoy it every year."

I remembered the times I had taken that trip in my youth. Starting in New York, we'd go outside in the ocean as far as Cape May, New Jersey, where the sheltered waters began. "Outside" was a word full of terror as well as excitement in those days. My father made me screw shut the portholes of our little schooner especially tight, and I got butterflies in my stomach even before we hit the slow ocean swells. Usually we started at dawn, and I tried to pretend I was too busy to eat breakfast. Once we had a strong fair wind and got all the way to the mouth of Chesapeake Bay before putting in. Next there was Norfolk, Virginia, where the great battleships had lain at anchor. Elizabeth City, Morehead City and Charleston came next. Within a few days we would be in Thunderbolt, Georgia, a sleepy town where you could at the time buy all the oysters and shrimp you could eat for fifty cents. The canals through swamp country were full of black water which reflected the Spanish moss hanging from the branches of the cypress trees on the nearby banks. It was silly to hope that the trip would offer the same excitement to me now that it had then.

"Do you know the Bahamas well?" the broker asked.

"No. I've visited Nassau and Eleuthera, but never aboard a small boat."

"There's a lot of development in some places, but most of the out islands haven't changed much since Blackbeard's time."

He had no way of knowing the appeal the out islands had for me. As a boy I had never sailed farther than the Florida Keys because my mother got seasick and my father had a bad heart which made him afraid to venture far from civilization. I too got seasick and scared, but that somehow had made me more resentful than ever of our inability to leave the coast.

"The Bahamas aren't much," my father often said. "There's nothing over there."

I loved my father and rarely questioned what he said, but often when we lay anchored in the bay near Miami, I gazed eastward over the horizon when the moon came up, and I wanted to go there.

"Be sure to take spare propellers and shafts with you if you go," the broker was saying now. "The charts still aren't very accurate, and there are plenty of coral heads."

I have no idea what we ate for lunch that day. When it was over, we took a taxi to the garage of my apartment, and while they were bringing out my car, I called Betty and asked her to come down. Almost immediately she appeared in a yellow summer dress, a small woman whose slender figure made her look even younger than her thirty-two years. Walking beside her was Jessica, who in a dress of similar colors looked to me like her mother viewed through the wrong end of a telescope. Coming down the dim corridor from the garage elevators, they looked like two lost children. Almost certainly they will be scared and seasick, just as my mother and I were, I thought, and for the first time I wondered whether it was really his bad heart which prevented my father from taking us to the Bahamas.

"You don't have to worry," I said with an urgency which must have surprised Betty. "We'll watch the weather and make short runs."

"On the way to Connecticut?" she asked brightly.

"After we get on the boat."

"I'm not worried."

Her voice sounded as though she meant it. In the three years we had been married she had consistently given me the compliment of assuming that I knew what I was doing, an attitude which always surprised me. It was also an attitude which made me work hard to prove she was right. If I get her on a boat and scare her and the baby half to death, I'm simply out of my mind, I thought, and resolved if necessary never to leave the canals of Florida.

During the drive to Stamford, where the *Bad Penny* was laid up, Jessica napped and the rest of us kept quiet to avoid waking her. It was a gray afternoon with a gusty wind whipping the leaves on the ground into brief frenzies, during which some of them swirled up and touched the limbs from which they had fallen. A small boat at sea would be rolling and pitching her guts out.

"Here we are," the broker said finally and turned into a boatyard. Immediately I saw the *Bad Penny,* her white and red hull looking sleek as it sat in its high cradle.

"I'll get a ladder," the broker said and disappeared.

"She's a beauty," Betty said as I gestured toward the vessel. "I don't know anything about boats, but she's got class."

Gently she woke up the baby.

"Where are we?" Jessica inquired grumpily.

"We're going to look at a boat."

"I don't want to."

Closing her eyes, the child began to whimper. At the other end of the yard the broker came out of a shed dragging a ladder, and I went to help him.

The deck was only about 12 feet above the ground, but the ladder looked rickety and did not rest very solidly against the cap rail. The broker ran nimbly up to hold the top.

"I'll stay here with Jessie," I said to Betty. "You go on up."

"I want to stay with you," the child said to her mother.

"Get on my back," Betty said, hoisting Jessie up. "Put your arms around my neck."

Before I had a chance to hold the bottom of the ladder, Betty skipped lightly up with the child clinging to her back. My 220 pounds went up more slowly. When I pulled myself on the deck of the boat, Jessica was sitting in the cockpit, reaching toward a chromium ship's bell.

"Don't touch *anything,*" Betty said to her.

The broker fumbled with some keys and slid open a hatch. Picking up the baby, I went down to a tiny cabin, followed by Betty. The portholes were small, and it was quite dark. There was the smell of a rust-streaked coal stove and mildew. As our eyes gradually got used to the gloom, we saw four narrow bunks heaped with piles of sails.

"If you sit down on one of the bunks, there'll be more room," the broker said, edging in. Somehow, no matter how we moved, the four of us were always touching one another.

"Is there another cabin?" Betty asked, her voice expressionless.

"I'm afraid this is about it. There's a storage compartment forward and the engine aft."

Betty said nothing, but in the dim light her white face took on a look of horror.

"I'm afraid that this isn't what we want at all," I said quickly to the broker. "We need more room. I'm afraid we'd all go nuts if we had to live here."

"Thank God!" Betty exploded. "I was scared to death that you were going to say this is wonderful."

"I want to go home," Jessie moaned.

"Don't make up your mind too hastily," the broker said. "This boat is beautifully constructed. She could take you anywhere."

"I would go mad," Betty said simply. "It would be like living in a small cave."

"It would seem roomier if all this stuff were properly stowed," the broker continued doggedly. "If you need more privacy, you could put in a partition. The owner wanted just one big compartment."

"Big?" Betty echoed hollowly.

"I'm afraid we couldn't put in a partition," I said. "I can hardly turn around now without turning black and blue."

"Well, she never was designed for living aboard," the broker said ruefully and, glancing at Betty, added, "Don't get discouraged. I think that right in this town I have something very different that you'll really like."

Jostling each other, we managed to back out of that tiny cabin and helped each other down the ladder. As we reached our car, the broker lit a cigarette and seemed to be glancing at me narrowly.

"Would you mind if I showed you a powerboat?" he asked.

"I'd never really thought of that." My voice sounded resentful.

"I think you've got a decision to make," he continued. "A sailboat small enough for you to handle alone can't possibly offer the comfort you'll want if you want to live aboard permanently, unless you're really willing to rough it. On the other hand, a power boat. . . ."

"I suppose we might as well look," I said. "We should consider every possibility."

"Go right down this street here and turn right," he said and, turning to Betty, added, "Now you're really going to see something."

Well, that's the way of the world, I thought gloomily. For a lifetime you dream of getting away from it all on a beautiful sailboat, but when it comes time to turn the fantasy into reality, you start settling for comfort and practicality. Instead of gliding on white wings into an azure cove, I would chug in with a noisy stinkpot.

"Right here," the broker said. "You can park over by that shed."

This was the showroom of a manufacturer of stock cruisers. As we followed the broker toward the largest, which had some red-carpeted wooden steps built beside it, my heart sank. Here was a craft of truly monumental ugliness, as fat as though she had been blown up like a rubber ball. A fat man shouldn't have to have a fat boat—he should be allowed a little grace. The bow of this craft looked like the face of a child with a bad case of the mumps, and the stern was as wide as the side of a barn. Betty and Jessie walked up the stairs with the broker. Before following them, I circled the hull, which was almost flat-bottomed and had virtually no keel. I would hate to take such a boat to the Bahamas, I thought—in any kind of a wind she would blow sideways almost as fast as she could move ahead. Was my plan to go to the Bahamas only another pipe dream which would fade as soon as I tried to be practical? This boat seemed designed for rivers and inland waterways, nothing more.

"Come on up," Betty called. "She's marvelous inside."

As soon as I got to the main cabin, I saw what she meant. Belowdecks, the boat looked more like a Hollywood apartment than anything designed to float. Thick blue carpets covered the deck, and on each side of wide plate-glass windows were lace curtains. Big rattan armchairs surrounded a marble-topped coffee table, and there was a galley that looked like a modern kitchenette, complete with a pink electric stove and a washing machine. Following the broker aft, we saw an astonishingly comfortable double bedroom with a vanity table surrounded by mirrors and a tiled bathroom with a shower.

"Gosh, we wouldn't exactly be roughing it here," Betty said and grabbed Jessica, who had started to jump up and down on one of the wide beds.

"Where are the engines?" I asked the broker.

"Under the deck of the main cabin."

Opening a tiny hatch, he showed me two cheaply converted automobile engines installed in such a way that it would be almost impossible to service them. The boat was shabbily constructed with plywood and straight, widely spaced frames. If driven into a head sea for any length of time, I suspected that she would start to disintegrate like a cardboard box.

Betty looked so enthusiastic as she opened the doors to linen closets and lockers for hanging clothes that I hated to say anything. Glancing at my lugubrious expression, the broker said, "These boats are a lot more able than they look. They take full advantage of materials which didn't exist a few years ago."

"What's her cruising range?"

"I guess that would depend on how fast you ran her. She can do twenty-five knots."

"How much fuel does she hold?"

"About one hundred and fifty gallons. That's more than most."

Appalled, I didn't say anything. Such boats get less than a mile from a gallon of gas. Apparently she was supposed never to go more than about 50 miles from port. And there was, I noticed, no generator for all that electrical equipment. When she was away from a marina, there would be no refrigeration, no cooking facilities, and no heat of any kind—not even many lights for long. A plug-in boat. Through the big glass ports I could see that her foredeck was innocent of anchors or any equipment for handling them. Suddenly I felt building up in me an absurdly exaggerated blaze of hatred for the craft. It wasn't just that this bloated monstrosity would prevent me from visiting distant islands, and even from anchoring in privacy near home; it was that her ugliness seemed some sort of projection of my fattening, middle-aged self. To a surprising degree, a man is the boat he chooses. As much as when he selects a wife, a man is dealing in mirror images or a desire to compensate for them when he chooses a boat. Perhaps I could satisfy my yearnings only with a graceful boat and a graceful woman, but that might be too much to expect. In small craft, comfort and grace rarely go together.

The satisfaction which so clearly glowed on Betty's face when she glanced about the luxurious cabin of this flimsy barge was not, I was sure, unusual—as the broker well knew, this boat had been designed to please women. Had I ever met a woman who would be happy for long in the Spartan quarters offered by a small sailing boat?

Yes, I had met a few, women who prided themselves on being as tough as men when it came to muscling a sail in, riding out a gale or even cussing a fouled anchor line. They were great for a cruise, but I had never been tempted to ask one of them to marry me. Instead, I had fallen in love with a dancing girl, a girl who liked to spend most of her spare time curled up on our "emperor-sized" bed listening to phonograph records, or playing the piano. If I had wanted to sail to distant places in a cockleshell, I couldn't have found a less likely companion.

Even if Betty did, through her devotion to me, force some change of character upon herself, what sense did it really make to take a two-year-old child into the danger and discomfort of a long voyage on a small sailboat? Sure, a few people had, but was I willing to face the risks not only of shipwreck and of prolonged seasickness but of the accidents which can so easily happen to a child on a violently rolling boat? Into my mind came, with terrifying clarity, the picture of a child's leg broken, a compound fracture with the bone sticking through the skin. How would I feel as I tried to bind that up alone, far from any doctor? And how would I feel if it was my leg which was broken, and I lay helpless while the boat rolled in the hollow of a rising sea?

My whole dream of taking Betty and the baby on a long voyage became ridiculous. If wanderlust had really got the best of me, I should buy this ugly boat and content myself with a leisurely trip down the inland waterway to Florida, the way so many other family men did. Or perhaps it would be more sensible to go whole hog and get a real houseboat, a cottage on a barge with flower boxes at the windows. The Bahamas would be out of the question, but there were plenty of canals, and perhaps we could float in a leisurely way down the Mississippi, as I had dreamed of doing ever since I read Mark Twain.

"The list price of this boat is thirty-seven thousand dollars," the broker said, apparently in answer to a question Betty had asked him.

In that case, an older model would be well within my price range. Of course, those two light gasoline engines would burn a ridiculous amount of fuel, maybe 150 gallons a day, and in doing a job heavier than they had been designed for, they could be expected to break down a lot, but like most owners of such craft, we would probably end up spending most of our time moored in some marina anyway. So ends many a dream, I thought, and if I wanted to complain about it, I should blame myself for yearning for incompatible delights.

"Is there anything else you want to see?" the broker asked.

"No," I said with a shrug.

"You don't like this boat, do you?" Betty asked, sitting down suddenly in one of the armchairs and taking Jessica on her lap.

"She's all right for what she's designed for."

"Plenty of people take these boats to the Bahamas," the broker said. "You just have to watch your weather."

I remembered an old commander in the Coast Guard who repeatedly used to say, "Half your battle for survival at sea is won or lost before you ever leave port. If you've got the right vessel, the right equipment and the right crew, all the odds will be in your favor. If not, you're just waiting for disaster."

Well, in my case, "the right vessel" would consist of plywood and glass, "the right crew" would consist of a pretty girl and a baby, and as far as I could see, this boat didn't have any "equipment" at all. If I headed offshore, disaster probably wouldn't keep me waiting long.

"A houseboat would give you even more room than this," I said to Betty.

"Are they seaworthy?"

"About as seaworthy as this. Instead of going to the Bahamas we could stick to the canals. Maybe we could float down the Mississippi."

"I'm afraid the Mississippi has changed since Huck Finn's time," the broker said. "A friend of mine just brought a boat down through there from the Great Lakes. There's a lot of industrial waste and sewage from the big cities. My friend said they ought to run the whole river through an enormous pipe underground."

"Sounds charming," Betty said, and I had a sharp vision of my family aboard an ugly little boat afloat in a sewer.

"But the *whole point* was to explore the islands," Betty said. "I've always wanted to go to the Bahamas."

"Bahamas," Jessie repeated, pronouncing the word perfectly. "Bahamas, Bahamas, Bahamas."

"*Plenty* of these boats have gone to the Bahamas," the broker repeated.

"Plenty of people have voluntarily gone over Niagara Falls in a barrel."

"If you want a real offshore powerboat, there are a lot I could show you. Take one of the North Sea trawler types."

"How much do they cost?"

"A few go for as little as fifty or sixty thousand."

Betty looked shocked. She had questioned the wisdom of spending as much as $20,000 on a boat.

"I'm afraid twenty-five thousand dollars is still our top," I said, and I saw that she winced.

"Could you give me a clearer idea of just what you expect to get for that?" the broker asked, and perhaps I imagined that the curve of his right eyebrow looked supercilious.

"Probably a powerboat, but one with a strong hull," I said. "Hopefully, a diesel engine with an adequate cruising range, instead of this light gasoline stuff. And I'd like a generator. I don't want to have to be at a dock every night."

"Maybe you can get all that in an older boat," the broker replied with a polite smile. "I'm afraid we don't handle much of that sort of thing. If I can locate anything in our files, I'll let you know, but why don't you try some of the smaller agencies?"

Obviously, he had given up on us. A professional salesman, he knew how to size people up, and his time was too valuable to waste on a man who wanted more than his money could buy.

Silently we walked to the car. In no mood for the celebratory dinner we had planned, we went straight back to New York, let the broker off at his office and returned to our apartment.

# 3 ⚓

That evening Betty played the piano until midnight. After several hours of pacing in the living room, I took a long hot bath and climbed into our enormous bed. Closing my eyes, I found that I was lulling myself to sleep with the fantasy of a tall schooner on a moonlit sea. Well, there was no use dreaming of that anymore. The music of the piano stopped, and Betty came in.

"I'm glad you didn't pressure me to buy that cabin cruiser we saw today," I said. "I know she was awfully comfortable."

"I don't want anything that's not safe. And she was ugly from the outside. She didn't have any class."

"She sure didn't. We have to remember that boats are like people, though—each has the advantages of its defects, and vice versa. If we get a sleek, graceful boat, she won't have anywhere near as much room."

"I don't need everything so fancy, as long as it isn't like that first boat we saw. That one really got me depressed."

"Yes."

"Did that broker discourage you?"

"A little."

"We'll find something," Betty said. "I'm sure of it. And don't let's settle for anything that can't make it to the islands."

It was almost eleven o'clock in the morning when I woke up.

Going to the living room, I came upon a scene of complete confusion. Every suitcase we owned and a variety of cardboard cartons were stacked in the middle of the Turkish rug, and Betty, helped by Jessica, was stacking books from the cases on the walls in huge piles beside them.

"What's going on?" I asked in bewilderment.

"Packing."

"Already? Shouldn't we wait till we get a boat?"

"Well, we are definitely going, aren't we? The landlord called, and I told him we were giving the apartment up. We've got only thirty days, and if we leave everything till the last moment. . . ."

"We can get professionals in to do this."

"You know how much they charge. Bert Ellis is going to take all the books in his station wagon. They have a new apartment with lots of shelves, and they're going to store our books until we have a place for them again."

Still talking, she went to the kitchen and got me a cup of coffee, while Jessica played with the books as though they were blocks.

"Why the suitcases so soon?" I asked, my voice sounding resentful.

"Bert is going to carry the books in them. He'll bring them back. He says he and Ellie will find space for our pictures too."

Taking a sip of coffee, I rubbed my face wearily. Betty, I suspected, was more upset than she had admitted by the great change we were making and by the difficulty in finding a suitable boat. It had always been her habit not to drink when she was depressed, and not to talk about it, but to throw herself feverishly into work.

"It's funny," she said as she dusted books and fitted them into a footlocker. "I never realized how many books about boats you have."

"People give them to me. Everybody knows that if it has an anchor printed on it, it's the perfect Christmas present for me."

"And most of our pictures are of boats or seascapes—the book-ends are made out of old running lights. . . ."

"I know. . . ."

"Will you clean out your fish tanks today? We can't possibly store all that complicated stuff. Leo Dienstag says he knows a school that can use them in a biology lab."

In a corner there were two huge aquariums in which I kept saltwater tropical fish, fussing with chemicals in order to create a tiny facsimile of the ocean in my living room. It had seemed a harmless hobby, but now all this preoccupation with the sea appeared ludicrous.

"I'll clean out the tanks tonight," I said gruffly.

"I'm glad we're going to get a boat," Betty said, straightening up, dustrag in hand. "By God, it's time you got the real thing."

After finishing my second cup of coffee and nibbling on some dry toast, I picked up a copy of the New York *Times* and turned to the sports section, where there were several columns of advertisements for boats. Most of them were for outboards, small sailboats or weekend cruising craft, but one advertisement in tiny type held my attention. "For Sale," it said. "Sixty-foot cruiser suitable for Florida, old but sound. $8,000." A Long Island telephone number followed.

"Hey, listen to this!" I said to Betty and read it to her.

"There's a catch to it."

"We might as well call up and find out."

The telephone was answered almost immediately by what sounded like a hearty old man.

"Could you tell me a little about the boat you're advertising?" I asked.

"She's a beauty!" he boomed. "Built in the days when they really built boats."

"When was that?"

"Nineteen twenty, but she was built to last. They really had the wood in those days, and the craftsmen."

"What kind of power does she have?"

"Lathrop diesels."

"And a generator?"

"Sure. Plus a radio telephone, a dinghy with an outboard, an electric anchor windlass, all Coast Guard equipment—she's got *everything* you need."

"Where is she?"

"Out in Northport. The first yard on your left as you come into town from New York. Just ask for the yacht *Sea Flower*. I'm the owner, and I'll be there. Stafford's the name—Commander Benjamin Stafford. To whom do I have the honor of speaking?"

I told him and promised to be there within two hours.

"Do you want to come?" I asked Betty.

She made a wry face.

"Bert and Ellie are going to come for the books this afternoon. Anyway, I think maybe you should look for a boat alone and call me when you find something suitable. It's so disappointing to find something wrong with everything we see."

Noticing that I looked unhappy, she added, "Anyway, you know how sick Jessie gets on long rides. I think she needs a rest today."

"On a boat I think she'll be better. She can run around and play and have her own bed and meals everywhere she goes."

"It sounds marvelous."

Betty was trying to be enthusiastic, but her sentence fell a little flat. Determinedly she took a huge dictionary from a pile and dusted it.

"Will we want to take this with us?" she asked.

"It would be hard to stow. I think I can get by with a small one."

Quickly I put on blue jeans and an old blue sweater which proved ridiculously small for me.

"That thing must have shrunk," Betty said tactfully and handed me a new cashmere which didn't look suitable for inspecting boats. "If you're going to Northport, you better stop in and see your sister."

"I hate to get this dirty," I said grumpily, "but I guess I don't have any work clothes that fit anymore."

That seemed a curious admission. Giving Betty and my daughter a hasty kiss, I hurried to the car.

It was a cloudy September day, cold enough to make the ragged men who sat on the benches near the entrance to Central Park turn up the collars of their coats. Certainly they would think I was fabulously lucky, a middle-aged man out to look for a yacht in which to sail south, but I didn't feel lucky—somehow the sight of our apartment beginning to disintegrate had left me badly shaken.

Anxious to see the *Sea Flower,* lovely sounding name, I drove fast, warily keeping a watch out for cops. The owner of the boat was or had been a commander of some sort, according to our conversation on the telephone. Perhaps he was a retired Coast Guard officer. Such a man could certainly be expected to have a good vessel.

The boatyard in Northport was a handsome one, with many beautiful boats moored to a complex network of piers.

"Can you tell me where I can find the *Sea Flower?*" I asked in the office.

A girl who was typing a letter stopped suddenly, and perhaps I imagined that both she and the manager of the yard looked at me oddly.

"Over there," the manager said. "At the small wharf behind that shed."

Picking my way across the tracks of marine railways, I found a rickety dock at the end of which a lovely old vessel with a black hull and white cabin was moored. Her stern resembled the tail of a seagull, not a barn, and although she was a power-boat, her bow was as graceful as that of a Gloucester fishing schooner of the past generation. From a distance of 500 yards, she seemed the embodiment of my dream, despite the fact that she had no sails, but as I hurried closer, she seemed to disinte-grate in front of my eyes. The paint was flaking from the top-sides, the decks had been clumsily covered with fiber glass which had begun to buckle, and all the bright work had been heavily encrusted with brown paint. I felt as though I had seen a beautiful blonde in the distance, hurried closer, and discovered a sick old woman in a wig. Here was a boat which clearly was little more than a derelict. Disappointed, not only for myself but by the sight of a kind of death, I would have hurried away if a thin old man in a blue coat that seemed much too big for him had not climbed out of a hatch.

"Hello!" he called, in that hearty voice. "Are you the fellow I'm expecting?"

"Yes," I replied a little weakly.

"Come aboard! But before you do, step back and take a look at the lines of this vessel."

"I have been admiring them."

"She was designed and built by George Lawley. Do you know what that means?"

"I used to work for Lawley," I said, sounding surprised.

"You did?"

"It was just a summer job when I was in college. I was a third-class blacksmith."

"Well, you know what a Lawley-built boat is! Not many do nowadays."

Walking across a creaking gangplank, I stepped aboard. Between the cap rail and the deck two of the frames by the gangway had rotted. Quickly I glanced away.

"She needs a little work, but she's a grand old boat," the commander said. "Come below."

Following him down a companionway, I found myself in a cabin paneled with mahogany which had turned almost black over the decades but still retained a certain elegance. Opening a locker with diamond-shaped, leaded glass panes, he took out a decanter of Scotch and two glasses with the yacht's name, *Sea Flower*, and two pennants inscribed in red and blue enamel.

"I'm afraid I can't offer you ice," he said. "The refrigerating machinery is being repaired. Will water be all right?"

"A little water will be fine."

"So you're going to buy a boat. I wish I were your age and bent on such an errand."

A shaft of light from a porthole hit his face as he leaned forward to give me my glass, and I saw that he was older than I had thought at first glance, perhaps well into his seventies.

"My wife and I bought this boat when I was about your age," he continued. "We had just been married. I quit the Navy and we went down to the Bahamas. My wife died last year. Except for the war, we lived aboard for almost thirty years."

"I envy you."

"It's a good life. You meet a lot of friendly people on the waterfront, a lot of interesting people. We sailed this boat all the way from Newfoundland to Panama. I'm too old for that sort of thing now, but the boat's not. She was built to last forever. Want to look around?"

Glass in hand, he led the way to the owner's stateroom in the stern. An oil portrait of a pretty young woman in a long dress and enormous green hat filled one bulkhead and was reflected in a cracked and frosted mirror which had been built over a vanity table with a skirt of faded red velvet. The deck had leaked, and the paneling over the bunks was stained and warped.

"She needs a little work, of course," he went on, staring around as though he were seeing the cabin for the first time. "I've had arthritis lately and haven't been able to keep up with her as much as I should. You'll find she's a grand sea boat, though. She'll ride easy as a gull in storms that send all the new boats to port."

"I'm sure."

"I'd start the engines for you, but I'm in the midst of replacing the injectors. I've got the old ones out, but I haven't had a chance to put the new ones in. Want to see the galley?"

We started forward, but when we went through the main cabin, he poured himself another drink and sank down on a bunk, propping himself up with a green silk pillow which had been fancily embroidered with the yacht's name. For an hour he told me about the cruises he and his wife had taken.

"When you get to the Bahamas you'll find you can hire native help for about a dollar a day," he said, as though times hadn't changed down there at all. "They're fine seamen, the Bahamians, and real gentlemen. If you like seafood and fruit you can live on practically nothing. . . ."

While he talked he drank, taking a full bottle of Haig and Haig from a case stowed in a locker where his naval uniforms hung.

"I've had a lot of people look at this boat," he said, a hurt looking coming into his eyes. "They don't understand her—there's not a sailor in a million of 'em. They pick around finding fault, but they don't stop to look at her lines and the way she's built. I wouldn't cheat you, mind you. I admit she needs work, but you know what a little scraping and painting can do. There is a spot of dry rot here and there, but the bad wood can be replaced easy enough, and it wouldn't cost much, especially if you took her to one of the yards in Maine or, better yet, Nova Scotia. You can't deny the price is right. You couldn't build a boat like this today, because all the great craftsmen are dead or as old as I am, but if you tried to replace her, it would cost you three hundred thousand bucks. That's what they're charging for new sixty-footers these days. Ask anybody. You'll find I'm right."

"I'm sure you are."

"Are you interested?" he asked, sitting up suddenly. "Is she your cup of tea?"

"She would be if I had the money to take care of her. Unfortunately, I don't."

"Well. . . ."

Leaning back on his pillow, he made a wry face.

"But you *like* her?" he asked, pouring himself another drink.

"She's an old beauty."

"Someday someone will come along who sees that and who has the money she needs. I figure it would take about twenty thousand bucks."

"Perhaps," I replied, reflecting that that would hardly get the carpenters started.

"I might come down a little in my price."

"I'm sorry. The lady should go to someone who can keep her in the style to which she has become accustomed. Thanks for the drink."

With a deprecatory wave of his hand, he sank back on his pillow and closed his eyes. Feeling as though I were leaving a tomb, I went ashore.

# 4 ⚓

Slowly I drove to my sister's house, which is high on a hill overlooking Northport Harbor. A nursery school teacher and the wife of a busy lawyer, my sister has never shared my love of boats. Now when she learned I was looking for one to buy as a home, she became as indignant as she used to when I pulled the cat's tail long ago.

"You're going to take Betty and Jessie to live on a boat?" she asked incredulously.

"Betty thinks it might be fun."

"You're both crazy. How are you going to keep a child that age from falling overboard?"

"We'll make her wear a life preserver."

"You think she'll be comfortable in that? Children hate life preservers. It's irresponsible to do such a thing. She'll be seasick and scared half to death most of the time. How long do you think Betty will really enjoy being cooped up on a boat?"

"I don't know," I replied, the depression from which I had already been suffering growing worse.

"Why do you have to do a thing like this? I should think that with a wonderful wife and a child as beautiful as that. . . ."

"I think an adventure like this—" I began helplessly. "If we don't do it now, we'll never—"

"I wouldn't say this if I didn't love you, but shouldn't you talk all this over with a psychiatrist first?"

"I'm tired of talking to psychiatrists. Why is anybody who wants to get away from New York supposed to be crazy? Why is it so sane to sit around being bored to death?"

"Don't let's fight," she said. "Sit down, and I'll get you a drink."

"I've got to get home. Betty's packing already."

Hastily I beat a retreat. When I returned to my apartment, most of my books had already disappeared and a young man I had never seen before was going out the door with my favorite armchair.

"That's Bill Gillespie," Betty said. "I met his wife in the laundry room. They just moved in, and they don't have enough furniture."

"But we shouldn't get rid of this stuff until we have a place to go."

"As we find opportunities to place the furniture, we should take them. Otherwise we're going to have an enormous moving and storage bill."

Going to the kitchen for a drink, I found that Betty had begun to wrap our fancy china in newspapers and was packing it in cardboard boxes. Already the well-ordered home we had had overlooking Central Park was a thing of the past.

I felt miserable. I had seen the destruction of my impractical dream and was witnessing the dismantling of our apartment. Impatiently I went to the telephone and consulted the classified section. If one expects to buy anything at less than the normal price, one has to be an aggressive, tireless shopper. Probably I would have to cover the waterfront from Maine to Florida if I wanted a really good buy.

During the next three weeks I did almost that, traveling by plane, train, bus and car. I saw converted fishing vessels, Chinese junks, and one monstrous catamaran which an enterprising dreamer had built in his backyard according to his own design, despite the fact that he had never sailed a boat in his life. Although I constantly repeated my specific requirements, eager brokers showed me everything in their files. When I complained about this to one weary agent, he smiled and said, "Experience has shown me that the only way to sell a man a boat is to keep him moving from one hull to another. Sooner or later he'll fall in love with one or just get tired enough to settle for something at hand. In either case, people often buy boats which have nothing to do with whatever it was they set out to seek."

What I needed was an agent who took my requirements seriously and was willing to spend the time checking with other brokers until he found something close. When I had just about given up hope, I found such a man. He was a stocky gentleman who had served aboard submarines during the war and obviously knew a lot about the water. His name was Ed Krammer.

"You want twin diesels," he summed up for me, lighting a cigar. "A generator and everything else you'll need for the Bahamas. A sound hull, of course. Something about fifty feet if you and your wife are going to handle her yourselves and are going to live aboard. All for twenty thousand dollars."

"Do you think I'm just dreaming?"

"You're on the thin edge of reality. Somewhere such a boat might exist. She'll be an old boat, of course, something out of fashion, but if we can find one that's had the proper care. . . ."

"Please try. The lease on my apartment is up in about a week."

"Give me a couple of days. Quit looking at all this junk people are showing you. Go home and rest. If I give you a call, it will be what you want. I'll go over our files with a fine-tooth comb and get our representatives in all the other cities to do the same. If I can't find your boat, you can be sure she doesn't exist."

Gratefully I took his advice. Our apartment didn't look like much of a home anymore. Betty had stripped it of all but what she considered the essentials, our enormous bed, a crib, her piano, a vacuum cleaner, a card table, three chairs and my desk.

Although she was determinedly cheerful, she was as restless as
I, and when she wasn't playing the piano she was prowling about
with the vacuum cleaner, an occupation in which she said she
found relaxation.

"Can you have a vacuum cleaner on a boat?" she asked me.

"Alongside the dock, I guess. Not many boats generate one
hundred and ten volts."

"Is it conceivable that we could take the piano?"

"Barely."

"I suppose that's silly anyway. Maybe I can get an accordion."

For three weeks I hadn't done any work, and I busied myself making some changes my publisher had asked for in the
manuscript of a novel I had just finished. Two days went by
without any word from Ed Krammer, and I went to a nearby
yacht basin to look at some houseboats I saw advertised in the
paper. They looked flimsy, more like house trailers than the sort
of craft about which I had dreamed, but they were comfortable
and relatively cheap. Maybe the only sensible course of action
was to settle for one of these and spend the winter floating
around the canals of Florida. Taking a handful of printed
pamphlets which offered photographs that made the cabin interiors look like enormous apartments, I went home and showed
them to Betty.

"A shantyboat," she said, examining the one which showed
the exterior of the craft. "Is that really what you want?"

"It's not a shantyboat; it's a houseboat."

"It looks like a shantyboat to me. Is it always practical to be
so practical? I know you, and you'll feel terrible every time
anyone sees you on a boat like this."

"How about you?"

Before she could answer, the telephone rang. It was Ed Krammer.

"I got the boat you want," he said in a matter-of-fact voice.
"She's in Maryland."

"Have you seen her?"

"About a year ago. Our Maryland man says she hasn't changed."

"Tell me about her."

"Length fifty-four feet. Two GM 4-71 diesels. Aboard the subs we used to call them Jimmy engines. They ain't fast and they ain't fancy, but they'll run till hell freezes over."

"That suits me."

"She's got a thirty-two-volt generator, radio telephone and all the rest of the stuff you'll need. The hull is beautiful. She was built like a violin by Nevins and has been lovingly maintained. For a long time she was owned by Guy Lombardo."

"What's the price?"

"Eighteen thousand. Till a few days ago she was listed at twenty-three."

"Why?"

"She's an old lady. Built in nineteen thirty. She's narrow—her beam is only a little over twelve feet. But wait till you see her. She's a sailor's boat. I'd buy her myself in a second if I had the dough."

"When can I see her?"

"I'll pick you up at your place at about nine in the morning. Bring your checkbook. The owner will want one thousand eight hundred dollars down and the rest subject to survey. She'll pass any inspection you care to give her. She was surveyed last year, and I've seen the report."

"You're a good salesman," I said.

"No, I'm a good broker. I found the right boat for your purpose. Take a look at her, and she'll do the selling herself."

"What kind of accommodations does she have?"

"A double stateroom aft with head and shower. A walkaround engine room under the bridge. Then a small deckhouse with a single bunk and a sofa that can pull out and sleep two. Next you've got a double stateroom with a head forward, the galley and the forecastle with crew's quarters. Everything is small, but she's got plenty of room for two couples to live aboard. On weekends she can sleep nine."

"I'll be interested to see her," I said, feeling that as a prospective purchaser I should avoid too much enthusiasm. "See you here tomorrow at nine."

Hanging up, I turned to Betty.

"I think we may have found the boat. Want to drive to Maryland tomorrow?"

"I'm supposed to take Jessie to the doctor for her shots in the morning, and in the afternoon, the dentist."

"Couldn't those appointments be changed?"

"I'd never get new ones before the end of the month. Anyway, I have this dream about your giving me a call when you've finally found the right boat. I don't want to get my hopes up until you've checked everything out first. Is that selfish of me?"

"No. Keep your fingers crossed. Maybe tomorrow will be the day."

# 5

⚓

Oxford, Maryland, is said by its admirers to be one of the most beautiful small towns in America, a sort of Williamsburg with the additional attraction of Chesapeake Bay's creeks. "Dainty, quainty Oxford," its detractors call it and say that the charm of a colonial fishing village has been made self-consciously precious by an influx of rich Yankees playing at being Southern gentlemen. None of this interested me when Ed Krammer and I arrived there early the next afternoon, which turned out to be a clear September day. All I wanted to see was the boat, which was named, Ed told me on the way down, the *Irish Mist*.

The name both pleased me and posed a small problem. Although Betty was born in Brooklyn, her father is Irish, and Betty had lived almost half her life in Dublin. We had gone there to be married, and everything Irish still retained for me a romantic charm which puzzled my wife. Although she was fiercely loyal to her family in Dublin and visited them often, she regarded Ireland as a country full of narrowminded poor people which anyone in his right mind tried to escape. The damp weather there was especially distasteful to her, and she would not regard it as a good omen to buy a boat called the *Irish Mist*.

"You might as well call her the *English Fog* or the *French*

*Drizzle,*" I could imagine Betty saying. "Or how about the *American Smog?* A man who would name a boat after a bloody mist must be a fool, and we better be careful of his boat."

I would have to promise to change the name of the boat immediately if we bought her, but still the words *Irish Mist* teased my imagination and put me in a pleasant frame of mind. When we arrived in Oxford I was exasperated when the people at two local boatyards didn't know where the *Irish Mist* was. Finally Ed went to a bar to telephone an associate in Baltimore, and we learned that the owner, a physician who had recently moved from New York to Oxford, kept the boat at a wharf on his private estate. It took us half an hour of driving about asking directions to find the place, but finally we went down a wooded road, passed an imposing white house built on a point extending into a small harbor, and got out of the car. There, lying at the end of the pier, was a graceful express cruiser which looked enormous to me. Her knifelike bow, painted a glossy light green, glistened in the sun. Even from a distance of several hundred yards, it was obvious that this was a boat which had received tender care. Her mahogany cap rails and hatches gleamed even brighter than the jade topsides and the white deckhouse. The bridge and the afterdeck were covered by awnings which matched the hull in color and which looked as though they had been designed for the tropics. Hanging in davits from her neatly rounded stern was a sailing dinghy wrapped in a fitted green canvas cover. The whole boat was mirrored in the still dark water of the little harbor, which caused ripples of light to play over her topsides.

"Didn't I say she was a beauty?" Ed asked.

Without taking time to answer, I hurried to the wharf and almost ran to the end of it. The decks were natural teak, untainted by paint, varnish, linoleum or fiber glass. In the stern was a cockpit much like that of a sailing yacht. Following me, Ed stepped into this and opened a hatch.

"This is the owner's cabin," he said.

On each side was a wide bunk with an innerspring mattress.

It wasn't as palatial as the quarters offered by the boats that looked like Hollywood apartments, but it was comfortable and there was a shower bath. Following Ed forward, I went into the deckhouse, which had two heavy bronze portholes like those of a Coast Guard cutter, instead of an expanse of vulnerable glass windows. It was small and the space was almost entirely taken by a bunk and a couch almost exactly the size of my wife's piano.

If we took that sofa out and replaced it with the piano, this would really please Betty, I thought, imagining a moonlit night in the Bahamas with her playing some of her favorite songs.

"You've got another double stateroom down here," Ed said, disappearing down a companionway. "The galley is not big, but there's a huge electric refrigerator built into the bulkhead, a good gas stove and a hot-water heater."

There were also some bookshelves, I saw as I followed him, and two cabinets with old-fashioned panes of leaded glass. Forward of the galley was a forecastle big enough to put up two youngsters of college age during vacations, with their own facilities for washing up. The interior was cream-colored with mahogany trim. No attempt had been made to decorate it like a house—it looked and felt like a comfortable, substantially built little ship.

Going back to the deckhouse, I rather weakly sank down on the sofa. It has been said that the essence of being a writer is to see what is going on and also to see oneself seeing it. Perhaps that is part of being anyone halfway intelligent, but even so there are times when I wish I could stop it, for what I was seeing now was a fool falling in love, losing every hint of judgment because of infatuation at first sight with a boat. Professional sailors rarely permit themselves such emotional excesses— they see a vessel as a specialized tool which will do some things well and other things badly. What I should be doing now was looking for weaknesses. I should be prying around in search of dry rot and asking questions about her machinery. It was absurd just to sit and stare at the graceful curve of her counter like a country boy introduced to a pretty girl for the first time, and it was worse than absurd to be afraid to look too closely for fear of finding weaknesses. For a long time I had been saying with high righteousness that people should love human beings, not things. In all sorts of ways I had preached against materialism, yet here I was, a heavy, middle-aged man fatuously caressing the smooth mahogany paneling of an ancient yacht. I was so excited that I was half-afraid to call Betty and tell her what I had found.

"Would you like to see the engine room?" Ed asked.

"Yes," I replied dutifully.

In promising a "walk-around engine room," Ed had obviously let his own enthusiasm, either for the boat or for salesmanship, run away with him. Climbing down a ladder, I found myself in a dark compartment, in only one small part of which I could stand. Ed flicked a switch, and in the glow of an electric bulb, I saw two engines, each of which was about three times the size of an automobile motor, and a great deal of auxiliary machinery, some of which whirred and buzzed in a way which alarmed my supremely unmechanical mind. The engines were streaked with rust and did not seem to have anything to do with the polished hull. There was a complex panel of electrical switches which made me aware that I would need a lot of instruction if I were to operate the boat alone. For a moment I imagined what might happen if we broke down and were drifting far from land, but I brushed that thought away and hurried back on deck.

"They look like fine engines," I heard myself say and realized more than ever that I was in the process of losing my sanity. Good enough the engines might be, but until I had an expert examine them, I wouldn't have a clue concerning their quality.

"Would you like to take a trial run?" Ed asked. "I believe the owner is up in the house."

"We might as well."

My impulse was to buy immediately without all these formalities. I felt curiously disloyal to the boat by seeking to test her in any way. Somehow it was like asking a pretty girl to go through a few dance steps and to chin herself a dozen times to prove whether she was suitable for marriage.

With difficulty I made myself look at the boat critically while Ed went to get the owner. Some of the chromium work was badly pitted—the three trumpets of the big air horn and the ship's bell would have to be replated and that would be expensive. Noticing two anchors, a davit and a husky electric windlass on the foredeck, I forgot about the minor weaknesses. Here, at least, was a boat which did not expect to be tied up in some marina every night.

"Good afternoon."

Turning, I saw a tall man with gray hair. They say that the happiest times in a yachtsman's life are when he buys a boat and when he sells one, but this man didn't look happy and his manner was barely polite. Perhaps he knew some dreadful defect in the boat that he was afraid I would discover. Perhaps he felt guilty at the prospect of sending me to sea in a vessel he knew was doomed. Whatever the reason, this cool, calm and collected man made no pretense at friendliness as he touched my hand and turned to the task of removing a green canvas cover from the wheel and engine controls.

"My wife's father is Irish," I said. "We visit Ireland a lot."

This fatuous remark was obviously uncalled for, and the look he gave me reflected that fact. Folding the canvas cover neatly, he stowed it under a seat and touched a starting button. The starboard engine came immediately to life, followed by the port engine. The boat trembled.

"You can cast off the lines," the owner said to Ed.

With cool enjoyment of his own considerable skill, the owner maneuvered his boat away from the wharf without touching her glossy paint to the pilings and headed out a narrow channel. When we got out farther, he shoved down the throttles and the *Irish Mist* leaped through the shining waters of the bay, leaving a lacy white wake astern.

"You been around boats much?" he asked me, as though there was no possibility that I had.

"A little. I commanded three ships in the Coast Guard during the war."

My voice was hostile, and my sentence sounded like a childish boast.

"Take her then."

Deciding to see how she turned, I moved the wheel a little.

"Hold it," he said. "There's not much water here. Better give her back for a while."

Relinquishing the helm, I sat on a high chair on the bridge. It had been just about twenty years since I had been on a boat of any size. Naturally, it would take some time to regain my confidence.

In deeper water the owner put the boat through her paces, demonstrating how quickly she could turn and how smoothly she encountered her own wake. There was no doubt that she was a nimble craft, even more graceful in motion than she looked at the wharf. Why was it that my joy in her passing her test was both heightened and complicated by the feeling that she would soon provide me with all sorts of tests of myself?

I watched the owner closely as he brought the *Irish Mist* smartly alongside his wharf. It would take practice, not the memories of my youth, to handle 25 tons alone so well.

"Thank you," I said to the owner. "I like your boat. I plan to ask my wife to come down and take a look at her tomorrow."

"Good," he said curtly and strode across the broad lawn toward his imposing house.

Before going ashore to call Betty, I decided to guess what questions she would ask about the boat and prepare myself to answer them.

"How big is the kitchen?" That was one thing she always wanted to know about a house or an apartment.

"I always carry this," Ed said professionally and handed me a steel tape. Going to the galley, I found that it measured 4 feet 4 inches by $2\frac{1}{2}$ feet. Somehow that didn't sound very good.

"It's professionally designed," Ed said. "Everything's built in. You just stand here in one place—you don't have to move your feet at all. Turn left and you can wash dishes in the sink. Turn forward and you can stir things on the stove. Turn right and you can take things from the icebox."

"I'm afraid my wife will turn all the way around and walk clean out."

"If a fancy galley is important to your wife, we could take down the bulkhead to the forecastle and expand it forward. At the price you're paying, you could afford to let your wife design her own galley."

"That's an idea. She'll also want to know about storage space."

"Well, you've got plenty of that."

Each of the double staterooms had lockers measuring about 2 by 3 feet for hanging clothes. That was good for a boat, but I doubted that Betty, who had four huge walk-in closets in our apartment, would be impressed. Most of the bunks had large drawers under them, and there was a bureau with five tiny drawers built under a mirror in each stateroom.

"In the Bahamas you won't need many clothes," Ed said helpfully.

Outside the sun was sinking behind a row of pines, and a cold breeze was springing up from the north. I shivered.

"Is there any way of heating this boat?" I asked.

"The stove will heat up the forward stateroom pretty well, especially if you leave the door of the oven open. In port, you can use regular electric heaters hooked up to shore current."

Slowly I let these words sink in. Despite the rich woodwork, life aboard this boat would be camping out after all, I reflected, and that was one thing I wouldn't want to do aboard a vessel I had bought for a home. If the stove heated the forward stateroom in cold weather, it would also do so in the blazing heat of the Bahamas. And during an autumnal cruise south we would freeze in the after cabin unless we were in a marina.

"How much would it cost to put in heat and air conditioning?"

"A thirty-two-volt system would run about four thousand dollars," Ed replied. "It probably would be more practical to exchange your thirty-two-volt generator for a hundred-and-ten-volt job. Then you could use regular home heating and air conditioning units, as well as toasters, irons, vacuum cleaners and all the rest of your household equipment."

"How much would that cost?"

"A new generator would run about three thousand dollars. I don't know what you could get for the one you've got. It's almost new."

"Is there a good boatyard near here?"

"Several."

"When we have her surveyed, we better get some estimates."

It was getting dark outside now, and Ed switched on a light in the deckhouse. The rising wind made the awnings flutter like a sail luffing. Turning up the collar of his coat, Ed said, "Do you know what I'd do if I were going to live aboard?"

"What?"

"I'd put a little soapstone fireplace right in this corner. They don't cost much, maybe a couple of hundred bucks. Then on cold nights you could all keep snug without the sound of the generator."

That was taking unfair advantage of my capacity to dream. Before my eyes, the crowded, drafty little deckhouse seemed to change. In place of the bulky green couch there was Betty's small upright piano, which would take much less room, and in the corner where Ed stood there was a glowing fireplace.

"Do you want to drive back tonight?" Ed asked, rudely breaking into my fantasy. "If you don't, there's a good inn near here. If your wife could fly to Washington, we could drive over to meet her in the morning."

"That sounds sensible."

The inn was aggressively old-fashioned and overcharming, but the rooms were comfortable and the bar was good. While I waited for a man to finish with the only pay telephone, I sipped a cold martini and made up a sort of sales pitch to give Betty. This was a mistake, I told myself suddenly. If I sounded too enthusiastic, she would feel that she had to approve of the boat even if she hated it. If she didn't like the *Irish Mist,* it would be better to learn that right away, rather than let her dissatisfaction seep out gradually or explode in one wretched scene when we were halfway south.

"The phone's free now," Ed said.

It seemed to take a long while before the soft-voiced Southern operator got my New York number.

"Hello?" Betty said suddenly. "Hello? Did you see the boat?"

"Yes."

"Do you like her?"

"I want you to make up your own mind. Can you get a sitter and take the ten o'clock shuttle plane to Washington?"

"Yes. What's the boat like?"

"It would be better if I didn't influence you."

"Don't be maddening! Tell me about her."

"She has a lousy galley. Hardly any room at all."

"What else?"

"There's practically no storage space, compared to anything you've ever seen."

"But you still want her, or you wouldn't ask me to fly down. Why?"

"Because she's beautiful," I said helplessly. "Because I'm in love."

Betty laughed.

"Buy her," she said.

"I'm not sure she's practical. In any case, we'll have to have her inspected by experts."

"I thought you were good at that."

"I told you, I'm in love. It's ridiculous, I know, but I would forgive her her weaknesses."

"Buy her," she said again. "It's the only way to live."

"I don't want to do anything crazy. We have to get all sorts of

estimates for changes. I want to put in heat and air conditioning. There's a place for your piano and for a fireplace."

"My piano and a *fireplace?*"

"You can even have your precious vacuum cleaner."

"Are you buying a boat or a hotel?"

"A powerboat as graceful as a sailing ship."

"Not a shantyboat?"

"No shantyboat this. I better warn you, though. She's named
the *Irish Mist,* and everything is all over green."

"God. Why is she named after a brand of booze?"

"Booze?"

"It's a kind I never liked. Americans buy it in Ireland for
gifts."

"I don't know. The owner isn't very communicative. I'll
meet you at the information desk of the Washington airport at
eleven. Forget everything I've said about the boat and judge
for yourself."

"I'll get a sitter for Jessie." There was a pause before she
added, "We're going to buy this boat, aren't we?"

"Not unless you like her. Remember, she's going to be your
home for at least three years."

"If you love her, that's important. You shouldn't try to mess
up a thing like this with too much common sense."

"Or too little."

"It would be no fun starting out on a boat we hated," Betty
said.

"Or on one which I loved and you hated."

"I don't know enough about boats to have much of an
opinion."

"Women don't have to know much about boats in order to
hate them."

She laughed.

"See you tomorrow," she said. "Look for a girl in red foul-
weather gear. It's raining here, and if it still is, I'm going to
wear that new outfit you bought me."

After asking me to talk to Jessica, who didn't make much sense, she hung up, and I returned to the table, where Ed had ordered me another drink. The specialty of the house was crab cakes and fried oysters. I couldn't remember when seafood had ever tasted so good.

# 6
⚓

That night Ed and I sat at the bar swapping sea stories until very late. Perhaps as a none too subtle form of salesmanship, he had taken to calling me Skipper, a title some of the men who joined us over a beer also gave me. It had been just about twenty years since anyone had called me that, and even when I was in command of a freighter in the South Pacific, I hadn't been at all sure I deserved it, but still the name seemed to ring with nostalgic charm and a dashing quality that hadn't changed with time. Oxford is a salty town. It is full of fishermen, retired naval officers and men who make a living servicing and sailing yachts. Some of the men in the bar had seen the *Irish Mist*, and when Ed expansively introduced me as the vessel's new owner, it seemed to me that I was accorded a degree of respect which was part of the boat's aura. Right away I saw what Betty meant when she said I would never be content to be known as the owner of a shantyboat. More than a house or a car, a boat gives an instant report on her owner's taste, experience, and dreams, as well as his pocketbook. The fat houseboat must belong to a practical, sedentary man, and the overpowered, flashily designed cruiser must be the property of a man who has been so busy making money that he has never had a chance to learn anything about the sea. The fact that some houseboats belong to lithe young couples who, in defiance of common sense, skate them over to the Bahamas, and that some experienced old salts love high-powered flashily designed cruisers has noth-thing to do with the inner truth of the matter. A codger who buys a graceful, tall-sparred yawl which he never moves away from its slip in the marina still receives credit for being a sailing man, as well he should.

And so because of the *Irish Mist* I was given the deference due a sailor with an eye for fine lines, expert craftsmanship, beautiful wood and seagoing equipment. At two in the morning I happily went to bed in a small room upstairs and fell into a dreamless sleep.

It was dawn when I awoke. My mouth felt dry, my head ached, and though I could think of no good reason, I felt as guilty and depressed as though I had been on a monstrous binge.

Going to the window of my room, I looked out over Chesa-peake Bay. A soft rain was falling, and in the first light of day the heavy clouds covering the sky looked as ominous as though they concealed hurricanes. Glancing at my watch, I saw that it was a little after six. In five hours Betty would be arriving in Washington. Now in the gray light of dawn before I had coffee, I had better have one look at the boat all by myself.

Quickly I dressed and, without waking Ed, stole down to the car. Within ten minutes I was driving down the narrow private road that belonged to the owner of the *Irish Mist*. As I ap-proached his big house, I slowed to a crawl to make as little noise as possible and put out my lights. Parking by the water's edge, I walked to a spot from which I could get a good view of the old yacht. There she was, moored in such a way that she seemed to be coming straight across the cove at me, looming out of the morning fog. Whatever the weaknesses of the boat might be, she still had that special kind of beauty which quickened my pulse and made me want her with unreasonable passion, the very quality that should be most important in a boat or a woman. Ignoring the rain, I lit my pipe and leaned against the glistening bark of a big tree. All my life, despite every effort to be practical, I had chosen women simply because they had the ability to excite me, and with occasional exceptions, the women I had known had always treated me well. Somewhere I had read that the mind acts as a giant computer, quickly sorting out facts fed into it over a lifetime in order to come up with a quick decision that appears irrational only at first. Because of differences in our age and background, many people had thought Betty and I had been foolish to marry, but after three years she still retained for me much the same sort of magic I saw in this boat, a kind of attraction no less powerful because it couldn't easily be expressed in words. Like the boat, Betty, who had been a professional dancer since the age of fourteen, was graceful, and like the boat, she had the ability to make a humdrum life turn into a romance, even though that was a word forty-six-year-old men weren't supposed to use. I was much happier with her than I would be with a woman who, whatever her beauty or other virtues, was unable to help me conquer the flatness of life, and I was suddenly sure that I would be happy with this boat, if only because it appeased my strange requirements for the raw materials of a dream. If the yacht had weaknesses, it would be more fun to learn how to live with them than it would be to set sail on a vessel which pleased nothing but my common sense. As Betty herself had said, the decision to live aboard a boat with a woman and child in the Bahamas is not in itself practical and should not be pursued in too practical a way. A vessel ugly enough to rob the dream of charm would be entirely self-defeating.

She's a grand old boat, I thought with a grin and climbed back into the car. Although I shut the door softly, some dogs started to bark. As I turned around, the tall figure of the owner of the boat appeared on the terrace. Dressed in a bathrobe, he stood staring first at me, then at the old boat at the end of the pier. Just before the trees cut me from his view, I saw him take shelter under the eaves of his house, where, like me, he could stand and smoke while he contemplated the sweet lines of his *Irish Mist.*

After a breakfast of ham and eggs served with old-fashioned Southern hominy grits, Ed and I started the two-hour drive to Washington. The rain was coming down hard now, and a north wind whipped it in almost horizontal sheets across the highway. It was a day on which one should sit and dream before a fire instead of preparing to venture to sea in a narrow yacht.

"It's a hell of a morning to ask a woman to look at a boat," Ed said moodily.

"Yes."

"Does she usually follow your lead?" he asked, obviously beginning to worry about his sale.

"Usually," I said, but then I remembered an apartment we had looked at in New York. Enthusiastic about its huge living room and its garden terrace, I had eagerly put down a deposit.

"Isn't it great?" I had said to Betty, and only then had I noticed that she was crying.

"Don't worry," she had said, clenching her teeth. "I'll learn to like it."

"What on earth is wrong with it?"

"There's just a living room and a terrace. There's practically no kitchen at all, and we'll have to sleep on a convertible couch in the living room. When the children visit, we'll all be in one room. . . ."

On that occasion, the real estate agent had been kind enough to give me my deposit back. Had I been overoptimistic in assuming that Betty would be willing to overlook the miserable cooking facilities aboard the *Irish Mist* and the staterooms which, after all, were no bigger than our apartment's bathrooms?

"The name of the boat is unfortunate," I said to Ed. "My wife is the only unsentimental person of Irish descent who ever lived."

"You should change it anyway."

"Why?"

"Well, in my business you see lots of men who love boats and lots of wives who frankly hate them. One way to get over that hurdle is to name your boat after your wife. That's an honor no woman can take lightly. It makes a woman feel pretty good to see her name in big gold letters on a boat's stern. Once that name is there, most women don't object so much to spending money on a boat."

"That's sneaky."

"But it works. No woman wants to see a boat that is named after her go in need of a coat of paint."

"I'll think about it. I also think I better begin by promising to put in a new galley. Maybe we could tear out a couple of bunks. We don't need so much sleeping space."

"When you talk to her, don't call it a galley," he said.

"Why?"

"Call it a kitchen. Most women hate nautical terminology. It makes them feel insecure or something, and they think a man who uses it is putting them on."

"Maybe you're right."

"Did you ever know a woman who really liked boats?"

"My mother didn't, and neither did my first wife. Let's talk about something else."

"You'd be surprised how many boats are sold after the first cruise," Ed continued morosely. "For Christ's sake, don't get out in rough weather right away. One little squall and I'd had it with my wife."

"I promised Betty that we'd plan a chicken cruise. If we watch the weather, I figure we might take short hops from island to island without ever getting caught in anything at all."

"Better stick to the canals at first."

"I plan to."

"And warn her about wakes. Not the Irish kind. When some of those fast sports fishermen or big tugs pass you, they can really set you rolling."

That I had not thought about when I had boasted to Betty about taking a long cruise without even spilling a teacup. I looked worried.

"Name the boat after her," Ed repeated.

# 7

⚓

The rain slowed us, and Betty was already waiting near the information booth of the Washington airport when we arrived. She was wearing the fancy foul-weather gear I had bought for her at Abercrombie and Fitch for our third wedding anniversary, and she was frowning.

"What's the matter?" I said apprehensively. "You look angry."

"I had a rotten flight."

"Was it rough?"

"No. Tell me, do I look ridiculous?"

In the red leather slacks and brilliant red vinyl jacket which Abercrombie and Fitch had declared to be fashionable for the yachting set, I thought she looked marvelous, especially with the salty old yellow sou'wester I had provided as a rain hat.

"You look adventurous."

"I thought so too, but nobody would sit beside me."

"What do you mean?"

"I was the first one on the plane. All these men came on, took one look at me and sat somewhere else. The seat beside me was the last one filled, and the man who finally took it looked everywhere else first."

"Most men nowadays are frightened by anything out of the ordinary."

"Nothing like that ever happened to me before. Am I getting old?"

"Hardly."

"I'm never going to wear these things again, even if they are practical."

Walking across the parking lot to the car, she was grateful for her foul-weather gear, however. Ed and I, in ordinary topcoats, were soaked.

"Great day for looking at a boat," he said with determined cheer.

The rain drummed so tightly on the steel roof that he had to shout.

"Why?" Betty asked.

"A boat is a snug place on a day like this. We'll make a cup of tea."

"Of course you're going to have to have a new kitchen," I added nervously. "We're going to put in a hundred-and-ten-volt generator. That will mean you can have a washing machine and anything else you want."

"Really?"

"When you see the boat, remember that she doesn't have to be painted green. Paint is cheap. She can be any color you want."

"Is she really named the *Irish Mist?*"

"I'm going to change it to *Betty,*" I said recklessly. "How would you like that?"

"I think that's a terrible name for a boat."

"A pretty boat like this deserves the name of a pretty girl," Ed said gallantly.

"The *Pretty Betty,*" I said with inspiration. "That's a marvelous name for a graceful boat."

"You're not being fair."

"Why not?" Ed and I asked simultaneously.

"Any woman would be flattered by that, and you know I never can stand up against flattery."

"The boat is like you," I said. "Honestly she is."

"Exactly how?"

"She's beautifully built and mysteriously exciting."

"They all told me I never should marry a writer."

"She will move gracefully."

"And she's getting old."

"This kind of boat never grows old," Ed said. "She will always be fashionable."

Reflecting that Betty, like most people, is usually optimistic immediately after a good meal, I stopped at a fancy restaurant just outside of Oxford and ordered steaks. While they were cooking, Ed and I sipped martinis and Betty toyed with a glass of sherry. Words came hard, and in long intervals of silence we could hear the rain, which seemed to be a lasting deluge.

"My father always liked to look at houses on rainy days," Betty said. "That's when you can tell if the roof and windows leak."

"They won't on this boat," Ed said. "She's tight as a drum."

His voice, I noticed, sounded forced, and he gulped his drink. I sneezed.

"Why didn't you wear your foul-weather gear?" Betty asked me accusingly.

"It wasn't raining when I left."

"Can you buy a change of clothes in Oxford?"

"Of course," Ed said.

The steaks looked good when they arrived, but after a few bites none of us felt hungry.

"Come on," Betty said, putting down her fork suddenly. "Let's go see this boat. I can't wait any longer."

"You've got to imagine what the galley, I mean, the kitchen, can be like," I said nervously as we got back into the car. "You've got to use your imagination."

"I thought that on a boat 'galley' was the right word for kitchen."

"You don't have to call it that. It doesn't make any difference."

"Everybody I know calls a kitchen on a boat a galley."

"I'm just trying to say that nautical terminology isn't important."

"We might as well start out right. I don't want to be lubberly."

"You don't want to be *what?*"

"Lubberly. My Scotch grandfather was a sailor. Didn't I tell you that? He was trained in the British Merchant Marine, and the worst thing he could call a person was *lubberly.*"

"I think your grandfather would like this boat," Ed said, brightening.

"My grandmother likes the idea of it," Betty continued, turning to me. "I called Grammy last night after talking to you, and do you know what she said?"

"What?" I asked, suddenly caring a great deal about the answer. On the few occasions I had visited Betty's Scotch grandmother in Brooklyn, the old lady had, without saying much, given me the impression that she somehow knew everything of any importance in the world, and I knew that all her children and grandchildren respected her in a way that is supposed to be common but isn't.

"She said Grampy used to talk about taking her to live on a boat, right up to the day he died. She said she didn't know that dreams could be inherited."

"You'll have to bring her aboard," Ed said.

"I asked her if she'd like that, but she said she's too old ever to leave her house now. There comes a time when memory takes the place of dreams, she said."

"Your grandmother sounds like a remarkable woman," Ed said. "I'll give you a snapshot of the boat to send her. We're almost there."

As we turned off the highway onto the private road leading to the pier where the *Irish Mist* was moored, Betty looked scared, and I guessed that she was wondering what she would do if she hated the boat at first sight. Her eyes widened when she saw the big house which belonged to the owner of the boat, and I suspected that she wished that we had come to look at that instead of an old yacht. Emerging from the trees, we came to the spot at the water's edge from which the boat was visible, and stopped. To me the *Irish Mist* had lost none of her charm. Even in the driving rain, her pale-green hull and white deckhouse gleamed, and her knifelike bow and low superstructure made her look as though she longed to escape the heavy lines which bound her to the dock.

"There she is," I said, waving a hand toward her with elaborate nonchalance.

Betty said nothing, but her face looked the way it did when the curtain went up on the first act of a good play. Getting out of the car, she walked to the pier with Ed and me following silently. The tide was in, and the boat was riding high, her deck even with the pier, and perhaps 4 feet away from it. There was no gangplank.

"Can we go aboard?" Betty asked.

"Yes," Ed and I replied simultaneously.

Betty paused and let her eyes travel from the stern to the bow and back again. The rain rattled loudly on the green awnings.

"I'll give you a hand," Ed said, jumping aboard.

I followed to help. We were both heavy men, and our weight served to heel the narrow old vessel just enough to dump on our heads a quantity of water which had gathered in a place where the awnings sagged. The shock of the cold water made me gasp, and I felt this was a terrible time for the boat to play a prank like that.

"Damn!" Ed said, rubbing the water from his eyes.

We were both afraid Betty would laugh at us or, worse, would be alarmed, but perhaps out of tact she stood staring at the bow, her face expressionless.

"I'll give you a hand," Ed repeated, reaching toward her. Taking hold of one of the lines, I started to pull the boat toward the dock.

"No need."

Betty, who weighs 112 pounds and who started her training as a dancer at the age of three, always moves effortlessly, and she arrived beside us on the deck without a jolt. Going to the stern, Ed slid open the hatch to the owner's stateroom. In the after cockpit she stood looking around for a moment before following him down. Her face seemed pale, her lipstick unusually bright. From her expression it was impossible to tell what she was thinking. Not wanting to crowd the little stateroom, I stood in the companionway.

"You can see that you've got plenty of room here," Ed said, his voice booming with a heartiness that seemed patently false. "The shower has hot and cold running water, and the toilet flushes electrically."

Without saying anything, Betty sat on one of the bunks and jounced up and down.

"Innerspring mattresses," Ed said.

Wordlessly Betty opened the door to the clothes locker and pulled open the drawers under the bunks.

"Plenty of storage space," Ed said.

"Show me the other cabins."

We went to the deckhouse. With the rain beating against the big glass ports, it was damp and the imitation green leather covering the couch felt clammy.

"We can replace that couch with your piano, and I plan to put a little fireplace in this corner," I said quickly. "We also will put in electric heaters."

"How much will that cost?"

"I asked the superintendent of the yard to stop in so we can get some estimates," Ed said. "He should be here any minute. Anyway, we're not talking about a lot of money, especially in view of the low asking price. If you set out to build a boat like this today, she would cost you more than two hundred thousand dollars, even if you could find the skilled craftsmen."

"Why is she going so cheap?"

"Do you want an honest broker's answer?" Ed asked.

"I'm not sure," I said.

He laughed.

"Fundamentally, this was designed as a rich man's boat. She cost about seventy thousand dollars to build, way back in nineteen hundred and thirty when that was a fortune, and she was meant to have a steward and professional captain. She's still in grand condition, but she's not a rich man's boat anymore. The rich want something new, something with more room, something faster. Yet she's not a poor man's boat either—anything fifty-four feet long, especially with all this brightwork, isn't cheap to keep up. And anything this size isn't handy for a novice. She's beautiful, but she isn't the easiest boat in the world to sell. What she needs is a man who has had experience enough to run her, who needs the room for living aboard, yet can't afford a new boat. . . ."

While she listened, I noticed that Betty was stroking the smooth mahogany paneling in the deckhouse with the fingers of her right hand, but she didn't say anything in reply to Ed. His voice trailed off. Silently Betty descended the four steps leading to the forward stateroom, poked the mattresses on the bunks and opened the door to the clothes locker. It smelled of mildew. Closing it, she started toward the door that led to the galley.

"There's one thing about the galley," I said. "It's so awful that you know it has to be changed right away."

"Don't forget its advantages," Ed said. "Professional cooks have turned out elaborate meals there for years. It's small but very practical. The refrigerator has enough room for a month's supply of frozen food."

Opening the door to the galley, Betty found that her nose almost touched the tiny Shipmate stove even before she went in.

"God!"

She made the one word ring with eloquence.

"We could take out the forward bulkhead and expand the galley right into the forecastle," I said.

"Where do people eat?" Betty asked.

"A table fits into the deck here, between these bunks. The owner will tell us where it is. I'll go see if he's in."

Looking nervous, Ed left. Betty opened the door to the oven, which looked as though one chicken would fill it, and peered into the refrigerator. Turning to the sink, which was less than a foot square, she said, "How do you wash dishes?"

"We can put in a bigger sink if we take this partition down. Look in here."

Opening a door, I stepped into the forecastle, a V-shaped compartment which was extremely narrow because of the knife-like bow. Two pipe berths were folded against the sides. Since there wasn't room for her to step in beside me, she stood in the doorway.

"What was this place for?" she asked.

"Crew's quarters. They have their own washing facilities and everything."

I showed her a folding sink and a toilet covered by a box.

"Do you mean two men had to live in here?"

"Sailors are used to cramped quarters."

"Rich people are bastards. No one but a bastard would make two men live up here."

"It will make a nice extension to the galley."

Before she could answer, there was a thump on deck and three men came into the forward stateroom, completely filling it. They were Ed, the owner and a short, stout man whom Ed introduced as the superintendent of a local boatyard.

"I want to make this into a modern galley," I said, finding myself talking very fast. "How much do you think it would cost to remove this bulkhead, take out the pipe berths and make room for a big sink and stove?"

"This galley has always worked out well," the owner said, sounding hurt.

"It's hard to give estimates without a detailed plan," the superintendent said, taking off a dripping blue cap and scratching his head. "Do you know what I advise?"

"What?" Betty asked.

"Don't make a lot of big changes right away. It would be wise to live with the boat for a while first. A new galley could run you anything from one to ten thousand."

Betty said nothing. Leaving the galley, she sat down on a bunk in the forward stateroom. Everyone looked at her.

"I think you're right," she said.

"We're buying this boat to live aboard, not just for a few weekends," I said. "We've got to have heat at least. How much would a new one-hundred-ten-volt generator cost?"

"We never needed that," the owner said. "The oven heats her pretty well."

"I'll get you some price lists," the superintendent said. "A new six-and-a-half-kilowatt diesel generator will run you about three thousand dollars installed."

"Do you have any tea aboard?" Ed asked the owner.

"I think there's some over the sink."

"Mind if I put a pot on?"

"Go ahead."

Betty edged past the three men and went on deck. I followed and found her standing under the dripping awning, looking down into the gray water of the bay.

"We don't have to get this boat," I said.

"Will we ever find better for the money?"

"We can find more room."

"But not with such beauty."

Reaching forward, she ran her fingers along a polished mahogany handrail.

"Probably not."

"We could make out all right here. Even with that galley. You can put up with anything if you really want to."

"If you turned out to be miserable. . . ."

"Can you take this boat to the Bahamas safely?"

"I think so."

"Can you fix this rail so Jessie won't fall through it?"

"We can lace canvas all around it."

She took a deep breath.

"Let's buy her."

"If it doesn't make you happy. . . ."

"Is this what you've always wanted? Is this some approximation of your dream?"

"This boat with you content aboard her, yes. Not with you miserable. That would be. . . ."

"I promised you to love, honor and obey, not to be happy, happy, happy all the time."

"You know what I mean."

"We could be proud of this boat. We're both foolish that way."

"Yes."

"I don't know anything about boats, but I love the way she looks. She's got real class. And she's so sleek. Is she very fast?"

"She used to be with gas engines, but not with these heavy diesels. They were designed for reliability and economy."

"Sleek, reliable and economical. That doesn't sound like such a bad combination."

"And uncomfortable. Let's not kid ourselves. Even aside from that terrible galley, there's not much space."

"That's not true. The three cabins could be very snug. They just need rugs and some decent curtains and . . ."

"How about washing the dishes in that sink?"

"We can use paper plates and throw them overboard."

I kissed her, moving clumsily to do so, and the awning spilled more water on us. She laughed.

"If fools can have such fun," I said, "I thank the Lord for not making me wise."

# 8

⚓

After that, as Betty remarked later, everything seemed to move like a crazily speeded-up movie. When we went below, the three men in the forward stateroom looked at us expectantly, sensing that some decision had been made.

"Could you come up on deck a moment?" I asked Ed.

He followed me to the helm while Betty sat down in the deckhouse.

"He's asking eighteen thousand," I said to Ed. "I suppose I should offer sixteen."

"He's just come down from twenty-three," Ed said uncomfortably. "The engines alone are worth at least ten. And a short while ago he got scared of metal fatigue and had all the fastenings below the waterline drawn and replaced. It cost him two thousand eight hundred dollars. He was just telling me."

I hesitated.

"Christ, look at the hull," Ed pressed on. "She looks as though she just came from the builder. And think of the equipment you're getting. A ship-to-shore radio. A Dyer dinghy with outboard and sailing rig. That alone is worth . . ."

"How about seventeen?"

"This guy has his pride—you can tell that by the way the boat is kept up. God knows how much he has put into her. It's hard to sell a boat at a loss. If you try to quibble. . . ."

"All right, give him the eighteen, conditional upon a survey. How soon can we have her inspected?"

"We'll have to find out. I'll make a few calls."

Suddenly I became aware of the urgency of time. In a few days the lease on our apartment would expire. In a month winter winds would start to howl down Chesapeake Bay. Within six weeks we should be in Florida.

"Let's get moving," I said.

Ed ducked into the deckhouse and took a printed contract from his pocket. The owner came to the companionway from the forward stateroom.

"I like your boat," I said. "I'll give you the eighteen thousand."

"Good."

His voice betrayed neither sorrow nor enthusiasm. Feeling that some sort of gesture was required, I put out my hand and he shook it perfunctorily.

"I suppose you'll need an inventory of all the equipment," he said.

"That's a lot of trouble. I'll trust you not to strip her."

"I'll want to take the ship's clock and barometer. Sentimentality, if you like."

"All right. If she passes the inspection, I may want to make some alterations before the change of title actually goes through. Will that be all right?"

"She'll pass the inspection. What do you intend to do to her?"

"Put canvas around the rail so my daughter won't fall overboard. Change the generator and the name."

"What are you going to call her?"

"The *Pretty Betty*. Private reasons."

"That figures," he said, his voice sounding curiously hurt, and I thought of all that green paint, the mystique of the Irish or some private dream of his own which he apparently felt was being spurned. Turning on his heel, he said to Ed, "I suppose you'll take care of the details," and strode ashore, his tall figure bent against the rain.

"You sign here and give me a check for one thousand eight hundred dollars," Ed said. "It will be returned if the survey doesn't go well."

I signed. His job done, Ed hurried off to get a bus for New York.

"Do you want me to haul her for the survey?" the superintendent of the yard asked.

"Yes. How long do you think it will take to put a canvas dodger around her and to put in a bigger generator?"

"A couple of weeks. Can you come over to the yard and go over some price lists?"

"Right away."

While I was in his yard, it became obvious to me that all work should be done at once, and I ordered a small fireplace made of soapstone and chromium and arranged to have the couch in the deckhouse pulled out to make room for our piano. The superintendent said he didn't know what the installation of the piano would cost, but somehow that instrument seemed an important part of my dream, and I plunged ahead.

It was almost dark when after one more visit to take detailed measurements of the cabins aboard the boat, we got in the car.

"There's one more thing," I said. "Before we go back to New York, we better make reservations at the inn here, starting the first of October. The boat won't be ready for us then, but we'll need a place to live, and I'll want to be nearby to keep an eye on the work."

"Won't that be expensive?"

"I'm trying my best not to worry about that. You can't live aboard a boat with workmen crawling all over her. It's no way to start."

The woman behind the desk at the inn gave me a blank to fill out. Before writing in the space for my address I hesitated and then wrote, "The yacht *Pretty Betty,* of New York."

"We have lots of yachtsmen staying here," the woman said, glancing at it.

"So," Betty said as we turned and headed toward the car. "What does that mean?"

"So we're yachtsmen. I never thought we'd end up that."

"I don't feel like a yachtsman."

"Don't be so modest. We have a yacht."

"Yachtsmen are silly people who wear white flannel trousers and blue jackets and don't have to make a living. And they go on cruises. I don't think we're doing that."

"Aren't we going on a cruise to the Bahamas?"

"Not really. People who take cruises have homes to come back to. We don't. We're really looking for a home."

"Yes," she said, and after we got in the car she added, "Do you think we might really make a permanent home in the Bahamas?"

"There are a lot of advantages," I said, trying to keep my tone light. "Aside from the weather, I mean. Jessie would grow up to be a sailing girl instead of a pasty-faced city kid."

"Yes."

"There would be no tax man to worry about—no income tax, no property tax, no inheritance tax, no taxes at all. And if my son lived with us, he wouldn't be drafted."

"Would you give up your American citizenship?"

She sounded disapproving.

"I don't know. Moving to the Bahamas isn't exactly defecting, I think."

"But we don't have to make up our minds for a long while."

"Not till Jessie has to be in school. Till then we can try one place after another. If we want to, we can even sail back to New York and tie right up at the Seventy-ninth Street pier."

"It's good to know that," she said and, putting her head back, slept.

It was after midnight when we returned to our apartment, which, with most of the furniture already gone, seemed to offer cold welcome. Exhausted, I went to bed. When I awoke in the morning it was to a scene of extreme confusion. Betty had emptied every closet and drawer and had laid all our clothes and personal possessions out in the middle of the bedroom and living room floors.

"Pick what you want to take with you," she said. "I just realized that the old chestnut of deciding what you would like to take to a desert island with you is no longer a joke."

"Can't I have some coffee first?"

"It's already made, but start thinking. I've called the Salvation Army man, and he is going to be here in an hour. There's no use storing all these clothes."

Going to the kitchen, I poured a cup of black coffee and put bread in the toaster.

"We can't take the toaster," she said. "There's no room in the galley for it. We'll have to use the broiler in the oven."

"All right."

"I figure you can take two good suits in case you have to fly somewhere for business. Will we need evening clothes?"

"No."

"I'm going to limit myself to five summer dresses and one outfit for cold weather. If we load up those little closets right away, it will be miserable."

"All right."

"Will we need overcoats?"

"Yes, it probably will be cold on the way down, and even in Florida. . . ."

"We can have two sweaters apiece. Look, I think we should sort everything into five piles: the first to take with us, the second to store, the third to give to relatives or friends, the fourth to give to the Salvation Army and the fifth to throw away. And be ruthless, please! We shouldn't start by loading the boat up like a hay cart."

With a curious kind of apathy my eye traveled over possessions that had accumulated and been dragged from one house to another for 20 years, ever since the end of the war. Some decisions were easy to make. Obviously the riding boots and the jodhpurs should be thrown away, unless the Salvation Army or some 220-pound horseman wanted them, which appeared unlikely. Most of the fancy sport coats were too small for me now— I had grown out of my dashing period, but I had several friends of my former size who were still in theirs. The binoculars I had bought for weekend cruising long ago would come in handy. My old Coast Guard uniforms would have to be discarded, for the boat did not offer room for sentimentality. Except a little, perhaps. The dress sword I had bought at the beginning of the war, when regulations still required it, but which I had never used in any parade, might make a fitting ornament if I could find a place to hang it in the deckhouse.

"Will I need my mink stole?" Betty asked.

"No. But maybe on cool nights in Palm Beach or Miami. . . ."

"It doesn't take much room."

Quickly I sorted out my belongings, keeping the pile that was to go with us as small as possible. The sight of so many clothes laid out for the Salvation Army man bothered me. It looked as though a relative had just died.

"We better pack the stuff we're going to take with us in cardboard boxes and store our suitcases," Betty said. "There's no place at all for them on the boat."

"I was going to tell you that."

"I'm worried about Jessie's toys."

"Where is Jessie?"

"With the people across the hall. She kept getting into things."

"You can take her favorite dolls and games and stuff. We can give her the whole forecastle."

"But not her pedal car, and she loves that. I've already arranged to leave it with Mona. Or give it to her. Jessie will be too old for it if we ever come back."

A look of sadness creased Betty's face, but she shook her head and it went away.

"We have to take the cat," she said. "I know I promised that we wouldn't, but with this we have to think of Jessie first. She's all excited about having kittens."

"Oh, Lord!"

"Don't lots of people on boats have cats?"

"Yes. If it's important to Jessie, we'll take the cat."

"Why don't you want to?"

"I hate the thought of a sandbox in a cramped space. You know how I am about the smell, even here. . . ."

"When I tried to tell her we were going to give the cat to Mona, she cried. After all, she's seeing so much disappear."

"We'll take the cat. When are the kittens due?"

"I don't know. Not right away, I hope. Do you want to take your electric typewriter?"

"I thought we could make a big table for it in the after stateroom. With the new generator. . . ."

"Fine. How about the great big encyclopedia?"

Before I had time to answer, the telephone rang. It proved to be a friend wanting to know exactly what we had to give away. While Betty was giving her the list, which sounded like a quick reading of the Sears, Roebuck catalog, the doorbell rang, and I let in the Salvation Army man, who stood scratching his head in astonishment at the Oriental bazaar confronting him.

Giving things away depresses me. When it comes to personal possessions, I am by nature a hoarder, while Betty is a born housecleaner.

"I like to see useless things go where they might conceivably do someone some good," she said, giving the Salvation Army man an opera cape my father had occasionally worn. A loud plaid jacket I had sported on many a suburban terrace when I was a young man followed. With her own clothes she was just as firm. The white woolen dress she had worn when we got married in the Dublin registry and the first dancing slippers she had bought as a young girl were added to the heap.

"There was a tribe of Indians on the West Coast that had

competitions to see who could burn the most possessions," I said wryly.

"They should have had a Salvation Army."

A black beaded dress she had bought in Paris while we were on our honeymoon landed on top of the heap. Feeling acutely uncomfortable, I said, "Can you handle the rest of this job alone?"

"If I have to. Why?"

"I've got to make some arrangements about paying for the boat. Anyway, Mort wants to see me."

"Coward."

"I hate to see the past disappear."

"You can't take it with you."

"Damn it, I'm not dying."

"If we're really going to start a new life, we have to kill the old one. That's why most people never really start anything new. They're chained by old lamps and bureaus left to them by their grandmothers."

"I feel dispossessed."

"Think of the boat," she said. "Think of the Bahamas. That's what I'm trying to do."

Mort Leavy, the lawyer and business manager who was trying to help me out of the financial troubles I had got into before I met him, looked glum when I told him I had just contracted to buy a yacht for $18,000.

"It's going to be my home," I said defensively. "Also my office."

"The tax people won't believe that. They never believe in boats."

"Half the yachts over forty feet long are owned by corporations. A guy who sells them fuel and sees their credit cards told me that."

"You've got to prove you entertain customers. Are you going to entertain your editors?"

"I hope not."

"The tax boys will never go for it. You're in trouble enough with them now."

As always, I wanted to shout *why?* but that was a long story involving not only prior lawyers but many foolishnesses of my own as well as the vast confusion of tax laws.

"In the Bahamas there are no taxes," I said wistfully.

"For the Bahamians. I think you're going to have to take out a loan."

"You mean I don't have eighteen thousand dollars? What happened to. . . ."

"I don't keep that kind of money liquid. How soon do you need it?"

"As soon as the boat passes her inspection. Maybe a week."

"If some of these decisions go against us, the tax boys could come after your boat. They generally leave you enough to live, but not on a yacht."

"I think I can live cheaper on the boat than in New York. How many people do you know who have a house that costs as little as eighteen thousand dollars?"

"Plenty. Give me some time to think about it. I'm sure we can work something out."

"The boat will give me all kinds of material for books," I said. "It's a business expense."

"The tax boys will never believe it. I told you, they get very suspicious about boats."

"I am not a free citizen. Ever since I first wrote a best seller, the Goddamn tax men. . . ."

"Please don't get started on that," Mort interrupted, looking pained.

"I'm not bitching about high taxes. I'm saying I never know where I stand. I never know my net worth."

"Don't ask them. They might tell you."

"After five novels, three of them best sellers, and two movies that made millions of dollars, I can't buy an eighteen-thousand-dollar home? I'd like to do an article—"

"I told you we'd find a way. Please don't stir up a big tax

thing. You've got to realize that no one will ever sympathize with you. Rich people crying about taxes just make the average guy glad."

"But as you have so well pointed out, I'm not rich."

"You live good, don't you? Who's planning to take off and go yachting in the Bahamas?"

"Me. About that I know I should be grateful."

The telephone rang, and some other client started shouting at Mort about taxes. Getting up, I waved a hand in farewell, and hunching the telephone receiver to his ear with his shoulder, he held out both hands in a gesture of helplessness.

"Things will work out," he said, either to me or to his other client. "Just give me a few days and I'll come up with a plan. . . ."

The thought of being cold broke in the Bahamas and having the boat attached by the tax men made my stomach churn. Walking rapidly to the Harvard Club, I went to the bar and ordered a martini.

"How's Captain Courageous?" an old friend asked.

"Fine. I just found the boat. Want to see a picture of her?"

Taking out my wallet like a fond father, I showed everyone near me a rather blurred photograph of the *Irish Mist* which Ed Krammer had given me.

"Boy," my friend said. "She's a real beauty!"

Several of the other men gave low whistles. After two more martinis I began to think of myself as a fearless adventurer dedicated to the pursuit of new worlds.

It was disappointing to find that around two thirty in the afternoon my friends had to go back to work. Since my office was now in cardboard boxes, I could not satisfy my conscience and my financial fears by emulating them. Instead I walked to Abercrombie and Fitch, a dangerous store for a man who loves boats and has just had a good lunch with three martinis. There I ordered a barometer of polished brass and a good ship's clock to match. They were expensive, but a sailor is always caught between the fear of financial folly and the need for nautical safety. It would be foolish to set to sea without a barometer, and the ship's clock, with its merry ring of bells which had nothing to do with the landsman's striking of the hour, was important to me, bringing back memories of the first cruise on which my parents had taken me, long ago, aboard a small schooner they had bought when I was thirteen years old.

"You better start by learning the bells," my mother had said. Although she got seasick easily, she had been born and brought up near the Naval Academy, which both her brother and her father had attended, and she knew how a ship's clock struck and many other interesting things.

Arranging for the barometer and clock to be mailed to the boat at Oxford, I went upstairs and ordered a full set of the newest charts for the Bahamas and the intra-coastal water route to Florida. Then there were navigation books to buy, tide and current tables, light lists and the *Nautical Almanac*, which I found I now only half-understood. Soon I should buy a chronometer and a sextant, but they were very expensive, and I decided to try some pawnshops around the waterfront.

It was six o'clock in the afternoon when I got back to the apartment, laden with packages. To my astonishment I found a boisterous party in progress.

"I called a few friends who I thought might want to take some of this stuff, and the word got around," Betty said, shouting in order to be heard above our portable record player, which sat in the middle of the pile of things to go with us. "Some of them brought bottles. They're giving us a farewell party."

The noise and confusion were such that I was tempted to grab Betty and the baby and leave forthwith. Instead I found a glass of bourbon being pushed into my hand and an eager crowd surrounding me.

The three martinis I had had for lunch had worn off, and in view of my hopes concerning the sobering effects of our cruise, I was reluctant to start drinking again. I was tired. The room was full of smoke, and the din of a new dance group on the phonograph was increased by a young woman, sitting on a pile of packing cases, who kept giving high, cackling laughs as though she had just laid the books which surrounded her. Here, surrounded by so many friends, as well as by the possessions I had accumulated over my entire adult life, I grew more and more morose, for clearly there was something deeply the matter with me. Betty, who passed from group to group, patting an arm here and kissing a cheek there, looked misty-eyed, as reluctant to say good-bye to her friends as she was eager to cast out ancient possessions, but I, vile from birth, felt just the opposite. Secretly I wanted to hoard every tattered garment that had hung unused in my closets for decades, but I could hardly wait to get rid of this collection of people to whom I had been sending Christmas cards and invitations to cocktail parties for so many years. Faded, frenetic, semialcoholic, gossipy, bubbling with excited reports about the business and sexual adventures of one another, my friends suddenly seemed to me to be at best worthy of compassion, at worst deserving of contempt.

"What's the matter?" Betty asked, passing me a bowl of peanuts. "You look miserable."

"I hate my friends."

My whisper was as hoarse and heavy as the snarl of a movie villain.

"Hush! What kind of way is that to talk?"

"A contemptible way, but I can't help it. Where did we ever find these people?"

"Be careful. Birds of a feather. . . ."

"I don't have feathers like Bert over there. What's the matter with his face?"

"Hush, he'll hear you!"

"He's so gray-looking and swollen."

"That happens if you drink so much that you stop eating."

Quickly I put my glass of bourbon down. Poor Bert, I thought—an advertising man facing his third divorce and near bankruptcy on a salary of $60,000 a year, he undoubtedly had reason enough to drink, and I should be admiring the grace

with which he was able to laugh and tell jokes at this farewell
party for an old friend.

"Skipper!" a fat man who had once been a poet and now
taught English in a business college said, lunging across the
room toward me. "We brought you a present!"

Accepting an elaborately wrapped parcel he held toward me,
I did my best to stammer out thanks while I tore the paper
from a child's yachting cap of the kind they sell at novelty shops,
with a little black visor and fake gold braid.

"Put it on," a tall, thin model shouted, waving an almost
skeletal arm in an imperious gesture.

The cap was absurdly small.

"Give us a grin," the model said and pointed a Polaroid
camera at me. "This is a moment we want to capture for eter-
nity."

I was tempted to grab her camera and smash it into her face,
an emotion which did not lose force because I knew it was
absurdly exaggerated. Hastily I reached for my drink, and the
picture she took showed me tilting up the glass, with that ridiculous cap askew on my graying head, in all ways a man who
looked as though he really belonged in that group.

The party lasted until late that night. Someone sent out for
Chinese food, a bowl of which was spilled on a red flannel
sport coat we had given to a bald man who filmed television
commercials. Exhausted by my attempts to be cheery and dulled
by too much bourbon, I went to Betty's and my room for a
quick nap, only to surprise a stout writer of detective stories
who had taken an aging editor of a women's magazine to my
bed. The encounter was all the more embarrassing because instead of making love, the woman was crying, emitting long,
racking sobs while the mystery writer hunched over her and
rubbed her back. Apparently they were both nude, and in the
dim light from the bathroom door, it looked as though his
figure was more feminine than hers. Fortunately they were so
engrossed in their private sorrow that they did not see me, and

I beat a hasty retreat to the kitchen, where Betty was serving hot coffee.

"I'm sorry they're staying so late," she whispered to me. "I didn't plan this."

"Nobody planned anything."

Cradling a cup of black coffee in my hands, I sat on a window ledge and stared at the beautiful view our apartment afforded of the downtown skyline.

"We can't say the city hasn't been good to us," Betty said, coming to sit beside me.

"No."

The woman who had been sitting all night on the packing cases gave her high cackling laugh again. Yes, I thought, this city has given me a career and a happy marriage, but God knows, it's time to leave. There was nothing in the world I wanted more than to cut and run.

# 9

⚓

$F$rantic though my desire to leave New York became, it was impossible to hurry the process. A retired merchant mariner in Oxford agreed to inspect the boat, but the yard was busy and could not promise to haul her out of the water for almost a week. Meanwhile I called Frank Bailey, who had been the engineering officer aboard the small tanker I had commanded in the South Pacific during the latter part of the war, and asked him if he could look at the *Irish Mist*'s engines and other mechanical equipment.

"Gosh, Skipper," he said, "I wish I could, but I just got out of the hospital, and now my wife's ready to go in."

He had, I knew, been dogged by ill health for many years, a fact which seemed incredible to me, for I still remembered him as a strong young man upon whom everyone aboard my ship had leaned.

"I wish you could go south with us," I said, recalling how cheerful he had been in the sweltering heat of the Philippines, even when the cargo pump on our tanker had broken down, flooding our bilges with gasoline. No one I had ever met knew more about engines than Frank or had such a curious ability to love them. To him they were not mysteries or maddeningly recalcitrant hunks of metal as they were to me.

"I wish I was well enough," he replied in his deep voice,

which hadn't changed at all since 1945. "What kind of engines have you got?"

I told him and added that they looked rusty, uncared-for over a period of years. He sighed like a mother hearing of a neglected child.

"How much are you paying for your boat?" he asked.

I told him.

"Do the engines run?"

"Yes."

"Any unusual sounds or heavy smoke?"

"Not that I noticed."

He sighed again.

"The only way I could really tell you about those engines is to take them all apart, and the doctor won't let me do anything like that. If you pay someone else to do it, it could cost you almost as much as repairs."

"What do you think I should do?"

"Take a chance and run 'em. Going down through the canals you can't get in much trouble. Keep an eye on the temperature gauges, and close them down if they heat up. By the time you get to Florida you ought to have a fairly good idea of what you've got."

"Is there any chance they might have to be completely replaced? They're about seven years old, and I have no idea how many hours are on them. The counters seem to have stopped."

He gave a deeper sigh this time.

"Yachtsmen," he said. "I suppose there are no engine room logs."

"No."

"Well, you're lucky you've got a good basic engine—they're a hard horse to kill. And you practically never have to replace *all* of a 4-71. They're available part by part, all over the world. It's unlikely that you'd have to spend more than three or four thousand bucks on them, unless they have to be hauled out and rebuilt."

"How much would that run?"

"Anything up to ten thousand, when you figure all the costs of taking them out and putting them in. Hell, maybe you'll be lucky and won't have to do anything. Buying secondhand diesels is like taking a ticket in a lottery. Here's hoping you win."

"Thanks," I said, unable to keep a little bitterness from my voice.

"If my wife gets better, I'll go over and take a look at them. Not that I'll be able to tell you much."

"Thanks," I said again, ashamed of asking so much from him during a crisis in his life. "Anyway, we can have a drink together."

"One. That's all my doctor allows."

Hanging up, I felt all my financial worries intensified. It was unlikely, he said, that I would have to spend more than three or four thousand dollars on the engines. How easily those figures had tripped off his tongue, and how easily they would have tripped off mine in the days when engine repairs had meant simply another government requisition.

Perhaps I should have stuck to sail after all, I told myself glumly. The *Irish Mist* was a mass of machinery, and in my years at sea I had always got along well with "the black gang" by never pretending that I knew anything at all about engines. With the pride of one who loved sail, I had boasted about my ignorance of everything mechanical, yet here I was ready to risk my family's life on my ability to keep two big diesels going. Beyond that, our comfort would depend on my skill at making the generator, the refrigeration plant, an air compressor, the electric toilets, and any number of other small motors work. Beginning to sweat, I walked down to a bookstore and bought some imposing volumes on the care and repair of diesel engines. Finding that I could make almost no sense out of them, I also bought a technical dictionary and went home to closet myself in my empty study.

How could I want to do something as much as I wanted to leave New York in order to live aboard a boat in the Bahamas and still be so terrified of it? There wasn't any answer to the question. And the realization that all my life I had been most afraid of what I most wanted didn't help.

As it turned out, the boatyard in Oxford was able to haul the *Irish Mist* for her survey ahead of schedule. At about three o'clock in the afternoon of the next day, the superintendent of the yard called and over the telephone introduced the inspector, who had a deep Southern voice.

"I checked her over pretty good," the man said. "I'll have a written report for you in a few days, but I thought you'd like to hear from me right away."

"What kind of condition is she in?"

"She's a fine old boat well-suited for her trade of plying semi-protected waters."

This, I knew, was an accurate statement, but I hated it.

"She can go anywhere" is the boast most yachtsmen like to make about their craft, however frail. But professionals know better, and almost all small motor yachts are suitable for, at best, semiprotected waters, into which category the Bahamas could be counted.

"The workmanship is superb," the old inspector continued. "I hope you're going to take care of her. In my business you realize she's one of the last of her breed. There just aren't any men alive who can build a boat like that anymore."

"I hope to take care of her."

"I can recommend her hull without reservations. Of course, it isn't my job to check the machinery."

"I'm going to take a chance on that."

As soon as I had hung up, I called Mort, my lawyer. He had found the cash for fulfilling my contract, but more money would have to be raised for impending tax bills.

"I'll get the check out right away," he said.

"Betty!" I called when I put the receiver down. "We've got a boat."

Coming from the kitchen, she put down a frying pan she had been drying.

"I guess the next step is to tell the family," she said.

We had agreed not to tell her father, my mother and my three grown children about our decision until we had actually bought a vessel. Oh, they knew we had been dreaming of living aboard a boat, and they even knew we had been looking for one, but we had so often talked about various schemes that concrete plans would surely come as a surprise. We guessed that such an abrupt and apparently quixotic change in our lives would alarm the old people and please the young ones, who could now look forward to seeing new parts of the world during Christmas, Easter and summer vacations.

Picking up the telephone, I called in turn my nineteen-year-old daughter, Lisa, at the University of Pennsylvania, my eighteen-year-old daughter, Rebecca, at Boston University, and my sixteen-and-a-half-year-old son at his boarding school in Vermont. When I told them we had actually bought a boat, they sounded dutifully delighted but not a little scared. Did they, like my sister, think that I was simply crazy? Children of any age want a stable father, I realized suddenly—adventures are fine for almost anyone but one's progenitor.

They tried to be enthusiastic, but their effort was apparent. Feeling guilty of crimes I could not name, I turned the telephone over to Betty, who began the long job of trying to get her father in Ireland while I set out to Gramercy Park to see my mother.

The closer I got to my mother's apartment, the more apprehensive I became. She was eighty that year and I was forty-six, but many things had not changed between us. Much of the time we still remained mysteries to each other, just as my own children and I remained largely unknown to each other despite all the powers of love.

I did not think that my mother would be much surprised to hear that I had bought a boat. For twenty years I had wanted to, and despite the fact that she herself was easily frightened by the water, the sea had played a large part in her life. Her father, John Danenhower, had been navigator of the famous

*Jeanette,* which on a naval expedition toward the North Pole in the 1870s had been caught in the ice for two years before sinking. My grandfather had been snow-blinded much of the time but had helped bring back the one small boat that survived. Blind and crippled, he had not lived long afterward, but his example had caused his son, my uncle, Sloan Danenhower, to take a World War I submarine far under the ice, just to prove it could be done.

At eighty my mother was fiercely independent. Despite long bouts of illness and despair, which she referred to as "this darn nervousness," she had lived alone for twenty-five years, ever since the death of my father, and she prided herself on never making demands. The same could not be said for her three middle-aged children. We all had busy lives and children of our own, but in the guise of worrying about our mother, we were always running back to her for long midnight conversations, because as long as she was there with her photographs of us as children and her tales of the amusing things our father had said, we ourselves were not growing old, and the world was still built upon a strict moral foundation.

At the door of her apartment my mother met me with a tremulous hug and asked Chester, the Negro man who has cooked, cleaned and driven for her ever since I can remember, to get us tea.

Chester told me the latest baseball scores while he took my coat. Sitting in front of a table her father had brought back from a cruise to China long before she was born, my mother said, "How's the work going?"

"Not much to do while the manuscript is being edited. Mother, I've bought a boat."

"How big?"

"Fifty-four feet. Big enough for Betty and Jessie and me to live aboard."

"Where?"

"We intend to go down the inland route to Florida. Then, maybe, the Bahamas."

"Well, you've always wanted to do that. . . ."

She gave me a smile that didn't seem forced.

"Yes."

"Are you happy about this?"

She was eyeing me sharply.

"Of course."

"You don't look happy. You look all upset."

"Of course, there always is strain involved in making decisions."

"Does Betty like the idea?"

"She seems to. I've promised not to get her into any rough water. At first we'll just be in the canals. Even in the Bahamas we plan to wait for the weather and stick to short hops."

"Then what are you worried about?"

"Money, partly. You know how it is with me and taxes."

She sighed.

"How much did the boat cost?"

I told her. "I'm probably going to have to put in a good deal more," I added gloomily.

"Do you need a loan?"

"I hope not."

"I hate to see you so worried. It's a family disease. No matter how much or how little we have, we all always worry about money."

"I know."

"If you get in trouble, I could give you a loan. I could sell some securities if you could give me the same interest I already get. With prices going up so—"

"Thank you," I said, touched all the more because I knew how much she feared poverty, how bewildered she was by inflation, the fluctuations of the securities in which her inheritance was invested, taxes and all the rest.

"I was never trained to make a living," she had told me only a few years before. "I'm too old to start now. Everything costs more and more every year. Why do people keep telling me that money isn't important?"

"Thank you," I said again. "I hope it won't be necessary, but if the need. . . ."

"Will I ever be able to come aboard?"

"You have a standing invitation. There's a nice double cabin aft with its own shower. I promise to keep to waters as quiet as a pond."

"Just when do you plan to get to Florida, anyway?"

"Early in December."

"You'll have the children with you over Christmas?"

"I hope so."

"When are you going to the Bahamas?"

"I haven't worked out all the details yet. I suppose it will depend on how the engines work out and on the weather."

"Could I join you in February? The winter always seems to get on my nerves then."

"It's a date!" I said, unable to mask all my astonishment. Somehow I had never imagined that my eighty-year-old seasick mother would sing "Take Me Along."

"Chester will be having his vacation then," she concluded. "I was wondering what I was going to do with myself."

"How did your mother take the news?" Betty asked me as soon as I got back to the apartment.

"She wants to come along."

"God!"

"It will only be a month. We can put her in the after cabin. . . ."

"I'm not worried about your mother."

"What is it?"

"Dad. He wants to come along too."

"Your *father?*"

Betty's father was an exuberant 225-pound Irishman whom she had once described as a "sort of Brendan Behan who doesn't write." On the two times we had visited Ireland and on the two occasions he had visited this country, we had filled each other with what could best be described as mixed emotions, all of them extreme. I simply could not imagine living with the man aboard a small boat, even without my eighty-year-old mother.

"I'm sorry," Betty said. "When I told him we were going to live on a boat in the Bahamas, he didn't say anything. There was just this terrible silence with the wires humming, and I remembered how much he has always wanted to spend a few months in the sun. You know how damp it gets in Ireland in the wintertime, and he hasn't been well lately. If he had begged, I think I could have been hardhearted, but when he just didn't say anything. . . ."

"I'm glad you couldn't be hardhearted."

"Do you think you can stand all this? I mean, here we were, going to get away from it all."

"They probably will be with us only a few weeks."

"He wants to come over for Christmas. He's so alone now. Ever since Mother died. . . ."

"Your father has never been alone in his life."

"Drinking companions and the women he meets in bars aren't all he needs. He just likes to pretend to be Ireland's answer to Maurice Chevalier. . . ."

"I shall be glad to have your father aboard, but I refuse to be sentimental about him. He will make this cruise into one long spree."

"He's on the wagon. He has been for weeks."

"He always is before he comes here. He just saves up."

"He promised to stay on the wagon. And he'll help you with the engines. He was trained as an engineer."

"Really?" I said. "I hadn't heard that."

"A locomotive engineer. He was an apprentice, back before the First World War. He said to be sure to tell you he doesn't know anything about modern marine diesels."

"He still will know more than I do. What the hell. You're good to my mother, and I'll try to get along with your father."

"Stop sounding noble."

"We'll have a hell of a good time together."

This, I thought, would sometimes be true.

That night I again found it impossible to sleep and paced the empty apartment until dawn gilded the roofs of the tall buildings on the other side of Central Park. It was not only financial worries and concern for remembering how to run a ship safely that kept me awake; it was fear that my older children would think Betty and I were running off irresponsibly, that I was, indeed, developing a scatterbrained pattern of life.

I was also thinking of the words of a friend of ours, a man who wrote television serials. "Well, I'll bid you good-bye, but not for long," he had said. "You'll soon get tired of this yachting kick, and next year you'll be back in New York. Even if you like it out there in the islands, you'll have to come back when your money runs out. Say what you want against America, it's still the only place where a guy with a typewriter can make real money. Like everyone else, you'll get tired of looking for the Ponderosa Ranch, and you'll come home to write about it or stare at it on TV."

Why did that speech upset me so much? In part, perhaps, because I suspected that he reflected the opinion of most of my friends. I knew that regardless of what messes these people had made of their own lives, they were not stupid when it came to judging others. To them I was just another guy who felt he had to escape the rat race for a while, but who would soon be back.

What was I looking for in the Bahamas, after all, and what chance did I actually have of finding it in any way that could last? A tropical Ponderosa Ranch with palm trees and cream-colored beaches—perhaps my friend was right and that was what I was looking for, an impossible dream of permanence and safety in a crazy world. And perhaps he was also right that I would soon return to New York defeated, eager to find an apartment by the great river of money which would gush in and gush out with a noise loud enough to drown out any cries of complaint. But at least I would have a year or two to try to seek my never-never land, and if I were strong enough, maybe it would be possible to find a better life by packing up my goods and leaving everything familiar behind. At least I had a goal now, however vague, and an opportunity to use all my strength and wit to pursue it. That was what I had been needing all along, wasn't it?

# 10 ⚓

That night, as though by predestination, our Siamese cat had four kittens. She delivered them in a cedar closet, cleaned up after herself and deposited them in our bed without waking Betty, me or Jessica, who had also joined us. When we awoke at about eight o'clock in the morning, there they were, two coal-black kittens and two gray ones that looked like the alley cat who had sneaked into our summer cottage.

Jessica was enchanted and forgot all about going to live on a boat.

"Do you think we should make them travel right away?" Betty asked.

"We'll put them in a nice box. There's no choice. The lease is up."

Tearing an old comforter, Betty prepared an elaborate traveling nest for the kittens and put it with the articles marked to go with us, a pile which now looked at me like one of the great pyramids, despite our ruthless sacrifices. While she was preparing breakfast, the driver of a truck I had hired from the boatyard at Oxford knocked at our door.

"What do you want me to take?" he asked in a soft Southern accent.

"We'll see to the cats and the clothes on hangers. You take the piano, all those boxes, the sewing machine and the vacuum cleaner."

While the men from the truck struggled with the piano, I sipped my coffee and thought.

"I'm taking care of the milkman, the postman and the newspaper deliveries," Betty said, busily scribbling notes. "Have you seen to the telephone?"

"I will just before we go. I might as well get the car packed first."

The man from the truck helped me to carry the remaining boxes and the clothes on hangers down to the garage. By ten thirty the apartment was completely empty, except for our big bed, which Betty's aunt and uncle were to call for, and the box of cats, which Betty insisted upon carrying herself.

"Don't forget the telephone," she said.

Picking up the receiver, I placed one last personal call to my agent, Willis Wing, the man who, other than myself, was chiefly responsible for my professional survival. He had long lent a sympathetic ear to my plans.

"Well, Willis," I said, "we're leaving."

"Right now?" he asked cheerfully.

"Right now. Everything is packed."

"Have a good voyage," he said. "I shall use you as an advertisement. All I'll have to do is point south when somebody asks, 'Where are the customers' yachts?' "

"You better keep the publishers interested, or we'll run out of fuel."

"Just keep the manuscripts coming, and keep me informed where you are."

"Oxford, Maryland, for now. When we finally start south I'll give you a schedule."

Perhaps catching a note of uncertainty in my voice, he said, "You know you're doing what practically everybody wants to do, don't you?"

"How come I'm the only one crazy enough to go ahead and do it?"

"The luck of the draw."

"Yes," I said, my voice sounding curiously hollow. "Goodbye, Willis. I'll keep in touch."

After calling the telephone company and asking them to discontinue my service, I turned to Betty and saw that she was buttoning Jessica into her overcoat.

"You carry the baby and I'll take the cats," Betty said briskly.

"I want Mommy to carry me!" Jessie protested as I picked her up.

"I can't," Betty said.

The cat was making a wretched sound, somewhere between a moan and a growl. Betty tied down the lid of the box, in which she had punched many holes. Before picking it up, she glanced around the empty apartment, and I knew she was feeling nostalgic regret, a pang of which grips her upon leaving any place, even a restaurant in which we have had a good meal.

"We had two good years here," she said.

"Yes."

I put the keys to the apartment on the stove where the superintendent could find them. Even the cat was quiet as we left.

It was almost five in the afternoon when we finally reached Oxford. As soon as we turned into the gates of the boatyard, I saw our yacht lying near the marine railways at the end of the wharf. Getting out of the car, the three of us walked toward her slowly, and I sensed that Betty, like me, was afraid that we would somehow be disappointed as we grew closer to our new home. With me, at least, the reverse was the case. The dock was low here, making the boat seem much larger than she had appeared alongside the former owner's tall pier. Outlined against the late afternoon sky, the fine old vessel looked powerful and rakish, presenting a silhouette much like the Coast Guard cutters I had known in my youth.

"They haven't put the canvas sides up yet," Betty said. "Jessie, take my hand. *You must be careful not to fall overboard!*"

Going aboard first, I took Jessie by the hands and swung her to the cockpit deck.

"Is this where we're going to live?" she asked dubiously.

"It's like a little house inside," Betty said and opened the hatch to the after cabin.

While she was showing her that, I walked forward to give the boat one more quick inspection. The hatch to the engine room was open, and looking down I could see a tangle of machinery and wires. Apparently the job of putting the new generator in had already started.

At that point, a fishing vessel, followed by a flock of gulls, came in from the bay, her wake causing our boat to roll lazily.

"I feel funny," Jessie said.

"It will be quiet again in a minute. Look at all those gulls."

Leaving the nets heaped on the fishing vessel, the gulls circled over our stern, calling eagerly to each other.

"Throw them this," I said to Jessie, handing her scraps of a sandwich one of the workmen must have left aboard the boat.

With Betty holding her waist, Jessie dropped the crusts into the water. Suddenly the gulls were all around us, almost brushing our ears with their wings as they vied with each other over the floating crumbs. Outlined against the sky, Betty stood with her arms encircling the waist of the child, while Jessie reached her hands out to the gulls, vainly trying to touch them.

"Awe, awe!" Betty called, imitating the cry of the gulls perfectly, and Jessie laughed.

"Are you a bird?" she asked.

"I don't know what I am," Betty said, and turning to me, she smiled. "I'm not a housewife anymore, that's for sure. What is my occupation?"

Before I could think of an answer, the beam of a watchman's flashlight traveled over the boat toward us and a gruff voice from the wharf called, "Hello there! Do you have permission to be aboard?"

"I'm the new owner," I said, the sentence sounding good. "Would you like to come aboard?"

"Don't mind if I do."

After scraping his heavy boots on the edge of the dock, the

watchman, a wizened man in denim trousers and an old Navy peacoat, swung himself onto the deck and walked toward us.

"Wilson's my name," I said, holding out my hand.

"Swenson. I hear you're going to take her south."

"That's right."

"To the islands?"

"To the islands," I said, and the phrase seemed to reverberate.

I had thought it would take about two weeks to get the boat ready, but at the end of a month we were still in Oxford. The golden days of October turned into the gray, windy days of November, and as the delays continued, I began to fear that ice would form in the bay before we could escape.

At first it appeared to me that the man responsible for the maddening slowness of work aboard our boat was the superintendent of the yard, whose slow Southern drawl soon began to infuriate me, but gradually I began to realize that Mr. Miller had been forced into the unhappy position of being only a spokesman for all the forces of nature and mankind which conspire against the creation and durability of a good boat. Every morning when I walked from the inn to my "yacht" (a word which still seemed pretentious and absurd to me), I expected to find miracles of progress, but instead I always found a growth of chaos presided over by Mr. Miller.

"I'm sorry," he always began, pulling the visor of his cap down as though seeking protection for his mournful face. "Things aren't going too well."

The details were endless. The first man he assigned to install the new generator went away and got drunk, apparently forever, a fact which did not surprise me too much when I saw the tiny corner into which he had to fit the large machine. The second mechanic quit a few days later because his wife had to go to the hospital.

The generator was not the only problem. "Are you sure you want to change the boat's name?" Mr. Miller asked the first week. "It's supposed to be bad luck, and there's usually a reason for sea superstitions."

As a surprise for Betty and as some small antidote to our feeling of homelessness, I had already bought stationery dashingly headed: The Motor Vessel *Pretty Betty,* and though my wife had demurred at the expense, she had speedily used it to write to all her relatives and friends.

"I still want to change the name," I said to Mr. Miller.

"Well, that means refinishing the entire transom," he replied, scratching his chin. "Then there are two life rings which will have to be relettered. Gold leaf don't come cheap, and anything else would change the style of the boat."

"How much will it cost?"

"The name's on the dinghy too, not to mention a lot of glassware, china and linens. She's a documented vessel—you'll have some legal folderol."

"What do you think the final bill will be?"

"I can't tell how much of a problem they'll have with the transom—maybe we won't have to go clear to the wood. You've got the trailboards too—I forgot them. All gold leaf on mahogany."

"How much?"

"The whole job will shoot hell out of a thousand dollars."

"Just to change her *name?*"

"That's why it's called bad luck."

Briefly I imagined asking Betty if she would mind retaining the name *Irish Mist.* When she learned the price of change, I was sure she would agree, but it's a hell of a thing to take a compliment back.

"I still want to change the name," I said. "Please do it as soon as you can."

The problem the next day was the piano, which now stood covered by a tarpaulin in a shed.

"You sure you want to have that piano aboard?" Mr. Miller asked me.

"Of course. I measured the space where that couch is. It will fit perfectly."

"Did you measure the door to the deckhouse?"

"Can't you take the legs off the piano?"

"Still won't fit. We'll have to take the bulkhead apart."

"That shouldn't be too much of a job."

"Wouldn't be on most boats, but you've got two layers of heavy mahogany here. I hate to cut it—you don't cut a patch out of a violin."

"Can't you disassemble the bulkhead and put it back together just as it was when it was built?"

"Mr. Nevins didn't use no short ends. The planks go clear across the end of the whole deckhouse. If we pull 'em, there'll be a big job building up the paint and varnish again. Then there's the paneling on the inside. . . ."

"How much will it cost?"

"Well, that's just the beginning. You've got the engine room hatch to consider—the piano will sit on the edge of it if you don't change something. And that piano weighs almost a thousand pounds. If you don't want her to carry away when the vessel gets to rolling, you'll need some heavy bronze straps."

"How much will the whole job be?"

"I haven't talked about the big ports yet."

"What about them?"

"You won't be able to close them when the piano is in place or open them if you close them first. The piano is a little higher than the couch. We'll have to change the handles."

"How much will the whole thing cost?"

"It will shoot hell out of a thousand dollars."

"I've finally learned how to budget changes for this boat. Everything will shoot—"

"I know it's terrible," Mr. Miller said. "And would you believe that my men have to get raises every year? There's not one of 'em that couldn't make more money building houses as it is."

"We still are going to have to install the piano," I said doggedly, for the piano was the thing Betty always mentioned first when she told people about the boat.

The radio telephone was the next big item—it needed so many repairs that Mr. Miller recommended a replacement.

"How much will it cost?" I asked warily.

"For the Bahamas you should have the best. Installed, it will shoot hell out of—"

"I know. Well, that's safety equipment, and we can't economize on that."

"While we're on that subject, do you want a whole safety check?"

"What do you mean?"

"I don't think you have a life raft, and the old ones weren't much good anyway compared to what they make nowadays. We ought to check your life preservers and weigh your $CO_2$ tanks. We ought to make sure your flares are fresh. Under the general heading of safety, I'd have the compass compensated—I don't know when it was done last, and the new generator might change it anyway. You only have one bilge pump, and that's electric. I'd add a hand one in case of emergencies."

"How much will all that cost?"

"I hate to say it, but those new life rafts alone will shoot hell out of—"

"I get the picture. Can you buy them secondhand?"

"Maybe. The ocean racers are all changing to the new barrel type of storage. If you don't mind folding—"

"Just get me anything that will float," I said and returned to the inn, where I set up my typewriter in a corner and began trying to write a magazine article on how to tell your children about sex.

After a month of this frustration, the woman who managed the inn told us that she no longer had any room for us.

"What's the matter?" I asked wearily. "Is it the sound of the typewriter, the baby running in the halls or the cats?"

"It's just the hunting season. It starts in a couple of days and we have men who make reservations months in advance."

"Is there another inn anywhere near here? Our boat is still a mess."

"Everything is filled up for the hunting season. If you're really desperate, I might find one small room without a bath on the third floor."

So it was that we found ourselves with a two-year-old child, five cats and a big electric typewriter in a room which measured exactly 7 by 9 feet.

"I think God meant this to be," Betty said, making a bed for the baby by fitting two chairs together.

"What did we do that was so terrible?"

"Nothing. God is doing us a favor."

*"How?"*

"If we moved from our big apartment directly to the boat, we would think the *Pretty Betty* was cramped. Now three whole staterooms and two private baths will be heaven, no matter how small they are."

"Maybe you're right. Would you mind giving up the dream of having everything just right before we moved aboard?"

"Anything would be better than this. At least we could put the cats out on the dock."

"They've just about got the deckhouse back together again. Everything is still a mess, but there's no reason why we couldn't make up the bunks."

"Let's get out of here," she said.

Despite our discomfort at the inn, I was apprehensive about moving Betty and the baby aboard the boat before everything was in readiness. Memories of chaotic weeks I had spent aboard vessels in shipyards during World War II were still surprisingly fresh, and there was some element of superstition which made me believe that a voyage must always continue as it starts. Besides, I was afraid that one of the laws of nature I have observed and privately listed as Wilson's Law Number 63A, would now go into effect, bringing disaster. Wilson's Law 63A is as follows: "All events which are supposed to be wildly happy turn out to be miserable."

Moving aboard one's yacht for the first time obviously was supposed to be a wildly happy occasion, and to avoid running afoul of Wilson's Law 63A, I had been determined that all would be in readiness before we spent our first night on the boat.

Looking back, I realize that we lucked right into Wilson's Law 63B: "All events which are supposed to be horrible turn out to be bearable and run an even chance of turning out to be pleasant."

Undoubtedly because we expected a good deal of confusion and discomfort when we moved aboard the boat, everything went beautifully. The piano was still in the middle of the deckhouse, the generator was not functioning, and the electric heaters had not been fastened to the bulkheads, but here at last was a home, where we were unpacking and settling in, not tearing everything apart.

It was about noon when we drove from the inn to the boatyard with our car full of cardboard cartons of clothes. With a wheelbarrow I carried everything to the dock and added to the pile the collection of packing cases the truck had taken from our apartment and left in a shed. Our first pleasant surprise was that the boat offered far more storage space than we had expected. The lockers and drawers were not big, but the more we explored, the more nooks and shelves we discovered. By two in the afternoon, all the cartons were empty, and the boat didn't seem crowded at all.

It was a gusty day with small craft warnings broadcast over the radio, and as the sun went down, it started to get really cold, but the new fireplace had been installed in the deckhouse, and some workmen had left a bushel basket of small blocks of wood and shavings collected from the floor of the carpentry shop. When I first lit a fire the cabin quickly filled with smoke, but as soon as I found how to use the damper, we got dancing flames and a delightful glow. Somehow this new warmth made us realize how tired we were, and we sank down on the couch beside the piano.

"I had planned to have a wonderful meal tonight, but I'm exhausted," Betty said.

"I saw some beans in a locker down there. That's all I need."

We had left the oven on to keep the forward cabin warm, and after puncturing the cans and stripping off the labels, Betty set them on a pie dish and pushed them in. By the time water was boiling for tea, they were hot.

"Is this all we're going to have?" Jessie asked, looking at hers dubiously.

"I'll get you a proper breakfast in the morning," Betty said.

"Do we have television here?"

"No," I said.

"I want to go back to New York," Jessica stated flatly.

"Hush," Betty said. "We're going to be very happy here."

Too tired to bother with sheets, we spread blankets on the berths in the forward cabin. Almost immediately Betty fell asleep with the baby sprawled on top of her. On the opposite bunk I stretched out, but I was far too keyed up to keep my eyes shut long.

Was it safe to leave a gas oven on all night?

Worried, I experimented with the electric heaters the workmen were preparing to attach to the bulkheads and found that I could connect them to the shore current. They hummed softly, and I turned off the gas. The embers in the fireplace were still glowing, and the deckhouse smelled pleasantly of burning pine and mahogany. Putting on a heavy sweater, I went on deck and was astonished by the brilliance of a half-moon which lay just at the end of a tattered banner of white clouds.

How strange to realize that during my years in New York I had forgotten what the sky looks like when there are no lights and no smoke to obscure it. The stars on this clear, cold night glittered with incredible brightness, and all around me were peaceful sounds, the distant murmuring of the geese in the marsh, the hum of the wind in the rigging of a yawl moored nearby, the lapping of the water against the piles of the wharf and the creak of our dock lines. The mahogany rail I ran my hand along as I walked toward the cockpit was slippery with dew. My fingers tingled, and suddenly I felt that all my senses had just come alive after years of being half dead. With a slight shiver, I sat down and stared at a wavering path of light which a planet, perhaps Venus, traced on the black water astern. Just beyond the edge of our awning, a falling star streaked for the horizon, and perhaps frightened by that or some fox on the prowl, the wild geese gave a cry of alarm followed by breathless silence. Without warning, my euphoria vanished and instead of staring at the sky, I found myself thinking of the mounting bills, the endless demands of the tax men and the approach of winter weather. When I finally left this yard, God knew what my bills would be, and I still would not have done anything to assure the quality of the most important part of my boat, the engines, which were still a mystery to me.

Deliberately I tried to cast off this pall, but that proved difficult. Going back to the deckhouse, I took a bottle from a locker and poured myself a stiff drink of Scotch. It was curious how the memory of those few moments of elation lingered, a new sensation, as different from my usual frame of mind as the brilliant sky was from city haze. The whiskey did not bring them back, but it killed some of my restlessness, and I went below. My narrow bunk was nowhere near as comfortable as the big bed we had left behind, but the creak of the dock lines and the lap of water against the hull made a good lullaby.

Perhaps with practice, moments like that will come again and will stay longer, I thought. At any rate, I felt I had learned a lot simply by realizing how much there was to hope for.

In the morning an influx of new worries made my momentary happiness appear almost ironic. Jessica awoke with a cough and soon developed a fever of 103 degrees. While Betty was calling the former owner of the boat to try to locate a pediatrician, Mr. Miller arrived with a sheaf of bills that showed that already we owed him more than $6,000.

"What do you think the total will be when everything is done?" I asked.

"About eight, I'd say. That ought to see you free and clear."

That would mean the boat had cost me about $26,000. Well, I had once talked about paying $25,000, and I certainly would have a lot to show for my money. I resolved to write to Mort about the new bills so I wouldn't have to talk to him. Perhaps the shock of all this expense had an effect on me, or perhaps I caught Jessica's cold. That night I too began to cough, and I acquired a bad case of that disease which is generally associated with traveling in Mexico.

The next two weeks were grim indeed, and it cheered me little to reflect that I had allowed the euphoria of our first hours aboard to trap me back into Wilson's Law Number 63A. The immediate joy of moving aboard had been so great that I had begun to expect too much, and my punishment was inevitable.

## 11

⚓

During the next week Jessie had a narrow brush with pneumonia and my illness continued. Only Betty retained any real vigor, and her face looked strained.

Still, there were some developments that were hopeful. Our boat gradually began to look like a vessel ready to leave for the Bahamas any day, and the loneliness we had felt ever since we had left New York was eased by our finding that there really was a sort of brotherhood of the waterfront, a fraternity for which we were now fully eligible.

Our first intimation of this came when a short, stout woman, the wife of a carpenter who lived on a converted landing barge nearby, struck up a conversation with Betty in the small shack where the boatyard had installed two coin washing machines and a dryer for the yachtsmen. Upon learning that Jessica was sick, this lady began dropping in almost every day with a Mason jar of soup or a batch of fresh cookies.

"Nothing like that ever happened to us in New York," I said to Betty.

"We didn't know any poor people in New York," Betty replied. "In Ireland people always bring food when you're sick. You just had to buy a yacht to find how most of the world lives."

The second acquaintance Betty made at the laundry room

was a tall, thin and aloof woman of indeterminate age who lived with her husband on a beautiful, big ketch which was also bound south. My theory that people choose boats which are curiously exact symbols of themselves certainly held true in this case. The man and wife were aristocratic even when they were dressed in blue jeans. The graceful, tall-sparred ketch represented the best that modern designers and boat builders can produce if they are given an unlimited budget. I guessed that the boat, which was not much larger than ours, had recently cost about $150,000, and she made all the talk about the disappearance of great craftsmen sound absurd.

Betty introduced me to the lady who owned this paragon of a boat, and though she was courteous, she made me feel uncomfortable in ways I couldn't explain. One reason was that the voyage to the Bahamas, which I regarded as a big adventure, obviously was nothing at all to this person, who made the trip every year. Secretly I had been regarding myself as something of a hero for venturing to sea with no one but a woman to help me, but this lady and her husband had been ranging up and down the entire Atlantic Coast for years without help and had done most of their cruising under sail. She knew so much about boats that she made me feel like a novice, and this sensation was so unpleasant that I found I could never remember her name, no matter how many times I was introduced to her. For some reason Betty, who usually is much better at remembering names than I am, shared this difficulty, and we took to referring to this gentle lady as though she were, in fact, her boat. We called her the Big Ketch.

"The Big Ketch was very nice this morning," Betty said one day. "I think that we just imagine she's snobbish. If she were on a smaller boat, we might like her."

After a trip to the laundry that afternoon, Betty came back wide-eyed.

"I found out who the Big Ketch is," she said. "Her father was Secretary of State. She doesn't like people to know. Anyway, I love the boatyard life. Where else could I do your shirts while discussing politics with the daughter of a Secretary of State?"

The Big Ketch, we found to our astonishment, had her troubles. Recently she and her husband had had their boat put in perfect condition by the yard and had begun what seemed to them a routine voyage to the Bahamas. Shortly after putting to sea, their expensive new diesel engine had come to a shuddering stop and had refused to start again. It had been a rough and windy night. With skill and courage, the man and wife, who were considerably older than I, had put sail on their vessel and returned to the boatyard. In the morning a mechanic had discovered that someone had poured sugar into their fuel tanks, a procedure guaranteed to gum up a diesel engine almost beyond repair. The big questions, of course, were who had committed this dangerous act of sabotage and why.

The Big Ketch and her husband said they had no idea. They had no known enemies, they told the insurance people, and they were obviously shocked at the discovery that someone wished them harm. For days the whole town of Oxford was humming with rumors of explanations, but no culprit and no satisfactory answer to the mystery were ever discovered.

The third person we met at Oxford was also bound south, but he had none of the self-confidence possessed by the Big Ketch. Although he was an athletic-appearing man who had once sailed a small sloop across the Atlantic single-handed, he was in the process of deciding that circumstances had made the trip to Florida impossible for the boat he was trying to deliver for a friend.

At first this was hard for me to understand. The boat was a Dutch boyer, a stubby, picturesque sailing vessel that looked a little like a huge wooden shoe. Although it was somewhat shorter than our boat, it was much wider and boasted four enormous staterooms, one of which had a fireplace which would do credit to an Adirondack lodge. Boyers were not designed for round-the-world voyages, but they are much more seaworthy than most small motor yachts, and I couldn't understand why an experienced sailor would be so gloomy about this one.

"We lashed the mast on deck because it's too tall to go under some of the bridges, and I don't like to mess around this time of the year outside alone," our new friend told me. "She's got only a small engine. I don't think it will push her against much of a wind, and this time of the year we're not liable to get good weather. We've waited too long."

"There always are letups in the weather," I protested, unwilling to admit that I too didn't like the idea of tackling Chesapeake Bay with a small craft in mid-November.

"Well, I'm going to try," he said with a shrug. "Wish me luck."

Early the next morning I saw him back the unwieldy craft away from the dock and head out of the harbor. At about four in the afternoon, I looked out a porthole and saw to my surprise that he was tying up again.

"What's the matter?" I asked.

"You can't feel it here, but it's blowing pretty good out there, right on the nose. I covered about five miles in six hours. Then I began losing oil pressure, so I came back in."

This procedure was repeated on two successive days. On the third day my new friend showed up with a black eye—he said he had drunk too much and had taken a bad fall. After that I didn't see him anymore, and a workman said the yard had orders to store the boyer for the winter.

"On the map Chesapeake Bay looks completely protected," Betty said. "Is it really that tough out there?"

"It can be in November. But our boat has much more power than that boyer. If we wait for the weather, we shouldn't have to worry."

My voice sounded more jaunty than I felt. That afternoon a big schooner put into the yard after having her foresail blown out in a squall.

"That bay can be a bitch," her skipper told me. "Don't let it fool you."

The art, of course, would be to wait for a break in the heavy fall gales, but when one finally came, our new generator was still incompletely wired. Because men were working on it every day, I had not been able to spend much time in the engine room trying to learn my way around, and there was no point in studying the old electrical system anyway, because much of it was being changed. When the man came to take the boat out and adjust the compass, I realized that although I had lived aboard the *Pretty Betty* for almost two weeks, I still hesitated to start the engines. Seeing my confusion, Mr. Miller assigned a young mechanic by the name of Carl Fluharty to help me.

Secretly I had been worried that the boat was too big for me to handle alone during the period that Betty would need to master her new trade of deckhand, but with Carl aboard to help with the lines as well as run the engines I felt confident. We moved smoothly away from the wharf, took our brief spin around the harbor and returned without difficulty.

"You really do know how to handle a boat, don't you?" Betty said to me. "I mean, I always knew you did, but I like to see you actually do it."

"She's an easy boat to handle," I replied, but there was a nagging doubt in my mind which kept me awake that night.

Something was wrong with my plan. All my instincts told me that I was headed for trouble.

The difficulty was, I realized, that circumstances were likely to make the first two days of our voyage the most troublesome of the whole trip to Florida. And most important of all, the first hours of steady operation would provide the first real test of the engines. In view of all this, it suddenly seemed obvious to me that it would be wise to hire a mechanic to go with us for two days, or maybe three, in case the weather turned bad. In addition to being on hand for emergencies, he could give me an intensive lesson in the handling of diesel engines which would be much more helpful under way than at the dock.

In the morning, I talked to Carl Fluharty, and he agreed to sign on at the rate of $25 a day for three days, in addition to his bus fare back from Norfolk. My budget was so completely out of hand that even this relatively small sum bothered me, and it hurt my pride a little to think that I was afraid to start alone, but the specter of drifting down a gale-swept bay on a dark night with stalled engines was a good antidote to vanity. A sailor, after all, is always playing a competitive game with the elements—one has to make every move exactly right if one expects to get home free. With Carl aboard to handle the diesels, I would be starting the game with a good hand, especially if I waited for the right weather reports.

"With all these preparations, I sort of get the feeling that we're starting out on a voyage around the world," Betty said. "After all, you said that tiny outboard motorboats often make this trip."

I laughed.

"They do, many of them without a bit of trouble. I know I'm dramatizing all the difficulties. Maybe I was sort of shell-shocked by weather when I was on the Greenland patrol. The first night I ever had command of my own ship, the wind blew more than a hundred and twenty miles an hour. I suppose that for the rest of my life I'll keep expecting that."

"Were you frightened?"

"Of course. Frightened enough to make every effort to keep the *Pretty Betty* out of that kind of weather."

"I bet that after all these preparations this whole trip is going to be a breeze."

"Knock on wood," I said, rapping our mahogany table.

"I never saw you so superstitious before."

"Just careful. The sea is a bad place to be cocky."

Betty smiled.

"You're confirming a theory I'm beginning to form," she said.

"What's that?"

"Life on a boat is just an intensification of life ashore. After all, we always live by God's sufferance, but usually we aren't so aware of it."

"That's true," I said.

That night I again had trouble sleeping, and I found myself brooding about Betty's theory. In the past week it had rained almost steadily, and although I had been reluctant to admit it even to myself, the irritations of life had certainly been intensified by the boat. All along I had been afraid that Betty would find the relatively cramped quarters uncomfortable, but it was I who found myself muttering about the narrow berths, the shower bath which wet only one shoulder at a time, and the galley, where I seemed to burn myself on the oven every time I reached for a dish. Now that she was recovering from her illness, Jessica was taking to climbing about the deck in a way that brought our hearts to our throats despite the new strips of canvas which had been laced around the rails.

*"Where's Jessica?"* became a question of terror every time we glanced around the cabin and didn't see her immediately. At night we locked doors to make sure she didn't wander on deck, but still we slept restlessly, constantly checking to make sure that she was in her bunk.

The next morning dawned so cold and gray that the Bahamas seemed no more than a fantasy. Finally the work on the new generator was finished, and we loaded the refrigerator with groceries just in case we were able to leave, but the weather reports coming over our new marine radio in a man's bored, flat monotone predicted nothing but sleet and winds gusting up to 40 knots. Instead of recovering, I found that my digestive troubles were getting worse. Too weak and discouraged even to pick up a book, I lay in my bunk and listened while Betty read endless nursery stories in an effort to keep Jessie quiet. At noon Mr. Miller called and, along with his final bill, gave us a package of mail which had been forwarded from New York. Afraid to open the bill, I leafed through a dozen letters from friends, all of whom congratulated me for having the courage to abandon the rat race in New York for a gay and carefree life on the bounding main.

"You lucky bastard," one old friend began, and ended with, "Enviously yours. . . ."

"Well, it's a consolation to know that *everybody's* miserable," Betty said when she had finished reading the mail.

"I'm still glad we left New York," I replied with a little effort.

"So am I. At least here we can be sure things will change. Once we get started, how long will it take to get into warm weather?"

"In about a week we ought to make South Carolina. You'll see the first palm trees there."

"The first hot, sunny day we get, let's anchor and just lie out on deck for hours."

"That's a deal," I said.

There was a brief silence.

"Do you notice that it's getting cold in here?" Betty asked.

Upon checking, I found that a fuse on the dock had blown, cutting out our electric heaters. Before going ashore to tell Mr. Miller, I flicked a switch and turned on our new generator, causing our heaters to turn red again.

"I do love having our own power supply," Betty said. "It makes me feel independent as hell."

Almost before she had finished speaking, our generator sputtered and stopped. When I tried to start it again, nothing happened.

"Independence," I said bitterly.

"We're lucky we're still in the yard. Maybe this bad weather is doing us a favor. At least you're going to have a chance to get all the kinks ironed out. . . ."

When he came aboard, Mr. Miller traced a short circuit in the new wiring, but still I was beginning to feel like an actor in a road company contracted to put on the play *Rain* twice a day endlessly. Feeling completely stir-crazy, Betty, the baby and I got in the car, which we had sold to a worker in the boatyard, subject to delivery on the day we finally sailed. Slowly we drove to Easton, the nearest town of any size, and sat through two cowboy movies. When the last shot was fired, we walked out into the night, and glancing up, I saw that the clouds were beginning to clear.

That evening the man who announced the weather reports said, "Fair, with light variable winds." I tried to call Carl to say we would sail at dawn, but no one answered his telephone.

"I'll keep calling," I said to Betty, but at midnight he still didn't answer. Setting my alarm clock for five in the morning, I went to sleep.

Before the alarm clock went off, I was awakened by the sound of someone jumping on deck. It was Carl, suitcase in hand. He hadn't got any message and he hadn't heard a weather report, but he had been brought up on the bay, and one glance at the sky had been enough.

"Good morning, Skipper," he said. "I think we've got your day."

While Betty prepared coffee, I put some briquettes in the fireplace and studied the harbor chart, before following Carl to the engine room, where he was checking the oil and the water in the heat exchangers. When we came back on deck, dawn was just beginning to tint a cloudless sky. It was cold enough to make us put wool jackets over our sweaters, but there was so little wind that the smoke from our fireplace went straight up to heaven, and the water in the harbor looked like polished black marble. The baby continued to sleep while Betty cooked scrambled eggs and sausages.

"We better start the engines and let them warm up while we eat," I said to Carl.

"That's not a good idea with diesels—they carbon up when they run too slow. Don't idle them. Just start them when you're ready to go."

Unwilling to waste a moment of daylight, we bolted our food.

"I'll start the engines," I said to Carl. "I might as well get used to it."

Except for the fact that there was no ignition key, the diesels started like gasoline engines. Their deep rumble did not wake Jessica, who slept with one arm over her eyes.

"What do you want me to do?" Betty asked. She had hurried so to get breakfast that she wore only a long red flannel bathrobe over her pajamas, and when she came on deck she shivered.

"Just watch Carl—in three days you'll have his job."

"You want all the lines off?" Carl asked.

"Might as well."

The *Pretty Betty* lay at the end of the wharf with her bow pointing out of the harbor. With no wind and no discernible current, there should have been no problem in getting under way, but my fingers were still tense as they touched the cold, hard rubber balls at the end of the engine controls. I had two throttles and two clutches to handle in addition to the wheel, and it would be possible, I realized, to get all mixed up, but practice would eventually make the process easy. The slender hull of the *Pretty Betty* reacted more quickly than I expected, and almost as soon as the clutches were engaged, her knifelike bow nudged a fender Carl was holding, and the stern swung clear.

"All engines back slow," I said Coast Guard fashion to a nonexistent quartermaster and changed the starboard clutch. Obediently the *Pretty Betty* pulled well clear of the wharf.

"Is that all there is to it?" Betty asked, her breath frosting.

"In a stiff wind or current it can be tougher."

"But all I have to do is coil up the lines?"

"That's about it."

"Big deal," Betty said with a laugh and, holding the collar of her bathrobe close around her neck, ducked below.

After shoving both clutches ahead, I inched the throttles down, and the beat of the engines increased.

"Don't push her beyond twelve hundred RPM until your temperature gauges get up to about one forty," Carl said, coming aft to stand at the wheel beside me. "This is your warming up."

"Right."

Just forward of the wheel the *Pretty Betty*'s big ship's compass glowed in the light from a small red bulb. On a fine mahogany desk at my left lay a new chart on which I had carefully drawn the course out of the harbor and down the bay. How long had it been since I had last brought a vessel out of a strange harbor in the first streaks of light, with every headland and island darkly mirrored around me and the low-lying mists of dawn obscuring the channel markers? No matter, I reflected as I steadied her on her first compass course—here at last I was in a world for which my youth had prepared me, no matter how confused the lingering shadows of night. In a crisp new log book I noted with a sharp, hard pencil: "6:43, got under way. Course, 248 true, speed, 7 knots."

"In eleven minutes we should pick up a nun on the starboard bow," I said to Carl.

"And what kind of talk is that?" Betty asked, sticking her head up the hatch.

"A nun is a conical red buoy."

"In Ireland that would be blasphemy. Do you want more coffee?"

"I'd love a cup."

"There's the nun," Carl said shortly, staring ahead through the binoculars.

"We'll see a can next, about two miles farther out."

Just as we cleared the harbor and entered a broad reach of Chesapeake Bay, the sun rose over a distant hill and burned off the mist. About three miles ahead of us a half-dozen big skipjacks lay, their limp sails turned to gold, their graceful white hulls mirrored in the still water.

"They must have been out trying to dredge oysters all night," Carl said. "This kind of calm doesn't do them any good."

"Why don't they get motors?" Betty asked. The baby was in her arms, blinking sleepily, looking astonished at the brilliant water surrounding us.

"Conservation laws," Carl said. "You can't drag for oysters

under power. They say that Maryland laws protect oysters, not men."

Glancing at the temperature gauges, Carl added, "You can shove her up to about eighteen hundred RPM now."

The stern settled a little as the *Pretty Betty* steadied to her cruising speed of 12 knots. Three big sea gulls wove back and forth across our wake, keeping a sharp eye out for any small fish we might scare up from the bottom. With the sun warming the air, we could no longer see each other's breath, and the sky turned from deep purple to a light blue still unmarred by any cloud. After glancing about the engine room, Carl came up and closed the hatch, reducing the noise to the point that it was possible to talk without raising one's voice. There wasn't much vibration, and in that dead calm, no pitching or rolling at all. Behind us our wake left a double row of lace doilies which seemed to stretch clear to the horizon. Settling down on a bench behind the wheel with the baby on her lap, Betty tucked a blanket around herself.

"This is the life," she said, taking a deep breath. "Will it be like this all the way south?"

"This is a miracle," I said. "We had no right to expect a June day in November."

Carl, I noticed, was studying the dials on the instrument panel.

"Anything the matter?" I asked.

"I don't know yet."

Quickly he opened the engine room hatch and disappeared, closing a wooden grate behind him.

"Everything sounds all right," I said worriedly to Betty.

"Skipper!" Carl called. "Can you look down here a minute?"

"Do you want me to take the wheel?" Betty asked.

"Will the baby be all right?"

"She's still half asleep. Jessie, you lie right here!"

Quickly Betty got up and went to the wheel, the skirt of her red robe fluttering in the wind caused by the motion of the boat.

"If you move the wheel right you go to the right," I said. "We're heading for that big lighthouse you can just see up ahead."

"It's just like a bloody big car. Go see what Carl wants."

Picking up the wooden grate over the engine room hatch, I looked down. The first thing I saw was that water was squirting from the after end of the port engine, drenching the new generator beside it.

"What's the matter?" I asked in alarm.

"The sealer in this raw water pump is bad. I don't think it's doing much harm. She's still getting enough water to keep her fairly cool."

"Can you fix it?"

"Not until I get some new seals. We can buy some in Norfolk tomorrow."

"Don't you think we should head back to Oxford?"

"Do you really want to waste this day?"

"Won't all that salt water ruin the generator?"

"Do you have a spare piece of canvas? We can hold down the spray."

In the lazaret I found an old hatch cover and passed it down. In a few minutes Carl fixed it in such a way that the squirting pump was draining directly into the bilge.

"It's not liable to get any worse," he said, climbing to the deck and wiping his face with a clean rag. "The main trouble with those engines is that they haven't been used in a long time. A lot of the seals have probably shriveled up and dried."

"I'm glad you came along," I said. "I would have been scared to death at the sight of that."

Taking a wet package of cigarettes from his shirt pocket, he found a dry one, lit it and threw the rest overboard. For a few minutes he stood watching puffs of smoke float up to the top of the windscreen, where the breeze caused by our motion whisked them away.

"Skipper," he said suddenly, "How long do you think it will take you to get to Florida?"

"I suppose that depends on how the engines hold out."

"If they give you no trouble. . . ."

"If we pushed it, I suppose we could make it in about eight or nine days, unless the weather turned really bad. But who wants to push it? I like some of those little Georgia and Carolina towns."

"How about two weeks?"

"That would be about right. Why?"

"I have a two-week vacation due at the yard. How would you like an engineer all the way down?"

"For twenty-five bucks a day?"

"I tell you," he said, throwing his cigarette overboard, "maybe we can make a deal. A lot of rich people want their boats delivered to Miami—they're always looking for someone to do the job. If I had taken the trip once, and if someone had showed me piloting and a little navigation, I could pick up quite a few bucks."

"In two weeks you could learn everything you needed for small yachts."

"Will you give me lessons on the chart work? I didn't finish much school."

"The chart work is easier than you think."

"Well, if you'll give me lessons and fly me home, I'll teach you how to put a new gasket in a raw water pump and a few other things about those engines. Is it a deal?"

"Wow!" Betty said. "You mean we got a free engineer for the whole trip?"

"That's right," Carl said with a grin. "I always wanted to be a yacht captain, and that's what I aim to be when I get back."

We shook hands, and in celebration Betty served bouillon and crackers, just the way they do on the Cunard Line. After Carl finished his, he took the wheel while I sipped mine. Although he didn't know theories of navigation, he had been brought up on the bay and was a fine helmsman. With nothing to worry about, I wandered forward and sat on the bow, bouillon cup in hand, watching the sharp edge of the green stem slice the smooth blue water. When the lighthouse came abeam, I checked the time and saw that we were doing a little better than 12 knots. A big bell buoy we passed seemed to be swimming down the bay alongside us, and I realized that with all the other good fortune of that day, we had a strong current pushing us on our way.

All morning the sky remained clear. At about four in the afternoon some white clouds spilled over the horizon astern and a brisk wind sprang up, but it served only to speed us on our way, and before it had time to roil the waters of the bay, I could see Norfolk Harbor ahead. As the sun sank, the rising wind was colder, and the clouds began to spread over the whole sky, banking the sunset like a fire with coals and making the western horizon look angry and ominous. The daylight faded so fast that for a few minutes I was afraid I would be left to grope my way into a strange wharf at night, perhaps in the midst of a rain squall, a job I always hated, but one orange cloud remained on the horizon to glare at us like an angry eye in the darkness, giving us enough light to pick out the channel markers in the Hampton River. As the last trace of day faded, we eased alongside the wharf of the Hampton Yacht Club, and leaving Jessica sitting on the captain's chair with me, Betty helped Carl put out the dock lines.

"She's all fast," Carl called from the bow.

I cut off the engines, and we all hurried below just as the first drops of rain began to rattle on the awnings.

"Well, that's a hundred and twenty miles under our belt," I said exuberantly. "Let it blow! We're done with Chesapeake Bay. Now we've got about a thousand miles of nice quiet canals!"

While Betty broiled steaks, Carl and I uncorked a bottle of Scotch. It was ridiculous to feel that I had just accomplished some enormous success, but my exuberance knew no bounds, and as the wind increased to a full gale outside our snug mooring, my exhilaration kept increasing. Maybe there wouldn't be another good day in Chesapeake Bay for the rest of the winter, but we had escaped, and my theory that I could cruise with a woman and child without spilling a cup of tea by waiting for the weather had thus far proved true, even in November. We had the unexpected assurance of having a good mechanic and deckhand aboard free for the rest of the trip south, and except for the small matter of a leaky water pump, the engines had performed well.

On deck the rain was starting to freeze, but our new electric heaters and the fireplace kept the cabins warm even when the gas range was turned off. Twelve hours of salt air and standing watch had left us ravenous enough to demand a second big steak from the freezer, and after that there was chocolate pudding with whipped cream and black coffee.

"How about a song?" I said to Betty. "We haven't really christened that piano."

"If you'll play, I'll do the dishes," Carl added.

"That's a deal any time."

She started to play "Body and Soul," one of my favorites, and it seemed to me that this was a night for which I had worked, dreamed and hoped all my life. The only trouble was that I was too exhausted to enjoy it for long. Without having the strength to do more than take off my shoes, I lay down on the bunk by the piano and fell fast asleep.

# 12

⚓

The next morning it was still blowing more than 30 knots and raining hard. It would not be particularly dangerous to continue into the canals, but our open bridge, which had been designed for the kind of sunny weather which it is the *Pretty Betty*'s profession to seek, would be an uncomfortable place for the helmsman. Happy to have the day for repairs, Carl put on olive-drab foul-weather clothes and took a bus into Norfolk to seek sealers for the engines.

Setting up her sewing machine in the deckhouse, Betty began to make new curtains. Restless and unreasonably irritated by the chatter of the sewing machine, I grabbed a book entitled *A Cruising Guide to the Southern Coast* and headed for the aftercabin.

As I emerged from the deckhouse, hunched against the rain which was slanting under the awnings, I was hailed by a tall man on the yacht club dock. He was wearing a yellow slicker and was smoking his pipe upside down.

"That's a beautiful boat you've got there," he said. "Are you headed south?"

"Yes," I replied. One of the joys of owning a good-looking vessel is receiving compliments, and I added, "Won't you come out of the rain?"

"Be glad to."

We went to the forward stateroom for coffee, and glancing at the mahogany molding on the beams overhead and the leaded glass panes in the cabinet doors, my new friend was properly appreciative.

"I've always wanted to take the inland route south," he said wistfully. "All I've got is a little sloop—I've just been bailing her out. But someday I aim to get something like this. . . ."

He went on, talking almost compulsively, the way strangers often do over a cup of coffee on boats, especially on rainy days.

"My wife would never do it, of course," he continued. "She can't see why I want to hang around the docks all the time, even in weather like this. I'm a salesman, electrical parts for big industry. It's not the kind of work I ever intended to do, but a friend of mine made a killing in it right after the war. I thought I might get in and get out fast to live the kind of life I want. . . ."

He talked for a long while, complaining about his wife and job in a way I had no right to criticize. Obviously he was an unhappy man who had chosen boats as his fantasy for escape, as I always had.

"I'm studying navigation in my spare time," he continued. "I suppose I'll never really use it, but I have a big compass on my boat. I had it compensated and everything. I even have a sextant."

Despite my attempts to be sympathetic, I soon grew bored with the salesman who hated his job and his wife so much. As soon as I was able to bid farewell to him, I went to squat in the engine room beside Carl while he put a new sealer in the water pump and tried to explain to me the cooling system of the engines. Now that I owned a motorboat and was committing the safety of my family to it, I felt it was time I conquered my lifelong aversion to everything mechanical. My intelligence did not appear to me to be less than that of Carl, who had left school in the ninth grade. There was only an attitude I had to conquer, this ridiculous aversion to grease and hot metal. There was no reason why I could not find in engines the same beauty I had once found in sail. Both sails and engines, after all, are machines designed to make the forces of nature push a boat where men want it to go. For this purpose sails harness the wind, while engines, with vastly more sophistication and efficiency, harness fire. Just as there is beauty in an efficient sail, so is there beauty in an engine kept immaculately clean, a marine motor with its intricate system of salt water cooling fresh water to protect the metal against corrosion, with its oil pressure giving as accurate an indication of health as blood pressure in a human. As though my engines were indeed patients made of flesh and blood, I was learning that their temperature was all-important, and much could be learned from the wheezing and sighs that emitted from their dark interiors.

The engines were also beautiful in their obedience, in their safety and in their reliability. Despite its apparent chaos, this engine room had been beautifully thought out. If a starting battery went dead, I did not have to curse and call a mechanic; there were all sorts of switches I could throw to draw on other sources of power to recharge it. The diesel oil was eager to explode when it got to the right place in the engines, but in the tanks it lay inert and, unlike gasoline, did not offer the constant danger of accidental explosion in case of leaks. There was no ignition system to go wrong, no spark plugs to replace, and as long as water and oil flowed through their iron veins properly to keep down their fever, these diesels could run months on end without stopping.

By any pragmatic test, the motors were truly a thing of beauty. With little noise or vibration, we had sliced along at 12 knots, about twice the speed most sailboats with auxiliary engines average under power. Because we were at our best in flat calms, when sailing vessels lie rolling over their reflections, we could make the most of smooth seas, but if the going did get rough, I was sure that these big diesels could push our narrow hull against winds and seas which would leave any sailing vessel chopping up and down in the same hole endlessly. Moreover, the engines did their job at remarkably little expense. We had burned just about 100 gallons of fuel on the 120-mile run from Norfolk, which figured out to a cost of about fourteen cents a mile, a figure not much more than that I used to get when I drove an automobile on an expense account, and here we were taking all our living accommodations with us.

Truly our diesels were noble flowerings of the ingenuity of man, but as I tried to fit the saltwater pump together under Carl's direction, I still could not help loathing them and everything else mechanical. As all engines had in the past, these seemed intent on making me look like a fool. For Carl the pump jumped together like a simple jigsaw puzzle. When I tried it, bolts refused to turn, washers got lost in the bilge, wrenches slipped, and my knuckles got skinned. My body ached from being bent around the generator, and grease soon spread from my hands to my face, hair and clothes. When I finally got the pump put together, it still leaked, sending triumphant geysers of water into my eyes, and Carl had to take it all apart again.

"I can't help it—I hate engines and they hate me," I said in a rage.

"You just need patience and self-confidence," Carl said.

I had neither. Sweat was trickling down my back and stinging my groin. Suffering from a sudden rush of claustrophobia, I bolted up the ladder from the engine room and went to the aftercabin for a shower.

Here I faced another problem. Although I didn't like to admit it to myself, my digestive troubles had continued ever since I had moved aboard the boat in Oxford, and I was developing new and alarming symptoms I had never suffered before and hesitated to describe even to Betty. The unattractive and agonizing truth was that my skin was beginning to split in all the most private seams of my body. Sweat stung me badly enough, but hot water and soap almost sent me up through the deck. Slathering myself with creams, oils and powders, I stretched out on a bunk.

In the morning the sky was clear, but the north wind still howled at better than 30 knots, and small craft storm warnings were up.

"What the hell," I said to Betty, my restlessness making me reckless. "We might roll a little crossing Norfolk Harbor, but after that we'll be in the big ditch. Let's go!"

The wind blew right on our beam, plastering us against the yacht club dock. It is always hard to pull away from a wharf in such circumstances without banging up the rails and the topsides, but I decided I was tired of being timid.

"Hang on to your forward spring line," I said to Carl. "I'll have to use a lot of power to kick her stern out."

When I eased the starboard throttle down, nothing much happened—the hull of the *Pretty Betty* is shaped a little like a pencil, and there is no broad curve in her bow on which she can pivot. If I had had more experience with her, I would have backed the port engine harder, but I was used to single-screw vessels and kept increasing the pressure on the spring line, pulling the bow in.

"Watch out!" Carl called. "You're bending the rail!"

Quickly I backed both engines, giving her half speed to haul her against the gale. There was a wrenching sound and she came clear. It was a clumsy, badly timed maneuver.

"You got a scratch about a foot long on the topside," Carl said, coming aft. "The forward stanchion on the rail tore loose. I think I can fix it."

"Damn!" I said. "Well, I've got to pay tuition as I learn how to handle her."

"I didn't say anything," Carl said.

He went below and a moment later reappeared.

"Did you switch off the shore current?"

"Yes."

"Well, you turned the dial too far. Always turn the constavolt off when you've got the big generator going. The way you had it, you were giving the batteries a double charge."

"Damn! Did it hurt anything?"

"I don't know yet, but probably not. It wasn't going on long enough."

Now my record of being the Perfect Sailor aboard the *Pretty*

*Betty* was marred, and I was unreasonably upset. Muttering curses at myself, I shoved the throttles down and headed across Norfolk Harbor. As we emerged from the shelter of the river, the full sweep of the wind and the long swells from the bay hit her, and the *Pretty Betty* began to dance. Baby in arms, Betty almost immediately appeared beside me.

"Everything's going crazy down there," she said accusingly.

"In an hour she'll be steady as a rock. Look!"

The view of the harbor ahead of us was magnificent. A gigantic aircraft carrier flanked by two destroyers was anchored on our starboard bow, and the sun glinted on tall white towers all around the glittering green bay.

"It's quite a sight," Betty said as we entered the main channel, ducked around the stern of a fat tanker and passed a tug with a string of barges. The view ahead was confusing, for a lot of channels went in different directions, and no entrance to our canal was visible.

"How do you know where to go?" Betty asked, the surprise in her voice stemming, I believed, from the fact that I commonly got lost while driving a car and spent much time asking directions.

"It's simple. We just follow the compass courses from buoy to buoy."

Threading our way up a narrow river, we came to a low iron bridge, the first we had encountered on our journey.

"How do we get through there?" Betty asked.

"They'll open it for us."

"They never will. It's impossible."

Touching a button by the wheel, I let our air horn blow three long blasts. It was the first time we had heard it, and the baby covered her ears with her hands.

Almost immediately sirens sounded on the bridge, cars came to a halt, and the great iron arch rose before us. Serenely we steamed through.

"Kings and queens couldn't do it better," Betty said. "Everybody makes way for us! It's like some great puffed-up dream of self-importance!"

With surprising suddenness, the city of Norfolk disappeared almost as soon as we got through the bridge. Within a few minutes we were in the Dismal Swamp Canal, which didn't look as though it had changed a bit since George Washington surveyed it. The narrow channel, bordered by a forest of cypress, juniper, black gum and pine, was motionless and black as a macadam highway.

"I don't see anything dismal about this," Betty said. "It's fascinating."

"There are plenty of snakes, alligators and bears in there, they say."

"Where?" Jessie asked eagerly. "I can't see them."

"We'd have to take the dinghy and explore it. Maybe we will someday when the weather is warmer."

There was a moment of silence, broken only by the steady throb of the engines.

"It's beautiful," Betty said finally, "but I have a lot of work to do below. Where did you put the kitty litter?"

"In the forecastle."

She and the baby disappeared, and I was left sitting high in the captain's chair at the wheel, monarch of all I surveyed. If I leaned forward in just the right way, my unusual affliction of the skin did not pain me much. The channel was so straight that I hardly had to touch the helm, and in the shelter of the swamp, the gales of Chesapeake Bay could hardly be felt at all. Here there was no need to keep glancing apprehensively at the sky or to keep careful track of buoys and compass courses. There was, in fact, nothing to worry about at all, for even if the engines failed, we would only have to tie up to the bank and wait for a tow. Many people complain about the trip through the canals being a great bore, but it was pleasant, sitting there in the cold November sun, watching the miles of swampland spin by without any worries. After an hour, my only problem was to stay awake.

Suddenly there was a shriek from the cabin below. Unable to leave the wheel and run to see what had happened, I stood paralyzed.

"What's the matter?" I shouted.

Betty stuck her head up the hatch.

"Oh, this damn boat!" she yelled. "Son of a. . . ."

"What happened?"

"I burned myself on that Goddamn oven, and when I jumped back, I hit a can of bacon grease I'd left by the sink, and it spilled *all over*. . . ."

"Are you hurt?"

"No, but Jessie is down there tracking it all over now, and that isn't all."

"What else?"

"When I picked up the bag of kitty litter, it was damp and the bottom came out of it. That stuff is all over too."

"Call Carl," I said. "I'll clean it up."

"No, it's my job."

Still muttering oaths, Betty went below. A moment later there was another shriek, followed by a string of words I had never heard Betty use before, and a loud banging which sounded as though she were hurling pots and pans. Turning to call Carl, I saw him stick his head up the hatch from the after cabin. The cursing became a crescendo, and he ducked back in again.

"Carl!" I shouted.

"What the hell is happening?" he asked, reappearing.

"I don't know. Take the wheel."

Hurrying below, I found Betty sitting on a bunk with her head in her hands sobbing while Jessie embraced her legs. The galley and forward stateroom were smeared with a combination of bacon grease, kitty litter and water. The cat was perched high on a bookshelf, trying to clean herself and one of her growing kittens. An empty bucket rolled on the deck.

"Are you hurt?" I asked again.

"Yes. Christ, I don't know. I ache all over. No, Jessie, I'm all right. I got scared, that's all."

"What else happened?"

"I filled that bucket so I could clean up the mess. Then I slipped in that damn grease and fell. Just when I was trying to get up in all that grease, two cats jumped right in front of me, and the whole brood tracked grease all over the bunks. I was so mad I threw the frying pan at them. Oh, everything is such a mess. Damn this boat!"

Sitting beside her, I picked up the baby and put her on my lap. I tried to comfort Betty, but her words sent a chill through me. Had her rage at the narrow bunks, the lavatories in which one had to be something of a contortionist to sit down, and that torture chamber of a galley been building up all through the weeks of rain at Oxford until it couldn't be contained anymore? Would it be only a matter of time before she, like every woman I had ever known well, would pride herself on saying how much she hated boats? If so, I probably had a short cruise ahead, or a lonely one.

"You lie down," I said with more solicitude than I had ever shown in similar crises in our apartment. "I'll get everything all cleaned up in no time."

"You can't clean it up. It's impossible. Sink the boat. Kill all the cats."

"I've got a bag of rags in the engine room. The kittens are old enough to go now. We can start trying to find them homes."

"Good," Jessie said enigmatically, leaving me wondering whether she was glad we were not going to kill the kittens or delighted that we would be rid of them.

When I came back with the rags, Betty and the baby were lying down together. Filling the bucket with water and detergent, I got clumsily on my knees, stretching the various cracks in my groin so wretchedly that I involuntarily let out a groan.

"What's the matter?" Betty asked.

"I've got a new kind of disease."

"Where does it hurt?"

"Well, you know how when you're doing your dancing exercises, you sometimes do the split?"

"Yes."

"Well, it's as though I tried it and really did—I split."

"You're kidding."

"I wish I were. I split in several places."

"We'll have to stop and see a doctor. How long has this been going on?"

"About a week."

"I thought you'd been acting funny. Here, let me help you with that mess."

Getting on her knees, she grabbed a handful of rags.

"Boy!" she said as she dipped them in the mixture of bacon grease and kitty litter. "So this is yachting!"

"Betty. . . ."

"Is it still hurting?"

"No, but do you really hate the boat?"

"I love it. Where else could you and I be praying together like this?"

I didn't say anything, but apparently my face looked hurt.

"Stop it," she said.

"Stop what?"

"Looking stricken like that. You know one thing I hate about the boat?"

"What?"

"Pretending I'm marvelously happy all the time. I've felt I had to put on some kind of a big act ever since we first moved aboard."

"I didn't know you were putting on an act."

"Stop looking stricken! You have to face the truth."

"I don't want to."

"Ever since we left New York, I've felt that you were always watching me, trying to see if I'm really happy."

Wringing out her rag, Betty added more detergent to the water.

"It will be awkward if you are miserable. We'll have to sell the boat."

"I knew that was what you were thinking! So I've tried to

look happy, happy, happy all the time. It's been killing me."

"But now the truth is out in all its hideousness. You hate the boat."

"Sometimes I do. Who the hell would like to live in three connected hall closets? That's about the amount of space we've got."

"Do you want to move ashore?"

"I didn't say that! I'm miserable there lots of times too, bored out of my skull, just the way you are. I think the boat is exciting, but it's also miserable sometimes. Can't I complain, *ever?*"

"Yes," I said.

"Not if you are going to keep looking so *stricken.* Get up and lie down. Are you still splitting?"

"I'm afraid so."

"Is it bleeding?"

"I don't know. Much of it is where I can't see it."

"Take off your pants. I want to inspect this thing."

"No!"

"Don't be ridiculous. Maybe some Noxema would help."

She started tugging at my trousers, and finding that any movement was excruciating, I collapsed on the bunk and didn't resist.

"My God!" she said a few moments later. "You must be in agony."

"Does it look terrible?"

"It looks as though someone took a red hot poker to you. What's the next town we're going to pass through?"

"Elizabeth City. We should be there about four o'clock."

"We'll call a doctor. You shouldn't move. Can Carl get us alongside a dock all right?"

"I'm supposed to be the captain around here," I said and, feeling stagily heroic, struggled to my feet and went to the wheel.

That afternoon the pain increased to the point where I found that no single position was comfortable for more than a few seconds, and I wound up prancing around the wheel while I steered in a way which made Carl look at me with astonishment. Before I was able to explain my predicament, he went to the engine room, and I heard a string of oaths that made those Betty had used seem innocuous.

"What's the matter?" I shouted.

His head was dripping with water when he stuck it up the hatch.

"Now *both* engines are spurting. I guess I didn't put that sealer in right, and the starboard pump has let go too."

So now I've got two bad engines and a mechanic who can't fix them and I can't stand, sit or lie down without going out of my mind with pain, I thought bitterly. Boy, this is the life.

"What are you going to do?" I asked Carl.

"Get some new sealers in Elizabeth City."

When we finally tied up at a wharf in that town, I stretched out on the couch in the deckhouse. Three bearded young men on a little black schooner ahead of us helped handle our dock lines, and Carl asked them aboard.

"You fellows want a drink?" I asked somewhat weakly as Betty went ashore to call a physician.

They did, and moving gingerly, I opened a bottle of Scotch. It was surprising, I discovered, to find that this famous painkiller actually killed pain—after three stiff drinks, I had forgotten all about my embarrassing complaint and was eagerly discussing the route through the Bahamas the men on the schooner planned to take. After three more drinks, the details of navigation no longer seemed important, and we all started singing songs that one of the men had learned in the islands.

"Here he is," Betty said. "He can hardly move."

She was standing at the door to the deckhouse with a baldheaded man who carried a small black bag, and her words seemed monumentally inappropriate, for my new friends and I were prancing about in a bad imitation of a calypso.

"I see," the doctor said dryly. "Do you have a cabin where I can examine him?"

We went below, and the doctor prescribed, among other

things, that I soak the affected areas in medicated hot water three times a day. Since we had no bathtub, this was difficult, but I plugged up the base of the shower, filled it and wedged myself awkwardly in.

That night nothing seemed ridiculous or unbearable, but in the morning as I crouched in the tiny shower built into a corner of the after stateroom and tried to soak my aching bottom in hot water while keeping a rag packed with cracked ice on my head, I felt that I had finally reached the nadir of a long disreputable career. Even Carl's assurance that he had now succeeded in fixing the water pumps on the engines didn't help much, until I reflected that nothing was stopping us now from continuing our voyage south except my physical condition, which probably would be as painful at the wharf as it would be under way. Struggling out of the shower, I dressed quickly and went to the galley.

"Will you be able to leave in five minutes?" I asked Betty.

"The doctor said you should rest."

"I don't want to rest. I want to get out of here!"

It was ridiculous how the joy of leaving a place persisted, even though it was fairly clear that my troubles were not exactly earthbound, but this reflection did not calm my restlessness, my absurd urgency to get south.

"He said you've got to stay still as possible until your skin gets a chance to heal."

"It can heal under way, can't it? I won't move from the wheel."

"It's not safe for you to try to run a boat the way you are. What if there was some emergency?"

That shaft hit home—if there was anything I was dedicated to, it was the cause of safety at sea, and it was undoubtedly true that if circumstances required me in my present condition to be active for long, I would prove ineffective.

"All right, we'll lay over for a day," I said and climbed onto the cool fresh sheets Betty had spread over a bunk for me.

To take my mind off my troubles, I continued my reading of

*A Cruising Guide to the Southern Coast.* This proved to be a mistake. The next leg of our journey was to take us across Albemarle Sound, which the author described as "the most unpleasant body of water on the Atlantic Coast."

"The tumbling seas that came racing down from the north were choppy, irregular and steep," he wrote, describing a recent crossing. "Albemarle Sound flung itself in a frenzy against Sun Dog."

"What's the matter with you?" Betty asked, coming in from the galley. "Is the pain getting worse?"

I put the book down.

"No. I'm afraid of crossing Albemarle Sound."

"Why?"

"It's a terrible body of water. It's only twelve miles wide, but this book makes it sound worse than the Atlantic and Pacific oceans combined."

"I thought you sailed these waters often when you were a boy."

"I did, but apparently I survived all sorts of perils without even knowing it."

Betty picked up the book.

"Don't read it," I said. "Get me a drink."

"I thought that once you got on the boat. . . ."

"Never mind. I have to prepare myself for Albemarle Sound."

Hastily she scanned the pages I had left open while I poured myself a glass of Scotch.

"How can a body of water only twelve miles wide be that terrible?" she asked.

"Any shallow bay can kick up in a squall. They write those 'yachtsmen's guides' for people in very small boats who expect smooth water all the time."

"Then there's really no danger?"

"Of course not. *Pretty Betty* can cross the damn sound in less than an hour, and we won't start if it's rough."

Looking unconvinced, she went to the forecastle, where she was arranging hooks for Jessica's toys. I lay sipping my whiskey, trying to find a position in which my ridiculous affliction was bearable. It was clear that the descriptions of Albemarle Sound had made me absurdly apprehensive. Was this how "getting away from it all" was bound to end up for me, this business of lying around full of more fear and restlessness than I had suffered in New York?

Maybe, I thought darkly, the mysterious rebellion of the tenderest tissue of my skin was psychosomatic, the way everything was supposed to be nowadays. Maybe my spirit had become so eroded during twenty years of lying about the shore that it deliberately crippled my body to prevent it from going to sea. And how about this glass of whiskey in my hand? Since moving aboard the boat, I had continued to drink at night in port, but I had been too busy during the days to need alcohol. Yet here I was at eleven o'clock in the morning immobilized and lapping it up again.

I tried to tell myself that after the excitement of moving aboard the boat, there was bound to be a letdown and that the change in daily routine, diet and water could be expected to cause all sorts of temporary physical ills. A few days in the sun of the Bahamas could be expected to cure all that.

If we ever get there, a dark voice deep within me echoed. If my health holds out, if the engines don't keep on giving trouble, if Betty's patience endures. . . .

"Skipper?"

It was Carl, standing at the open hatch.

"Good morning, Carl."

"How are you feeling?"

"A little better."

"I wondered if this would be a good time for a lesson in navigation."

"Sure," I said, reflecting that this would be a fine chance to divert my thinking to more constructive channels.

The next day I was up at dawn, and though I was still in considerable pain, I was so restless that I told Betty I felt much better and to make sure the galley was secured for the rigors of Albemarle Sound. It was a gray day with a stiff wind continuing from the north, a fact which delighted my bearded friends on the little black schooner. Hoisting their sails, they went scudding away, leaving a wake of beer cans glinting behind them. Moving in a gingerly fashion I tried to disguise, I went to the captain's chair and started the engines while Carl cast off the lines.

"Can I take the wheel?" Carl asked as soon as we were free of the wharf. "I'd like to steer that compass course I laid out and see if it works."

There was a slight chop in Albemarle Sound, but the *Pretty Betty* did not seem unduly impressed. With her long bow neatly cleaving the muddy waves, she soon passed the little schooner, and in about twenty minutes we could see the beacon marking the channel on the other side. Before long we were slicing through the smooth black waters of the Alligator River.

"When do we get to Albemarle Sound?" Betty asked, bringing up hot coffee.

"We just crossed it."

She laughed.

"May all our fears turn out to be so absurd," she said.

# 13

⚓

The next week proved to be so pleasant that even my aching bottom and my penchant for manufacturing worries could not ruin it. The weather turned bright, and under sparkling skies we went winging down through the Carolinas and into Georgia. Much of the intracoastal waterway here consisted of meandering rivers, not straight-banked canals, and every five minutes there was a different view, sometimes of majestic oaks already bearded with Spanish moss, sometimes of lonely beaches backed by marsh and sometimes of small towns that went staggering as far as they could out to sea with weather-beaten shacks on barnacle-encrusted piles. It was a pleasant voyage with little for the helmsman to do but follow the compass courses already marked on charts and check the buoys off as we passed them. Much of the time Carl stood beside me, staring at the charts as though he were trying to memorize them.

The voyage went so smoothly that only the troubles of other people kept us on our toes. One morning, when we decided to rest at a pleasant wharf near a grove of giant oaks in South Carolina, we saw three expensive yachts cast off their lines to continue their trip south, and by noon they had all limped back again. One, a brand-new yacht which had cost more than $100,000, had suffered a dangerous fire in the engine room caused by a badly installed electrical system. A second boat, only a few years old, had burned out the bearings in one engine, and a third had hit a submerged log, tearing off a propeller. The next day, shortly before we reached Charleston, we rounded a bend in the channel and came upon a boat much like our own which had missed a channel marker and run hard aground on a mudbank. When we arrived, the tide had dropped enough to leave her high and dry, miserably lying over on her side. There wasn't much to do until the tide came up again, and the professional skipper who was trying to deliver her to her owner glumly refused our offer of assistance and waved us on.

"What's the matter with these people?" Betty asked. "I thought this was supposed to be a simple trip."

"It is," I said. "That professional skipper probably was so bored that he was just nodding at the wheel. If he had been driving a car, he would be dead by now."

"But what about all the boats that break down?"

"The longest trip most yachts take is the trip south," Carl said. "They lie at marinas all summer and then they go to some place in Florida to tie up all winter. Nobody takes care of their machinery, and when they try to use it, they break down."

"They're not fortunate enough to have a resident engineer," I said.

"Or an old Coast Guard officer as skipper," Carl added with a smile.

The mutual congratulations were a mistake. Almost immediately our port engine developed new trouble. It started losing fresh water and heated up dangerously unless we replenished its supply every few hours.

"What's the matter this time?" I asked Carl.

"I don't know. I can fix it unless it's something like a cracked block."

"A *cracked block?*"

"Maybe it's the heat exchanger. We'll just have to keep checking and see."

Every night Carl dismantled a different part of the engine, looking for the mysterious leak, but he couldn't find it. As long as we kept feeding the engine water as though it were a thirsty horse, it continued to grumble along steadily, and I tried to make myself believe that soon some minor, easily repaired leak would be discovered.

That night we tied up at a big marina whose owner helped us to solve one of our problems: he took all our cats but the mother. "I'll let my kids take their pick, and there are plenty of families here who will take the others," he said. "Rats are getting to be a problem."

Jessie bid each of the kittens a fond farewell, but she seemed as relieved as her parents by the new peace aboard the boat.

At Charleston, South Carolina, we stopped for three days. Already the mornings were warm enough to make coats and sweaters unnecessary, and feeling that we had reached our goal of summer weather, we decided to do some sight-seeing and wait for our mail to catch up with us. The first morning I enjoyed walking along the battery, examining the stately old mansions I remembered visiting as a boy, but the grand old hotel where we had stayed had been torn down, and all the people whose names I remembered were no longer in the telephone book.

On the third morning a large package of envelopes awaited us at the general delivery window of the post office. One of them was a short note from Betty's father, Bob Stephens, who had booked passage on a Cunard liner and was prepared to meet us anywhere in Florida in two weeks.

"Tell him to go to Daytona," I said. "I don't want to go any farther south until the hurricane season is over, and there are lots of people I want to look up there."

Betty sent him a cable telling him we would be lying at the Daytona Boat Works, and when she came back from the telephone, I noticed that she looked unusually cheerful.

"What did your father do to make you so glad to see him all the time?" I asked somewhat grumpily, for I hadn't received any mail from my children, despite postcards I had sent at every stop, and I was feeling neglected.

"*Everybody* is always glad to see my father come," Betty replied. "Sometimes, I confess, they are even gladder to see him go, but you've got to admit that it's always fun to see him come through the door. Life is never boring when he's around."

"Someone told me once that the way to find a good wife is to find a girl who loves her father and whose father is somewhat like yourself."

"In a lot of ways you do resemble each other. You're both big. He always told me to find a man who had some real bulk."

"And we both drink too much," I said sourly.

"You exaggerate that. Anyway, you're not like him in that. You don't throw people around when you get drunk."

"I try not to," I said and hoped that all the secret forebodings I had about the visit of Betty's father would prove to be another Albemarle Sound.

What did I actually know of Bob Stephens, and why was I full of such an odd mixture of almost unwilling happiness and deep foreboding at his arrival?

When I had first met Betty, she had not seen her father in several years, for she had been working in New York and he had been living in Dublin, but she had talked about him constantly. Robert Stephens had been born the youngest son of a large and fairly prosperous Protestant family in Dublin shortly after the turn of the century. By his own account he had been a hell-raiser starting fairly early, but he also had been a champion oarsman in the Dublin rowing clubs and had helped his brothers build a small factory which specialized in chromium plating. Faded photographs Betty showed me in a much-thumbed family album showed a muscular, jaunty young Irishman who looked as though he had never known a moment of self-doubt.

In 1926 or thereabouts, Bob Stephens came to America, not as an immigrant but as a tourist who had every expectation of returning to his home. In New York he met Jessie McSkimming, the daughter of a Scotch sailor who had settled near the Brooklyn shipyards with a bride he had brought from the old country. Jessie was popular, Jessie was vivacious, Jessie in the old family album looked like Betty dressed up in the style of the twenties for a masquerade ball, and Bob had apparently fallen in love with her completely, just as I had with her daughter about thirty years later.

But their life was difficult, almost from the beginning. In Ireland Bob was considered an engineer, but he didn't have the academic degrees to be thought one in the United States. And Jessie tried but couldn't get used to living in Dublin. They moved back and forth across the Atlantic a lot before Bob decided to cut his ties in Ireland and live permanently in New York.

About that time the Great Depression hit. Convinced by batteries of personnel men that his talents as an engineer were unwanted in America, Bob sold vacuum cleaners door to door and worked as a conductor on the Long Island Railroad, and during one desperate period this great, exuberantly proud man delivered telegrams on a bicycle. Nothing seemed to work for him. He tried tending bar, managing an apartment house and breaking up barrels of hard glue with a sledge hammer in a factory. Meanwhile his wife became executive secretary to a man they both knew who was a vice-president of a large corporation. From time to time Bob went back to Ireland to try to get started all over again there, and Betty was brought up regarding Dublin as a sort of suburb of Brooklyn.

Shortly after World War II, a period he had spent mostly in Dublin, Bob discovered that his wife had some sort of heart trouble that did not have a hopeful prognosis. Although he hated Brooklyn, he stayed there to be near her. Still frustrated in his attempts to get a good job in America, he bought a small tailor shop near their home, despite the fact that he had never threaded a needle or pressed a pair of pants in his life. One way or another, he made a living while Jessie went through a series of operations and temporary recoveries which lasted for seven years.

Then Jessie died. Apparently a broken man, Bob went home

to his beloved Ireland, leaving behind his daughter, who had inherited her mother's mysterious ability to cope with America. For a while Betty worried about him, but almost immediately he started a new little factory in Dublin, and when I met Betty he was riding high, manufacturing all the bus seats and most of the steel furniture in Eire.

Betty had always regarded him as a hero for three reasons. First of all, he had obviously loved her mother, his devotion never fading through thick and a great deal of thin. Second, he was a man who loved life, even when his luck was as low as it could get, and he had a knack of making the people around him love it too. And third, he was a man who had always made her proud to have him as a father, even when he was delivering telegrams on a bicycle. He had a mysterious quality which kept any man from looking down on him. I first met Bob when we went to Ireland to get married. The moment he sprang from the crowd at the Dublin airport to greet us, I saw what Betty meant. With snow-white hair, a pink, glowing face and a vast, barrel-like body, he was an impressive figure even before he began talking. A Niagara Falls of words, he had a voice full of the peculiar charm of the Dubliner. Without a brogue, which the Irish consider their equivalent of Cockney, his diction was almost that of an upper-class Londoner set to Irish music, full of cadences and rhythms which made ordinary English sound dead. I was charmed, and I couldn't understand why Betty kept eyeing us speculatively as though she expected us to square off and fight any minute.

"I knew you would like him when you first met him," she said when we were alone together. "It's the long run I'm worried about."

"Why?"

"Well, there are some things I didn't tell you about. Try to remember that he's *Irish*. Ireland is much closer to Europe than America and it has its own peculiar problems."

"Like what?"

"Irishmen are a lot more repressed than Americans four-fifths of the time and a lot more explosive the other fifth."

"Your father doesn't seem either repressed or explosive."

"He's lived off and on in America for almost thirty years, and you never know what facet of him is coming up next. Just take it easy and try to be understanding."

During a tour of Ireland we took together, I was more amused than alarmed by Bob's character. Obviously the gentleman was a lady's man—as a prosperous widower of such unusual appearance he was pursued by women everywhere he went. And his attitude toward women was entirely different from that of anyone I had ever known.

First of all, he had apparently never met an ugly woman in his life. To him even an ancient crone had a sparkle in her eye.

"Now there goes a bit of glamour!" he'd say as we were walking down the street, and turning with astonishment, I would see only a stout middle-aged housewife on her way to market.

Women apparently sensed that he felt that way about them, and gaunt spinsters turned coquettish when he flashed them a smile.

Since Bob obviously did so much for women, I should not have been surprised to learn that he expected a great deal in return. Without the necessity of his raising his voice, women fetched and carried for him, drove him about in cars, got his meals and laughed endlessly at his long jokes. The only emotions this inspired in me were envy and admiration, except when he made Betty one of his subjects.

"Wash this for me," he'd say, tossing her a bundle of dirty linen.

"Mail this for me," he'd say to Betty when he finished a letter. "Find out how many stamps it needs."

This was only the start of a steady procession of demands. All my life I had known men, including my own father, who did their best to wait on women hand and foot. Perhaps I was learning something. Since Betty obviously had no objections, I held my peace.

"I think your father is charming," I said to Betty when we flew back to New York. "I don't see why you thought we'd ever have any trouble getting along."

"He's at his best in Ireland. That's why I wanted you to see him there first. He doesn't drink much there, and he knows just how far he can go."

"Do you expect him to visit us?"

"He said some time next year."

When Bob first came to New York to see us, Jessica was only a few months old. The apartment we had at the time was too small for guests, so we gave it to him and moved a few blocks away to my mother's apartment, which she had vacated for the summer. There we asked him to join us for meals.

The day after he arrived, Bob announced that he didn't like spending his nights alone and moved in with us. I myself am incapable of handling solitude, and I didn't mind this until I discovered that he did not regard the arrival of a new baby as an event which should occupy a great deal of his daughter's time. The bundles of laundry were still tossed at her with the greatest nonchalance, and at any time of the day or night he saw nothing wrong in saying, "Betty, would you mind getting me a cup of tea?"

That was a period when Betty was suffering the exhaustion which often follows the exuberance of giving birth, and I tried to protect her by getting the tea as often as I could myself, hoping he would get the idea that American men are capable of putting a kettle on to boil. This was a hint he did not take. When he wasn't calling for more tea, he was writing letters, each one of which he took to Betty with a request that it be stamped and mailed. I myself was touchy and overwrought after the excitement of Jessie's arrival and a stint of hard work. It wasn't long before I thought I would explode every time he presented my wife with another little chore.

The first small climax came when he interrupted her with more letters for Ireland while she was nursing the baby.

"Bob," I said, trying to keep my voice scrupulously polite. "Betty is very busy with the baby now, and she's not feeling strong. There is a letter chute out by the elevators."

"I don't have any stamps," he said in surprise.

"You can buy them in any drugstore."

"I don't know how much postage they need."

"There is a post office just down the block."

"All right," he said with an air of vastly injured dignity and, putting his letters down on a table, walked out of the room.

"You hurt his feelings," Betty said to me, using a note of accusation entirely foreign to her nature.

It was important not to upset her while she was nursing, I had been told. Choking a little, I too left the room.

The next morning the letters remained on the table.

"I'll mail them when I go out for the groceries," Betty said. "There's no use in building a federal case. . . ."

"Then he'll know he's beaten us down. He's making this a test."

"He is or you are? The two of you are just as stubborn. . . ."

"Why can't he mail his own Goddamn letters and take care of his own Goddamn laundry and dry cleaning and tea at a time like this?"

"You know you're not supposed to get me upset."

"All right, I'll mail his Goddamn letters!"

"No, I will!"

She grabbed them from me.

"You're not supposed to be going out for groceries anyway," I shouted. "They're supposed to be delivered."

"Then leave the letters there," she retorted. "I'm not going to have you running his errands if it makes you furious."

"Am I crazy to want him to mail his own Goddamn letters?"

"He doesn't know where anything is in this country."

"I thought he lived here almost thirty years."

"Leave the letters there," she said wearily. "He'll get around to mailing them."

The next morning the letters remained on the corner of the table, and at breakfast it seemed to me that we all kept glancing at them as though they were evidence of some crime we wished could be concealed. I went out for a business appointment, and when I came back they had disappeared. Betty said her father had finally taken care of them.

During the next few days Bob did not in my hearing ask his daughter to mail more letters, but my irritation at him kept growing. The reflection that this was only classic in-law trouble did not help. Despite the fact that we had provided him with his own apartment only a short distance away, he did not recognize our desire to be alone as much as a minute. Day after day he sat sipping tea or pacing up and down the living room jingling the change in his pockets and singing scraps of the lyrics of different songs, which he pieced together oddly and set to melodies having nothing to do with any of them. "In the deep purple night I sang that stardust of a song to my wild Irish rose," he caroled happily one afternoon, fitting it all into the melody of "Let Me Call You Sweetheart."

At night he slept on the couch in the living room and filled the whole apartment with thunderous snores. Asleep or awake, he was omnipresent—one could never forget for an instant that he was there.

"He's just lonely," Betty said. "After all, he came here just to see us. . . ."

"For twenty-four hours a day? For *how long?*"

"We told him he could stay as long as he liked."

"How am I going to get any work done?"

"The main trouble is he doesn't have any friends here. Maybe if I could introduce him to a nice woman. . . ."

Among our friends was an actress of uncertain age who dropped in to see us one day.

"Is that your father?" she whispered to Betty. "He's *beautiful!*"

A glint came into Betty's eye, and there was more whispering. That night Bob got all dressed up and left the apartment just before dinner. The next day he said he was going to start sleeping in our old apartment.

"Well, that was simple, wasn't it?" Betty asked me triumphantly.

As it turned out, it wasn't. The following afternoon we got an impassioned telephone call from the actress.

"What's the matter with him?" she demanded shrilly. "He called me up at *four o'clock in the morning!* He said he couldn't sleep and he wanted me to come up and cook him some breakfast."

"You've got to understand—he's Irish," Betty said wearily.

"Well, I'm Jewish," the actress said, and the rest was unprintable.

"Dad," Betty said when her father returned to our apartment a few hours later, "in this country you can't call a woman up at four in the morning and ask her to get your breakfast, especially when you've just met her."

*"Did she say that?"*

Standing in the middle of our living room, Bob glanced up at the ceiling, obviously appealing to God as his witness. A look of the most incredible virtue shone from his pink face, haloed by his snow-white hair. He looked like a venerable priest waiting for the inspiration which would allow him to give an unusually moving prayer.

*"Did she say that?"* he again asked, his voice rising with incredulity.

"She did," I unkindly grunted.

"Well, I did nothing of the kind! The woman must be daft. Now what would make her accuse a man of a thing like that?"

"How can he work himself up to such a pitch of indignation when he lies?" I whispered to Betty when we finally escaped the Case for the Defense and huddled in our bedroom.

"He doesn't know he's lying. He really thinks he's innocent."

"How does he accomplish that?"

"Well, he probably didn't ask her to fix his breakfast—he probably asked her to get him some tea and crumpets. That's not breakfast to him—breakfast is six eggs, sausages and all the rest."

"But does he really think he can demand tea and crumpets at four in the—"

"He probably didn't know it was four. Perhaps he had been drinking, and he just woke up and wanted tea, so he called the first woman who was handy. He never looks at his watch when he's hungry. When Mother was sick and he was between jobs, I was out dancing professionally until three every morning, but he often woke me up at four for tea and crumpets."

"I'm beginning to hate the old bastard."

"You won't when you understand him. He only did it when he was drinking. Sometimes he brought everyone in the bar with him home for breakfast."

"And expected you to get up and cook it when you'd been working all night?"

"I never minded. Everyone was always so convivial. When Mother was sick, she used to like to hear them all laughing."

"At four in the morning?"

"There are times in your life when you value laughter at any hour, even at four in the morning. It's a hell of a lot better than waking up and hearing a man crying."

"I'm sorry," I said.

"It's all right. You won't hate him when you come to understand him as I do."

The trouble was my powers of understanding were not as good as Betty's. When I got an invitation to lecture at a college in New Jersey during a three-day seminar, I thought this would give us an opportunity for a brief escape from her father, who had again taken up residence in our apartment.

"We can't leave him behind," Betty said when I broached the idea to her. "He'd be terribly hurt."

"Well, at least we'll be living in a big dormitory," I replied grumpily. "He'll have a room of his own, hopefully with sound-proof walls."

So Betty, her father, the baby and I all got in our car and set out to a small New Jersey town to discuss literature. Always before I had survived occasions of this kind, seriously telling students to double-space their manuscripts and reassuring them that most editors really do read everything submitted, but I had never before contracted to give a course like this one, which required some seven hours of talk. How in the name of heaven was I to piece out my meager store of transferable knowledge over such an interminable time?

While I tried to answer this riddle, Bob occupied himself by giving me directions in territory he had never before seen and singing his interminable repertoire of mixed-up melodies and lyrics.

When we finally got to the college, I was happy to discover that Betty and I were given a room some way down the hall from her father. Before I had a chance to make many notes for my lectures, the first of the faculty cocktail parties began. A great lover of any party, Bob armed himself with a glass of Scotch and soon drew an admiring crowd around him. With his lilting speech, his inexhaustible supply of Irish humor, his handsome, animated face and his crown of snow-white hair, he was obviously far better suited for the role of literary lion than I was. Hearing that a novelist was in their midst, most people assumed that here at last was a man worthy of the title, and without consciously practicing any deception, Bob fulfilled their expectations better than I ever could. When an ancient lady shyly showed him some poetry she had written, instead of groaning inwardly as I would have done, he declaimed it with relish, his incredible diction making every line sound like Shakespeare, and putting his arm around her thin shoulders, he assured her she was a genius who deserved world fame. Charmed, all the old ladies in the vicinity crept forward, like children learning that someone has just built a fire on the hearth of a cold house. Grabbing drinks from a white-coated waiter every time they were passed, Bob was soon pressing elbows and patting shoulders in the fond style that had brought him friends in so many Dublin pubs.

"I'm worried," Betty said, approaching me in a corner.

"Why? I should pay him to give my lectures. I'd soon be so famous I wouldn't even have to write anymore."

"He's all right now, but he's drinking too much. This can get sticky awfully fast."

"I never saw him drink too much in Ireland."

"But here he's like an American visiting Paris. We have to watch out. I'm afraid all this adulation will go to his head even more than the booze."

"What do you want me to do?"

"Pray."

"Can I do it in my room? I really ought to be outlining my lectures, and it's obvious I'm not needed here."

"You run along. I'll bring him back to his room as soon as I can."

At a student's desk in the dormitory I sat with pencil in hand.

"Double-space manuscripts," I wrote in a small spiral notebook.

"Yes, editors really do read everything submitted, or at least enough of it to tell whether they can use it. That's their business.

"No, it is not necessary to have an agent when you submit your first piece. Most good agents won't take you anyway until you have sold a few things."

There, I'd said it—everything I knew about writing which could conceivably help a talented beginner, and I had no idea what could aid a person with no talent, whatever that mysterious word meant.

"What is talent?"

That sentence looked fairly good at the top of a page, and perhaps I could talk about it for several hours before admitting that I didn't know the answer. Of course I should have come better prepared, but always before, I had despaired of making detailed notes come to life and had relied on my ability to think on my feet. What would happen if that mysterious skill had in truth deserted me? It would mean the end of my lecturing career, which should be a relief—unless I also found I couldn't write profitably anymore. Then where would be my reserve program for survival, the comforting thought that even if I couldn't write, I could teach?

Gone—gone the way money disappeared, driven before the cold winds of divorce, high living, taxes and the rash kind of investments lawyers recommended as an escape from the upper brackets of taxation. Was the whole world simply a device calculated to reduce fools to penury?

Betty could always work—she had told me that during many a midnight sinking spell. Would she end by supporting me, as she had for so long helped to support her father? Was a mysterious financial weakness the real thing that she recognized we held in common?

No, we were not alike in that, for in Ireland Bob always prospered, but where would I find a nice little country which recognized my talents? Now was no time to brood about that. I had to get loosened up so that I could talk on my feet within a couple of hours. Perhaps a drink would help. Despite the much publicized terrors of alcohol, it often was preferable to panic, an almost tangible substance it well knew how to dissolve.

Taking a bottle of Scotch from my suitcase, I poured myself a stiff drink and lay down on my bed. In a few minutes the warm glow started and my supply of anecdotes began to seem funny.

"Sloan?" Betty said, sticking her head in the door a few minutes later.

"What's up?"

"I really think we have to get Dad out of there. Can we tell him we have to go to a restaurant for dinner?"

"We're supposed to go to some professor's house. What's he doing?"

"He's reached the fanny-patting stage. Some of the deans' wives are not entranced."

"For God's sake! I'll go tell him to cut it out. Doesn't he know he's in a small college town?"

"You mustn't lecture him. He'll get furious, and then. . . ."

"What?"

"You don't know him when he gets like this. He starts throwing people around."

"He won't throw me around. That's one advantage of getting fat."

"You mustn't lecture him! You have to realize that he doesn't know he's offending anybody. When he gets like this he thinks a pat on the fanny is just a perfectly normal expression of affection. If you call him on it, he will feel terribly insulted, and you must never insult an Irishman when he's drunk."

"Let him alone then. I've never known a dean's wife who can't take care of herself."

"But I'm worried about your reputation. Most of the people there think he's you."

"They'll find out better at the lecture tonight," I said grimly.

"Half the people there won't go to the lecture. They're community leaders who just came to the party."

"Who gives a damn what they think?"

"They're talking about getting up a fund for giving writers part-time jobs. It might be a good opportunity. . . ."

"Oh, hell, we'll take him to a restaurant then," I said and drained my glass before putting it down. Betty didn't say anything, but I saw that her eye went to the bottle of Scotch on the table, registering the fact that it was no longer full.

Getting Bob to go to a restaurant proved impossible. He was now the center of a crowd which hung on his every word and waited with baited breath for every gesture. The atmosphere in the big room was tense and he was talking a little thickly, but he said he was having much too good a time to go, and obviously there was no way to remove him without a scene. I went back to my room for another drink.

Somehow that night I got through the lecture. Without worrying about whether it had been good, I was delighted that it was over and eagerly went to a party being held by someone described as a Friend of the University. The Friend had opened his commodious ranch house, and the party had spilled from the living room onto a flagstone terrace which surrounded a swimming pool. Betty kept running between me and her father, who was now holding court in the living room. Although at the time I thought that the concern on her face was caused solely by Bob, it came to me afterward that she was distracted because she knew we were both getting drunk.

Alcohol of course affects individuals in many different ways. Betty had told me that it made Bob expansive, affectionate in progressively more demonstrative ways and physically violent if crossed. Usually it made me confident, sleepy and verbally violent whether crossed or not. The climax of the evening was predictable to anyone who knew both men well, which is why Betty soon began to look tormented.

The woman who ignited the explosive mixture was a well-meaning old soul who got me aside and said that I really ought to do something about my father-in-law, because charming as he was, he was saying and doing things that were getting some of the ladies quite upset. Deciding that I had had enough of this situation, I brushed by Betty, broke into the throng surrounding Bob and asked if I could talk to him alone outside.

"What's up, lad?" he asked as we went out the front door. Some of the people on the nearby terrace eyed us curiously.

"I'll tell you what's up," I said succinctly. "I've been getting complaints about you. You've got to watch your language and your hands when you come with me to visit a college town."

"What do you mean?" he bellowed and glanced up at the sky again, seeking divine guidance with which to protest his innocence.

"I'm getting complaints," I said again, perhaps a little thickly.

"Who's complaining?" Bob demanded, and before I could stop him, he strode back into the crowded living room. Turning from the window where she had been watching us, Betty looked aghast.

"Ladies and gentlemen!" Bob boomed. "I want to ask you a question."

There was a sudden silence while he stood behind a chair, gripping the top of it as though it were a lectern.

"My son-in-law here says I have been offending people," Bob said with a voice full of sweet reason. "Now all I want to know is, who? *Whom* have I offended? Will anyone who feels injured step up, please?"

No one moved, and except for an awkward shuffling there was no sound in the room. Deathly pale, Betty stood with her hand to her throat.

Cold anger, the New England schoolmaster's horror of anything approaching a scene, obliterated whatever sense of propriety I myself had left. I don't know exactly what happened, or how we got there, but suddenly we were standing in a tiny downstairs washroom and I was shaking my finger in Bob's face, shouting, "I'll tell you who you've offended, you've offended me!"

Behind me the door opened and Betty shoved herself into the lavatory.

"No!" she said, but I had just got started.

"All day you've been blackening my reputation and your daughter's reputation!" I thundered.

"How?" he demanded in genuine bewilderment.

"Because you have no idea of how to behave like a gentleman and everything you do makes it worse! Why the hell don't you go back to Ireland where you belong?"

I saw it then, coming from the floor—Bob's fist, which looked almost as big as his head. I ducked, and simultaneously Betty screamed. The fist crashed into the plaster above my head, and suddenly every man at the party seemed to be trying to squeeze into the tiny room and jump on the two of us without killing Betty. The brawl spilled out of the lavatory into a hall. It ended when about a dozen men jammed Bob against a wall, two of them hanging on to each limb, while the rest pushed against his middle. The old man was breathing hoarsely.

"He has a bad heart!" Betty shouted.

Suddenly Bob stopped struggling, and the men let him go.

"I didn't *do* anything!" he panted as Betty took his arm and slowly led him to a chair.

"You shouldn't have talked to him like that!" Betty said to me. "Especially not where people could hear!"

Suddenly furious at her as much as at him, I walked out on the terrace where the Friend of the University had put out some bathing trunks for the use of anyone who wanted to go swimming. Grabbing a pair of these, I went back to the lavatory and changed. For the rest of the evening I dived and swam furiously from one end of the pool to the other, trying to exhaust the chaotic emotions which filled me. That night I had to finish the bottle of Scotch in order to get to sleep.

In the morning I awoke with a violent headache, a mounting dread that my second marriage too was heading for disaster, the knowledge that I had to give two lectures that day on the art of fiction writing, and a fury at Bob which seemed to be mounting, not subsiding. Betty's bed was empty, and neither she nor the baby was in the room. Grabbing a towel, I went to the men's room at the end of the hall.

There I found Bob, singing in the shower at the top of his lungs.

"Good morning, lad!" he boomed heartily. "Well, we had quite a night, didn't we?"

"Yeah," I said glumly, thinking of the stories now sweeping the campus and of the audience I would soon have to face. Taking off my pajamas, I saw that the entire right side of my body was black and blue.

"I guess we showed these college lads a thing or two," Bob shouted above the rush of water and continued to soap himself vigorously.

"Yeah," I said and, deciding against a shower at that time, walked silently back to my room.

Except when I had to get up and lecture, I spent the next three days lying in my bed somberly drinking, and the episode ended with Bob's telling Betty she had married a lousy drunk and had better take the baby and go back to Ireland with him. When he himself finally returned to Ireland the following month, I found myself blessing the Atlantic Ocean, that most beautiful body of water, the empress of all the seas, which was now to separate us.

A year later we visited Ireland, and as Betty had predicted, he was an entirely different man there. "He's always easier to handle when he has a woman with him," Betty had observed.

But now, according to the letter Betty had just received, he was coming to America alone to visit us on our new yacht in the glorious Florida sunshine. For most of a month we would be confined to a space 54 feet long and 12 feet wide. I had found no way on earth to get along with him, and I doubted if we would improve our relationship at sea.

Originally, I had thought our voyage would be mostly a test of seamanship, my ability to avoid storms and to navigate, but suddenly it seemed obvious to me that the examination was going far beyond that. Betty, her father and I would have to learn to understand each other better than we ever had been able to ashore. Perhaps it would help if I started out by regarding Bob as some great natural phenomenon like a typhoon, which builds up violence in predictable ways, spins furiously in known directions and then subsides.

# 14

⚓

Wearily I went to bed, but my restless desire to press on with the voyage awoke me shortly before dawn, and by the time Betty got up to make coffee, we were 5 miles past Charleston, South Carolina. This was swamp country, full of tall blue herons darting in and out of the morning mist. The surroundings were peaceful, but the engines of the *Pretty Betty* soon began to raise hell again. The sealers in the water pump which Carl had replaced held, but now others gave way, and the fresh water in both engines was mysteriously disappearing.

"I'm afraid you better stop pretty soon for some major repairs," Carl said, emerging from the engine room with his face blackened by grease. "I don't have the tools or spare parts to do much here."

Looking dejected, he came and stood by the chart table.

"The hell of it is, I ought to be leaving you in Jacksonville," he continued. "If I don't get back to my job and my wife pretty soon, I won't have either. I know it's a hell of a thing to run out. . . ."

As though the *Pretty Betty* heard him, everything else started to break down almost at once. In his last days aboard the boat, Carl fixed the outboard motor on the dinghy, stopped a leak in the pipe bringing hot water to a lavatory sink and showed me how to replace four different cartridge fuses which blew periodically, bringing everything electrical to a full halt.

Limping along at reduced speed with the engines needing constant refills of fresh water, with the saltwater pumps spurting like stuck pigs, and with my groin burning in such a way I couldn't sit still for more than a few seconds, we pressed on with our heroic voyage south. About noon the wind piped up to a near gale, whipping the tall swamp grass into wavelike undulations, and I noticed that a strong current which had been pushing us had now changed, taking away what little speed we had. By about four in the afternoon the job of piloting the boat through crooked, tide-swept channels had exhausted me, and I decided to anchor for the night. Catching the general malaise, our brand-new generator refused to start, and Carl, who had been repairing machinery since dawn, said it too needed new parts.

"It's good that the anchor goes down by gravity," I said disgustedly and, steering to the middle of a quiet bay, walked forward to throw it over the rail myself.

"Cut the engines," I called to Carl.

He did, and the sudden silence, broken only by the splash of the anchor and the calls of some redwing blackbirds darting through the nearby swamp, was curiously healing. Luckily, our galley range used bottled gas, and we had the little fireplace to ward off the evening chill. Putting a piece of frozen shrimp on a hook, I dropped a line over and decided to be philosophical. In a few minutes Jessie came with a line her mother had given her and sat down by my side.

"Daddy, why is everything broken?" she asked.

"I don't know. It is the way of boats."

"Does your bottom still hurt you?"

"A little."

"Don't worry, Daddy. I'll take care of you."

Attracted by our package of shrimp, the cat approached, and as it crawled across Jessie's legs, she shoved it roughly away and poked it.

"Don't hurt the cat," I said.

"I like to hurt the cat."

"Don't say things like that. It bothers me."

"I like to bother you."

Well, there it was, I thought: the long and short of human perversity and kindness, all wrapped up in one rather precocious two-year-old. Reeling in my line, I went to bed. That night the wind blew up to 50 miles an hour, but there was scarcely a ripple on the still black water of the swamp, and the *Pretty Betty*'s anchor at least held as anchors are supposed to do.

The next morning we found that some of the salt water escaping from the port engine's water pump had gotten into the oil of the clutch. On one engine we struggled along to Fernandina Beach. It was a gray day with the temperature dipping into the forties, and our cheer when we crossed the Florida line was rather feeble. It was November 21, just ten days since we had left Maryland, and, I reflected sourly, my old friend Frank Bailey had been right when he said that by the time we got to Florida we would know what kind of engines we had.

The marina in Fernandina Beach was crowded, and in backing into a slip with one engine, I narrowly missed amputating the gleaming stern of a hundred-thousand-dollar Chris-Craft. Even when we got tied up, a heavy swell sweeping through the inlet kept the *Pretty Betty* rolling hard enough to send dishes skittering. Jessie said she felt ill, and Betty was tight-lipped as she pursued plates in the galley.

"I don't want to lie here for major repairs," I said to Carl. "Can you get that clutch fixed up enough to get to Jacksonville?"

"I'll borrow a pump to change the oil. While I'm doing that, do you want to go into town by bus and get some new sealers? I'd like to have one more go at those saltwater pumps."

It proved impossible to find a taxi, so I hitchhiked to the city. Feeling more like a bum than a yachtsman, I returned to the boat with the new parts that afternoon and collapsed in my bunk.

"I fixed some of it, but you still need the port pump rebuilt,"

Carl said that night, sponging his bruised knuckles with alcohol.

"How much will that cost?"

"Maybe a hundred dollars. Don't worry about that. Worry about the fresh water you're losing. I don't have any idea what they'll find is causing that."

With one engine and a strong following wind, we got under way for Jacksonville Beach. This was Carl's last day, and in celebration of it, all the toilets stopped working and the lights dimmed out. After checking out the whole circuit, Carl found that the Constavolt, a malignant-looking device in an inaccessible corner of the engine room, had blown a big cartridge fuse. He had repaired the generator, but when he started that new machine, it heated up. With no electricity we couldn't flush the toilets, and the cabins began to stink.

"I hate to leave you like this," Carl said wearily when we moored. "I feel terrible. I've never really been trained for major diesel repairs, and you need special tools and parts."

"You've already done about two thousand dollars' worth of work for seventy-five dollars," I said. "What is there to feel bad about?"

"I enjoyed the trip. I'd give my right arm if I could go on to the Bahamas with you."

"You're kidding," Betty said.

"You'll be all right when you get all this machinery settled down. Basically you've got fine engines. It's just that they haven't been used in. . . ."

"How about that brand-new generator?" Betty asked.

"You just have to get the bugs out of it."

"Or out of us," Betty said and, glancing at me, added, "Maybe Dad will be able to do something. He built his whole factory in Ireland with his own two hands."

As soon as we landed in Jacksonville, we called a mechanic, and after showing him around the engine room, I rented a car and drove Carl to the airport. On the way back to the boat, I stopped to see a physician who informed me that I had a serious infection which had started with a fungus like athlete's foot.

"Use this ointment and be sure not to get any water on it," he said.

"But the last doctor told me to take three baths a day!"

"He was wrong. Do as I say, and it will clear up."

Returning to the boat, I tried the ointment and it hurt so much that I bit my tongue. Clenching my fists, I poured myself a shot of whiskey and went to the deckhouse where the mechanic was waiting.

"I can fix everything but this business about your losing fresh water," he began.

"But you're a specialist!" I bellowed, in no mood for equivocation. "I thought diesel engines were a relatively simple mechanism. Why can't trained mechanics fix them?"

"Oh, I can fix them all right, if you want to haul them out of the boat and let me take them back to the shop. I'm trying to save you money."

"How?"

"You can run them by adding water every few hours. Before you do anything drastic, try some of the compounds that are supposed to stop leaks. Maybe there's a pinhole in the block or a loose freeze plug. If it's something minor like that, you may be able to fix it for a few cents."

"What if the blocks are cracked?"

"I don't think they are, but if I'm wrong, you'll know soon enough. The compounds won't work and the leaks will get worse."

"Where is the water going? Will it ruin the pistons and all the rest?"

"I think it's shooting right out with the exhaust. There isn't a drop of water in your oil. That's one good sign."

"There was water in the clutch oil."

"That's a whole different system, and apparently you found the cause of that. You've come a thousand miles without doing any damage. Run the engines a little more and see how they work out."

The next day was Thanksgiving. Deciding not to try to cook a turkey in our tiny galley, we rented a car and drove to St. Augustine, where we had dinner in the huge, elaborate old Ponce de Leon Hotel, where I had often stayed with my parents when I was a young boy and where I had attended Advanced Officers Training School during the war. Now it was deserted and dilapidated. An ancient waiter said it was soon to be converted into some sort of college, and he served us a fine dinner as though he were giving us the last meal on the *Titanic*. After our pumpkin pie, we telephoned the older children, who were spending the holiday with their mother in New Jersey.

"How's the cruise going?" Becky asked.

"Fine!" Betty said bravely. "We're having a wonderful time!"

"You don't know how I envy you," Lisa said. "It's freezing here!"

"Well, we've got sun," I replied.

"How's the fishing?" David asked.

"Marvelous!" I found myself bellowing.

"Have fun," he said. "Everybody I tell about you admires you for getting away from it all."

In our rented car I got a speeding ticket, and when the policeman learned my address, he said I was a lucky fellow to be living on a yacht. Giving him a look of pure hatred, I paid my fine at the desk of the police station and left.

The next day we settled bills for something like $200 of engine repairs and left for Daytona. It was the first time Betty had handled the dock lines alone, but she had learned a lot from watching Carl. During our maneuvers Jessica sat on the captain's chair while I stood at the wheel. She had been told that she had to be very good in order to let her parents take care of the boat, and she cried only a little.

The trip to Daytona went well despite the pain I was experiencing. Somehow the new ointment had made matters much worse, and by the time we sailed down the Halifax River past the house in which I had spent most of my youth, I was doing such a jig at the wheel that I didn't even pick up the binoculars. As soon as we docked at the Daytona Boat Works, I went up to see another doctor, who gave me a new kind of salve, ultraviolet light treatments and permission to take baths. As I walked down the pier where we were moored, the first thing I saw was the cat, which was dripping wet.

"What happened to the cat?" I asked Betty in astonishment.

"The cat!" she exclaimed, and then I noticed that she too was dripping wet.

"Mommy fell overboard," Jessie said, "and then the cat did. They were sinking right to the top."

Often I had worried about Jessie falling overboard, and I had moved about the boat with exaggerated caution myself, but I had never imagined that two such surefooted creatures as Betty and the cat would slip. That's what had happened, however. Putting on some sandals with leather soles to go ashore for the mail, Betty had put one foot on the rail to step to the pier and had suddenly found herself in the water. There had been a lot of excitement, and no one knew how the cat had fallen in. Suddenly it too had tumbled from the spot on the bow where it had been watching, but almost immediately it had shot up a tall pile to safety. Betty had not been so fortunate, because there was no ladder and the piles were encrusted with barnacles which cut her hands. No one had been nearby. For several minutes Betty had swum back and forth, calling for help and at the same time trying to reassure Jessica, who kept shouting at her not to sink to the top. She had been able to hear men talking in a big yacht moored nearby, but apparently they had been unable to hear her. After a few moments, some boy heard her and threw her a line. Scratched and bruised, Betty had just crawled over the edge of the pier when I arrived to ask what had happened to the cat.

Apparently Betty had hit the hull of the boat going down, for her whole right shoulder was black and blue. After I comforted her, I undertook to lecture her about Safety at Sea.

"It's always one hand for the ship, one hand for yourself," I said, and stepping backward to illustrate by putting one hand on the wheel and one hand on a stanchion, I found myself treading air, for I had neglected to close the engineroom hatch. Fortunately my bulk was such that I stuck at the shoulders like a jack-in-the-box, but I had bruised myself and I couldn't understand why Jessie and Betty laughed uproariously.

For dinner that night Betty prepared whiting that an enthusiastic fisherman had given us. We were both so stiff that we moved about the cabin like octogenarians.

"Anyway," Betty said, "Jessie isn't accident-prone. She's a better sailor than any of us."

At that moment all my superstitious dread of making congratulatory or optimistic statements at sea was proved reasonable forever. While she was talking, Betty took the hot broiler of fish out of the oven and put it on some coasters on the cabin table. Jessie, who had been standing on the starboard bunk, moved closer and leaned against the galley door, which had been fastened in the open position with a clip at its base. Suddenly the door came free and Jessie tumbled directly onto the hot broiler of fish, where the grease was still sputtering. There were two piercing shrieks, one from the child and one from her mother. The griddle fell to the floor with the baby still on top of it. Reaching over the table, I picked Jessie up, but she had serious burns on both her thighs and her arms. Grabbing her from me, Betty rocked her back and forth, trying to still her cries while I went for a doctor.

It was late that night before the baby, swaddled in bandages, went to sleep. Pouring myself two shots of Scotch, I lay stiffly down, and Betty, in the bunk on the other side of the stateroom, uncorked a bottle of aspirin.

"It's been quite a day," I said.

"Yes. The doctor said she'll be all right."

There was a pause.

"Betty," I said with sudden courage, "do you hate the boat?"

"It's not a good time to ask that."

"I know it's been rough these last few days. But when we get the engines straightened out. . . ."

"Don't worry," she said. "I'm not going to panic because we have a few bad days."

"The trip down the inland waterway doesn't offer much in exchange for all the discomfort. When we get over to the Bahamas. . . ."

"Do they have doctors there?"

"In Nassau and most of the big settlements, sure. . . ."

"How about mechanics?"

"In Nassau and the big settlements. . . ."

"How about the out islands?"

"We'll be sure the engines are all fixed up before we go there."

"What if we had been there when Jessie fell?"

"I'd call for a seaplane with the radio telephone. They'd have her in Nassau in a few minutes."

"If the weather was good."

"That's right. But we have a pretty fair medical kit."

"We've got to be more careful. We just can't let accidents happen."

"And at the same time we've got to relax," I said, forcing a laugh.

"I know I've been something of a bitch lately."

"We've both been irritable. After all, we've had some provocation."

She sighed and then smiled.

"I forgot," she said.

"What?"

"Dad will be here day after tomorrow. The dockmaster brought me a radiogram."

"Well, that's good," I said, unable to keep a note of irony from my voice.

"Yes, it is good," Betty said. "Nobody can be gloomy for long when Dad is around. You'll see what I mean. He's at his best when the whole world is going to hell."

# 15

⚓

The next morning was bright as summer, and Betty and I decided to wash down the boat, which was showing many signs of just having completed an inland voyage of about a thousand miles. In boating magazines I had been enviously reading for years about the joys of scrubbing decks, varnishing and touching up the paint, but my groin still burned, my back still ached, and I was still too fat to make kneeling on our narrow decks with a pail of water and a stiff-bristled brush any great delight.

"The hell with it," I said about noon. "Let's rent a car and I'll show you my old hometown."

There was no answer. While I was concentrating on hard manual labor, Betty had apparently taken Jessie and gone ashore. Disgruntled, I poured myself a drink and sat down in a folding armchair under the bigger of the two awnings. An hour went by before I saw my daughter and wife walking toward me on the dock. Both carried bags of groceries.

"A lady from a big schooner gave us a ride in her car," Betty said breathlessly. "It was wonderful. They've asked us aboard for dinner, and you'll feel much better when you meet them."

"Why?"

"They're worse off than we are."

"In what way?"

"They're *miserable*. She keeps saying they never should have left Chicago."

"What's their trouble?"

"They have *four* children, two of them twins about Jessie's age, and the oldest is eight. And they have this bloody big sailboat that can't go down the inland route. They have to stay out in the open ocean all the time."

"Her husband must be quite a sailor."

"He's *horrible*. He says he likes rough weather because it's the only time all the kids lie down and shut up."

"The world is full of miserable people," I said happily. "We're not the only ones."

"I'm trying to figure out," Betty said as she put hamburgers in an electric frying pan, "whether most of the people on the waterfront are slightly crazy or whether there's something about us that simply attracts nuts. Everybody we've met lately is either crazy or has crazy things happen to them."

"We used to meet a lot of odd people ashore too."

"Not this odd. If you ever write a book about this trip, I have a great title for you."

"What?"

"*Chock Full o' Nuts.*"

Her feeling that we seemed to be meeting a lot of highly unusual people was increased an hour later, when we drove to a fine restaurant I remembered in Ormond Beach, the town 5 miles north of Daytona where I was brought up. While we were having lunch there, a dapper-appearing man of about my age asked if he could take a photograph of Jessica. This flattered us, and we struck up a conversation. In a few minutes he introduced us to a beautiful, dark-haired young woman at his table, and we all had coffee together.

"Where do you live?" the man asked me.

"On a boat."

This information, I had found, triggers all sorts of curious reactions in strangers.

"*Really?*" this man replied, using the word most usually employed for the occasion, and then he went on, as so many people do, to say that he had always wanted to live on a boat. This observation often leads to a short autobiography, but the life stories I have heard have rarely been as bizarre as this man's.

"I'm crazy," he began. "I mean, officially I'm crazy—I get a pension for it. I broke down in the Korean war, and have a ninety percent disability. I just got out of the loony bin, and the post office, where I used to work, is also going to give me a pension. There's no reason why I couldn't live on a boat."

"You certainly seem to have the main qualifications," Betty said.

"I'm getting a whole new start in life," the man continued. "I'm going to be a painter, like Van Gogh. He was crazy too. Did you know that?"

"I'd heard a rumor," Betty said. "Did he live on a boat too, after he had cut his ear off and all that?"

"I don't know, but he loved pretty girls the way I do. I always wanted to know a really pretty girl, but before I got out of the loony bin, I was too shy and didn't know how to go about it. Actually, it's simple. Do you know how I met this beautiful young lady here?"

"In a taxi dance hall," the beautiful young lady said. "Usually I don't work those places. I have a nightclub act, sort of an exotic dance, but I needed something between engagements."

"I used to be a dancer," Betty said sympathetically. "I was often between engagements."

"Did you ever work a taxi dance hall?"

"I was a secretary. I was lucky—my mother made me get the training."

"Believe me, typing is better," the beautiful young lady said.

"How can you say that?" the dapper man inquired. "If you had been typing, I never would have met you."

The beautiful young lady shrugged.

"After three dances, I asked her to go to Florida and she went," the dapper man said in triumph.

"Sailors had been stepping on my feet all night," the beautiful young lady said to Betty and shrugged again.

"You act like you don't like it here," the dapper man said. "I've bought you three dresses and two pairs of shoes. I've spent hundreds of dollars. . . ."

They fell to bickering, and this man who described himself as a crazy painter and his exotic dancer soon began to sound like any unhappily married suburban couple going over their budget together. When Betty, Jessica and I finally excused ourselves, they were so wrapped up in their deadly arguments that they hardly saw us go.

"I feel sorry for them," Betty said. "That's the trouble with living in sin. When you get into a big fight you can't even threaten divorce."

There was a moment of silence, and though it was quite warm, Betty shivered.

"I shouldn't joke about it," she added. "They're so miserable. I wonder why he wanted a picture of Jessie, anyway?"

Getting in the car, we began driving slowly around Ormond Beach, where there had been so much new building that I soon got lost, despite the many years I had spent in the town long ago. Seeking the river, I finally found the huge old Ormond Hotel, which hadn't changed much over the decades. Across the street from it was the Casements, the house in which John D. Rockefeller, Sr., had spent the winters of his old age. Beginning there the River Road, a narrow lane over the top of which the branches of great live oaks met, paralleled the shore.

Nothing here had changed at all, except that Mr. Rockefeller's house was now a part of the hotel.

"Is this near where you used to live?" Betty asked.

"Just about half a mile down that road."

"Let's go," she said. "I've always wanted to see the house."

Somehow I had forgotten how beautiful that little road was, and how eerie, with the bright sun obscured by the Spanish moss in the thick branches overhead. No one said anything as I crawled along in low gear, noting that a rotted wharf where I had tied my first small sailboat had been replaced and that a rock garden my mother had built near the water had disappeared. Pulling off the road in front of a large white house with a brick front, I said, "There it is."

"I had no idea it was so spectacular," Betty said.

"I never used to think of it as that. In my youth I was rather miffed that the Rockefellers had a bigger place."

But the house was truly spectacular, I saw now, not in its size or design but in its setting. On each side of the front terrace was a live oak about 4 feet in diameter, trees my father had said were there when Indians camped by the river and left mounds of shells. The white brick front and the iron trelliswork with which my father had disguised an ugly old wooden house gave the whole scene a flavor of old New Orleans as I had seen it in antique prints.

"Can we go in the house?" Jessie asked.

"I don't know the present owners."

There was a short silence during which Jessie watched a green lizard crawl onto the hood of the car and lie there, distending a pink membrane under its throat. Before I could get out of the car to try to catch it for her, it ran away.

Suddenly the door of the big house opened and a strange woman of middle age walked out and paused on the terrace, looking at our parked car curiously. Embarrassed, I started the engine and drove off.

"It's funny," Betty said.

"What?"

"Your father was an editor and a writer, wasn't he? And your mother's people were naval officers. So you end up a writer on a boat. It's all so curiously inevitable."

"Perhaps."

"A writer on a boat with a mad Irishman about to visit him. Try to understand him, darling. His weaknesses are different from those of your people, but so are his strengths."

The radiogram had not told Betty at exactly what time to expect her father, and on the day he was to arrive I felt curiously fidgety.

"When was his boat supposed to dock?" I asked.

"He didn't say."

"Wouldn't he send us a telegram from New York when he found what plane he was supposed to take?"

"Dad doesn't spend money that way. He told us the day and the place he's going to meet us. Why isn't that enough?"

She was serenely seated at her piano composing a song, picking out a melody with her left hand while she painstakingly inscribed notes on a blank score with her right. On the deck by her feet Jessica busily scribbled with a crayon on another blank sheet of lined music paper.

"I'm writing a red song," Jessie said.

"Better try the blues, baby," Betty said. "There's more money in it."

Restlessly I got up and, walking to the galley, stood looking around.

"What are you doing?" Betty asked.

"I'm going to take this Goddamn door down before it hurts Jessie again."

"Oh, come on. You know how you are with carpentry."

"I can take a door down!"

"But the places where the hinges were will look awful. Remember what the man who inspected the boat said: she is a museum piece and we have to take care of her."

"But this door represents a whole different era," I said, shoving it with my toe. "Cooking was supposed to be invisible because it was done by professionals. Now that it's done by wives, the galley is supposed to be part of the living area. It was ridiculous to lock the cook up in a space the size of a hall closet anyway. This boat may be a museum piece, but in part it's living testimony of man's inhumanity to man."

"Just taking the door down won't help much."

"Shut up, Daddy," Jessie said. "We're trying to work."

"Don't say 'Shut up' to your father," Betty said. "I never said that to my father in my life. Don't think that just because you're being brought up to be an American—"

Jessie stuck her tongue out at her.

"You're an American, all right. Do you know what would happen to children in Ireland if they even thought of sticking a tongue out at their mother?"

Crayoning serenely, Jessica didn't seem interested.

"I'll go aft and let you alone in a minute," I said. "I'm trying to figure out what to do with this galley."

"We can't afford to do anything. I'm Irish enough to accept that. Just think good thoughts while you're in it, and everything will be all right."

"Damn it, I'm an American and I'll find a way to change it. If we took the whole upper half of this bulkhead out, as well as getting rid of the door, you could get some air and talk to people while you were fixing dinner. And if we put a big shelf over the lower half of the bulkhead, you would have some counter space."

"That would shoot hell out of a thousand dollars. You know that everything we do to this boat does."

"I could do it myself. If we're going to live on a boat, I have to learn how to handle tools. Isn't this as good a time as any to start?"

"Wait till Dad gets here. He's really good with tools. I told you, he built his whole factory with his own two hands."

"I don't want this galley built with cinder blocks!"

"He can work with wood too, and formica. All those steel tables he builds have formica tops."

Unreasonably annoyed by her conviction that her father would be more effective, I said, "What's such a big deal about cutting out half of a wooden wall?"

"How would you start?"

Her eyes were challenging.

"I'd inspect the wall thoroughly to make sure no wires or

pipes crossed the place I was to cut. This can't be a structural bulkhead, because the door cuts it in half vertically anyway."

"But how would you actually start?"

"I'd take a yardstick and draw a line right across here. Then I'd start to cut."

"That's what I was afraid you'd do."

"How would your old man begin?" I asked in exasperation.

"He'd measure me to see how high that line should be drawn, if we're going to build a counter on it."

"All right, I'll do that."

"Then he'd put newspapers down to protect the deck from the mess."

"You're quibbling."

"And he wouldn't start by sawing. He'd unscrew all that beautiful molding first, because some of it could be put back on the raw edge."

"Well, I could do that."

"And he wouldn't start by borrowing or buying some little handsaw. That's heavy mahogany about an inch thick—I know, because I've banged my elbows against it plenty of times. He'd rent a power saw with some gadget that would make it easy to cut a straight line."

"Well, that's a good idea."

"And he wouldn't do anything until he drew a detailed plan first."

"I could just work it out as I went along!"

"What are you going to do about the top of the wall, where it joins the ceiling?"

"I think that if I hit it with a hammer, it would come loose."

"Oh, God! Please don't."

"What would he do?"

"I don't know. Maybe it should be cut about two inches from the top. Then if we put some of that mahogany molding over it, it would match the other beams that go across."

"I guess I better wait for him," I said disconsolately and went to the after cabin. The electric typewriter I had brought to Oxford had proved too bulky, and I had sold it to the boatyard. In its place I had bought a small portable machine, much like the one on which I had written my first book, a little-known novel called *Voyage to Somewhere* which I had composed in the basement of an apartment house in Cambridge, Massachusetts, just twenty years ago. Now I got out this small machine and set it up on a built-in stool opposite a folding aluminum chair. This was about the kind of arrangement I had had when I was starting out, and there was comfort in the simplicity of it. Somehow I had never known elaborate studios to work out very well for me or any of the other writers I had known. This little typewriter rocking under my heavy blows could be part of a new start, professionally as well as every other way. Now I was just writing letters to my children, but in time perhaps something else in me would grow. *Voyage to Somewhere*—despite the fact that the book hadn't amounted to much, the title still appealed to me, and I wished it was fresh so I could use it all over again.

# 16

⚓

That afternoon Betty prepared a dinner of roast beef, but still her father did not come.

"Why doesn't he wire?" I again inquired irritably.

"He knows we'll wait for him," she said, serenely wrapping up the leftover beef in aluminum foil. "Maybe he had trouble getting a plane out right away. It can be hard this time of the year."

My family had always traveled exactly on schedule, sending out frequent wires and telephone messages to announce safe arrivals or the slightest delay, and my annoyance at not knowing precisely when Bob would arrive was increased by my inability to explain the mysterious need I had for such precision. In my heart I suspected that Bob had taken to celebrating on the Cunard liner, as Betty said he often did, and would continue his spree endlessly in New York while we waited in Daytona, cooking up festive meals every evening. That night I had trouble getting to sleep and sat in my tall captain's chair, drink in hand, watching the moonlight sparkle on the muddy waters of the Halifax River. Suddenly it occurred to me that Bob might still be with us in February when Mother arrived. What kind of shipmates would they be together?

My mind boggled at the very idea. When he was sober, Bob would be courtly, of course, and Mother would say, as she had when she had met him in the Adirondacks, that he was an *extremely* charming Irishman, but when Bob got to drinking and asking friends aboard, there would be more earthy humor, fanny-patting and other shenanigans than I thought Mother had seen in all her eighty years.

"That terrible Mr. Cryden!"

The sentence popped into my mind as clearly as though Mother had just uttered it in a firmly disapproving voice.

"That terrible Mr. Cryden" had lived in a tall white house by the river. Every time we passed it on the way to school, Mother had said, "That's where that terrible Mr. Cryden lives." The tone of her voice had been such that the shadows of the big trees surrounding the old mansion had seemed sinister to me, and the black Cadillac parked in that driveway had always looked to me like a gangster's car.

"What did Mr. Cryden do?" I finally plucked up enough courage to ask.

"You're too young to understand."

For about ten years I let it go at that, but finally when I came home from college, we took a drive past the old house.

"Is that where that terrible Mr. Cryden lives?" I asked my mother.

"He's dead now. We shouldn't speak evil of the dead."

"But what did he actually do?"

"It's nothing that need concern you now."

"But I've always been curious. Was he a gangster?"

"No! He was a retired stockbroker."

"Well, why was he so terrible?"

"He behaved irresponsibly when he drank."

"Did he hit people?"

"No."

"Well, what did he do?"

Haltingly, with considerable embarrassment and many circumlocutions, my mother described that terrible Mr. Cryden's single crime. She and Dad had asked him and his wife to dinner, shortly after the end of Prohibition. My father, who had declined to serve any alcohol while Prohibition was in effect because, he said, it was wrong to break the law under any circumstances, had laid in a store of fine liquors and had served cocktails in the huge, formal living room. Standing in front of our fireplace with some other friends, that terrible Mr. Cryden had imbibed too many, "a fact which did not become evident," my mother told me, "until dinner was served."

"Then what happened?" I asked, fascinated.

"He committed an indiscretion."

*"How?"*

"He took my arm to escort me into dinner, and at first I thought he was all right, except that he was laughing too loudly."

"What did he do?" I pressed on relentlessly.

"He, he made an inexcusably vulgar gesture. He committed an affront against my person. Your father was furious. If he hadn't had a bad heart, he would have thrown him bodily out of the house."

It took considerably more questioning before I finally was certain of what had happened. The terrible Mr. Cryden, who must also have been the bravest of all men, had goosed my mother, right in the entrance to the dining room, causing her to leap forward and spill a tall goblet on the table. Because of his bad heart, my father had not hit him, but he had delivered a strong lecture to him. Apparently the meal had been completed in silence, and that terrible Mr. Cryden had never been invited back again.

Now what would Mother do if she were dining with Bob in our tiny deckhouse, and as Betty would say, the devil got into the old man? Undoubtedly he would have more sense than to commit an affront against my mother's person, but as Betty had told me, he considered a slap on the bottom a perfectly normal expression of affection, and if we had friends aboard, anything could happen. Would my mother give him a stern lecture, as my father had to his guest, and as I had once tried to do with Bob myself? How would Bob handle a sternly lecturing old woman, and what would Betty do if she felt her father was being imperiled again?

It was best not to cross these bridges until I found them burning under me, I reflected, refilling my glass and carrying it to my bunk with me.

"You still awake?" Betty asked, turning over sleepily.

"I can't seem to sleep."

"Whew!"

"What's the matter?"

"I can't help it—I hate the smell of booze. It's always been the stink of trouble in my life."

"I'm sorry."

"Try to cut it out, won't you? I don't know if Dad will be drinking or not, but if I have to live here with the two of you going at it. . . ."

"I'll try."

"Will you say a prayer with me?"

Betty says she's not religious, but she still seems to feel better when she says prayers.

"I'll try," I said again.

"Please, God, let us have peace on this boat together, and let us help each other, not tear each other apart."

"Amen."

"Say it. Say the whole thing!"

"Please, God, let us have peace on this boat together, and let us help each other, not tear each other apart."

"Amen. Thank you. I love you, darling, and I always will, no matter what."

With a sigh, Betty went back to sleep. In the engine room compartment the refrigerating machinery whirred and seemed to develop a peculiar ticking sound.

Oh, Lord, I thought, now something else is breaking. I wonder if they have specialists in refrigerating machinery here in the yard?

The ticking speedily grew into a clacking.

"What's that?" Betty asked, waking up.

"The ice machine, I think."

"God, I suppose that will have to be replaced."

"Yes," I said grimly. "Probably it will shoot hell out of a thousand bucks."

"Maybe Dad can fix it. He used to fix refrigerators at home."

"Hell, maybe I can fix it myself," I said rebelliously as the sound got definitely worse and the baby suddenly sat up with a cry.

"At least we can turn it off," Betty said. "There's a switch in the dry food locker. It's all right, Jessie. Go back to sleep."

"Before I shut it off, I can at least take a look," I said, and arming myself with a flashlight, I went to the engine room. As the beam traveled over the two big diesels and the new generator, which was painted white, I had that angry, hopeless feeling I always have when confronted by balky machinery. The clacking sound came from a spot under a fuel tank forward of the engines in a nook even a midget would have difficulty reaching, but with desperation I wedged myself into a corner from which I could play the flashlight upon the source. There I saw a big electric motor driving a fan near a complicated coil of copper tubing. Apparently vibration had caused one section of the tubing to sag close enough to the fan to hit it, thus causing the peculiar noise. Jubilant at seeing something I might conceivably fix, I got down on my belly and crawled between the engines, over some batteries and onto a curiously sharp bilge pump. There I reached out, and holding the flashlight under my chin, I lay on my side and pushed the tubing back. It moved stiffly and seemed to stay in the correct position. Immediately the clacking sound stopped, and the fan purred as contentedly as a rescued kitten.

Extricating myself from the engine room, I skinned my knee badly on the bilge pump, but I didn't curse at all.

"Thank heaven, that racket stopped," Betty said sleepily as I walked into the forward stateroom. "Did you turn the thing off?"

"No," I said nonchalantly. "I fixed it."

"You did?" she asked, sitting up and snapping on a light.

"Yep. I fixed it myself. Permanently."

"You're a bloody genius! But, my God, look at you!"

Turning to a mirror, I saw that my face and pajamas were covered with black grease.

"Never mind," Betty said. "You fixed it, and there won't be any repair bill at all. Go take a hot shower and I'll have some clean pajamas waiting for you."

When I finally stretched out on my bunk that night, it seemed as though the world were mine. Pushing a tube back from a fan may seem to be a small thing, but after all, a repairman would have charged us $15 at least, just to come aboard, and if one small recalcitrant bit of metal had yielded to my hand, who knew what fantastic triumphs could lie ahead?

# 17

⚓

In the morning even the baby slept late. We were awakened by a knocking on the deckhouse door and Bob's bright, musical Irish voice calling, "Hello, aboard the *Pretty Betty!* Is anyone home?"

"Dad!" Betty called, and in her brief white sleeping costume, which looked more like a bikini than a nightgown, sprang up the companionway with me after her. There Bob stood with the sunlight glinting on his silvery hair, his pink face aglow, a beautiful man, as almost every woman he met said. He was wearing, I saw with envy, an expensive suit of blue silk which I had bought several years ago and had gained too much weight to wear, but this man of sixty-five had the figure of my younger self, and it looked made for him. Picking Betty up, he waltzed her around, thumped me heartily on the shoulder by way of greeting and said, "Now where is my darling Jessie? I have come four thousand miles to see her!"

At the top of the companionway Jessie's sleepy face appeared. Usually she is grumpy when she first wakes up, but like most females, she smiled when she saw Bob and ran to him.

"Faith, but she's my own Jessie newly risen from the grave!" Bob said, and tears sprang to both his and Betty's eyes as he picked the child up and kissed her forehead.

"I'm afraid the Irish are very emotional," Betty said to me with a smile.

"How about coffee?" I replied hastily. "Have you had breakfast yet, Bob?"

"There was a beautiful young lady on the airplane, and if her breakfast had been as good as her figure, I'd be far from hungry now, but all she gave me was a little tin tray with a doughnut that wouldn't make a fly wink if you put it in his eye. Do you have some eggs and a rasher of bacon?"

Leaning forward, he slapped Betty heartily on her rear.

"Sure, Dad!" she said.

"You talk with your father," I said. "I'll get breakfast for a change."

"And if you have a spot of tea I wouldn't be throwing it in your face."

"We even have crumpets," Betty said. "They make them frozen, ready for the oven here."

"Ah, it's good to be back in America with everything frozen, ready for the oven," Bob said, sitting down on the couch and stretching his legs.

"Did you bring me a present?" Jessie asked, something we have not been able to prevent her from saying to all new arrivals.

"And what kind of a present do you need after I bring you myself?"

Taking the child on his knee, Bob began telling her about the great ocean he had crossed, leading her to believe he had swum 4,000 miles through sharks and alligators in order to see her. Even in the galley, the sound of their laughter penetrated, obliterating the purr of the ice machine, a wonderful, uncontrollable sound which seemed to gush out of that man with force tangible enough to sweep all troubles before it.

After breakfast Bob wanted to be shown over the boat. Although his experience at sea had been confined to the Cunard Line, he had an old-fashioned, European appreciation of good craftsmanship and ran his fingertips lovingly over each piece of joinery much the way he kept patting both Jessie and Betty. The name of the boat obviously meant a lot to him, and he inspected the life rings, the mahogany trailboards and the stern—each place on which it was inscribed in fancy gold leaf—with special satisfaction.

"We have some beautiful stationery with the name engraved on it," Betty said. "My husband won't tell me what he paid for it. I think it cost more than the boat did."

"Could I see it?"

Betty gave him some stationery, and forthwith, Bob sat down to write all his friends and relatives in Ireland, pausing now and then to read aloud his glowing descriptions of Betty, the baby and the boat. When he had finished about six brief letters, he sealed them, addressed them and handed them to Betty.

"Mail these for me, pet," he said. "I'm tired. I think I'll take a little nap."

Lying down on the couch, he glanced at me, and perhaps I imagined that there was a triumphant gleam in his eye as Betty took stamps from a drawer, painstakingly affixed them and, carrying Jessie in her left arm, walked ashore to the mailbox. Stretching out with a sigh, Bob closed his eyes, and almost immediately the whole deckhouse reverberated with his snores.

Ashamed at myself for being annoyed by the resumption of the old battle about mailing letters and by the incredible grunting and rasping which sounded as though Bob enjoyed snoring as much as he did laughing, I went up to the captain's chair by the wheel. Regardless of the cramped quarters, I simply could not allow myself to build the tension between us which had existed in my mother's apartment in New York. Why couldn't I, like Betty, enjoy the man's strengths and accept his weaknesses with good humor? After all, if Betty didn't seem to mind the little chore of mailing his letters, why should I?

More than my inclination to regard his revels with Puritan disdain was involved, I concluded. Bob's personality was so strong that without apparent effort he had dominated every situation in which he had ever found himself. Women either succumbed to his charm or became furious, but they never ignored him, and if men got in his way, he either outtalked

them or, if all else failed, knocked them down with his huge
fists. The mere threat of this was enough to reduce most men to
acquiescent silence. Betty had told me that her grandfather and
uncles had never talked much when Bob was in the room and
that he was the only man alive who ever had made her strong
old Scotch grandmother forget for a moment that she was an
empress in her own house.

If Betty saw in me, as she often said she did, many resem-
blances to her father beyond a similarity of physique, perhaps it
was my inclination to assume that the world revolved around
myself. In one fashion or another, both Bob and I had grown
used to getting our own way, and we could not be together for
more than five minutes without finding ways to join battle and
see who was going to put the other down. The center of this
struggle was always Betty, whom we both regarded as our chief
asset in life. No wonder the girl was often reduced to tears
between us, for we tugged at her like two dogs on a bone.

But, of course, it was absurd of me to get involved in such a
contest. With a little self-confidence, a little maturity, I could
gracefully give way to the old man during his visit, and in so
doing could gain much more than I could lose.

"God," Betty said as she and Jessie hopped back aboard the
boat. "He really is the champion snorer of all time. I could hear
him a hundred yards down the dock."

"We'll get used to it."

"I think we better move into the after cabin. I was going to
put him there, but if I know Dad, he'll spend most of his time
right there on that couch."

There was a pause before she added, "Sloan?"

"Yes."

"I'm worried about him. He hasn't been well."

"He looks marvelous."

"While you were getting breakfast he told me his heart has
been acting up again. He's thinking of selling his business and
maybe moving over here."

"Well, he can always have a bunk aboard this boat," I said determinedly.

"We'll see how it works out. But I don't think we should ask him to do things like take down that galley wall or really fuss much with the engines. He's even worried about helping with the dock lines. He said I should tell you he can't move very fast."

"He can just sit in the cockpit. You've been doing pretty well."

"No, we've got to find little ways to make him think he's helping. I'll show him how to make the stern line fast to a cleat when I throw it to him from the wharf."

All that day Bob slept, recovering from the rigors of his journey. The condition of the skin in my groin, which had appeared to be improving, suddenly got worse, and the local doctor gave me a new kind of ointment.

"No one really knows what makes this sort of thing happen," he said to me cheerily. "We'll just have to try one thing after another until we find something that works."

"Let's get out of here," I said to Betty. "I don't know why, but I still have the feeling that progress consists of moving south."

That night I went to bed early while Betty was talking with her father in the deckhouse. Everyone was sleeping soundly when I awoke at dawn. The river was like molten glass, and a gentle tide was pushing the boat away from the wharf. There was no reason why I couldn't cast off the lines myself and get under way without waking anyone up, I decided and went to the engine room. Although I was still ignorant of almost everything mechanical, I was learning to enjoy the sensation of at least conducting a maintenance program right. Before starting the engines, I checked the oil, both with the big dipper sticks and in the clutches, and noted its color. Putting fresh water in the heat exchangers, I found that the compound we had poured in at Jacksonville Beach had apparently done some good, for the leakage had not been as great as it usually was. After checking over the generator, I pumped out the bilges, feeling a ridiculous sensation of accomplishment as I spun valves which had been a mystery to me a few weeks before. Hardly any water came either from the forward half of the boat or from the stern—regardless of her other difficulties, the *Pretty Betty* did not leak. The last item on my checklist was the switchboard, where we changed from shore current to the generators run off the main engines. Because it was damp and the engines hadn't been used in a few days, I decided to help the batteries by squirting a little ether into the air intakes, as Carl had shown me how to do. Going back on deck, I touched the starting buttons, and the big engines immediately came to life, making me feel as though I had just invented them.

After going to the after cabin to slather myself with my new ointment, I hopped ashore and disconnected our electrical cable, a chore I always imagined myself forgetting. As I started to cast off the mooring lines, the thought occurred to me that the current setting the vessel off the dock might push her away before I, in my weakened condition, could jump aboard. If that happened, the boat, with Betty, her father and Jessica still soundly asleep, would go merrily drifting down the river, and even if my shouting woke them up, as the starting of the engines had failed to do, I had not yet shown Betty much about handling the boat. Probably the current wouldn't move fast enough for that, but part of the challenge of seamanship lies in foreseeing trouble and taking steps to forestall it, the way a chess player thwarts his opponent. I realized that I should forsake my idea of getting under way alone and let Betty handle the deck lines while I stayed at the wheel, but for some reason the attraction of proving my independence was strong. Going back aboard the boat, I doubled up a stern line in such a way that I could release it from the deck. Hopping back to the wharf, I cast off all the other lines, tossed them to the bow and jumped back aboard myself. Standing in the after cockpit, I released the last line, allowing the boat to drift gently away from the dock. The water was deep here, and before going to the wheel, I took great satisfaction in coiling all the lines up neatly from bow to stern, as though a professional crew had been at work.

The sun was just climbing over the peninsula when I finally stepped up to the wheel, shoved both clutches ahead and drove the sharp bow of the *Pretty Betty* through the opalescent waters of the familiar channel. Soon we passed Bird Island. Pelicans were already circling up from the mangroves where they roosted to begin their day's work of fishing. After another few miles, the river narrowed and we entered a narrow, winding canal. Looming ahead was the first bridge. After a moment's hesitation I touched the button of our big air horn and blew three mighty blasts.

"What's up, lad? Is that a distress signal?"

Bob's head popped out of the deckhouse door, his big pink face startled, and I realized that although I had perhaps only half-realized it, I had been arranging a childish practical joke.

"It's just the bridge, Dad," Betty said, rising out of the after cabin. "Everything's all right."

The glance she shot at me was somewhat accusing, I thought, and I said, "I just thought that you guys were probably tired and I'd give you a chance to sleep."

"Where are we?" Bob asked, blinking in the sunlight which was reflected brightly by the still water.

"Daytona is about ten miles astern."

"Ah, this is the life, traveling without even having to get out of your bed," Bob said. "Betty, how about a spot of tea?"

Still glaring at me with small appreciation of my single-handed seamanship, Betty went forward. Ducking into the deckhouse, Bob emerged with one of my blue boating caps, which I generally hung over the fireplace.

"Mind if I use this, lad?" he said. "The visor might keep off the sun."

His pink skin could stand only a brief exposure to sunshine, and his pale blue eyes were unusually sensitive to light. The bridge was slow to open, and I simply nodded at him briefly as I hopped down from my tall chair to manipulate the clutches more easily. Apparently the bridge tender was waiting for a gap in the morning traffic before he blew his siren and put down the gates to stop cars. A fair tide was pushing us down on the bridge more rapidly than I had judged, and I pulled the clutches into reverse. Obediently the *Pretty Betty* waited, parting the current with her shapely stern.

"There he goes!" Bob said. "He's opening now."

Turning, I saw that he had climbed into the captain's chair and was studying the bridge through the binoculars.

"Right you are," I said and pushed the engines ahead.

Moving slowly with the current, the *Pretty Betty* started through the bridge. Many fishermen were leaning over the edge of it, and as we passed only a few feet from them, a woman in a straw hat waved at us.

"Good morning, Skipper!" she called. "You sure got a beautiful boat!"

"Thank you!" Bob replied before I could say anything, and doffing my cap to her, he half-stood on the rungs of the tall captain's chair to give her a gallant little bow.

Well, his response was more stirring than mine would have been, I reflected, and of course she thought he was skipper, this fine old white-haired man sitting on that commanding perch with a blue cap on his head and the strap of my binoculars around his neck. Just as most of the people at the little college in New Jersey had assumed he was the novelist when we went there together, it was predictable that everyone here would assume he was the captain or owner of this boat. His appearance simply fitted dramatic roles better than mine did.

"Now what do those red posts mean?" he asked, settling comfortably back in my chair.

"They're channel markers. You keep the red ones to the right going south."

"*Do* you, now?"

At the door to the companionway Betty appeared with two mugs of tea.

"Do you have any crumpets, pet?" Bob inquired.

"They're in the oven."

"And a rasher of bacon like we had yesterday would set well," Bob boomed. "Running a boat makes a man hungry, doesn't it, lad?"

# 18
⚓

Despite my determination to be self-confidently mature, I might have got angry at Bob that morning if the day hadn't developed into one of those magical ones which come along just often enough to make all the expense and trouble of running a boat worthwhile. Fair tides and fair winds really don't mean much to a motorboat in sheltered waters, but it always seemed a good omen when everything was quite literally going our way. The canals and inlets around New Smyrna and the Indian River, which the rushing currents swept us into that afternoon, have always seemed particularly beautiful to me, ever since I explored them in a 15-foot sloop with a tent for camping when I was a boy, and now they exceeded even my nostalgic memories. Nowhere in the world had I ever seen so many gaudy birds and such spectacular underwater activity. So many egrets perched in the mangroves of the little islands we passed that the spectacle seemed contrived. On one little tree I counted eighteen of the big white-crested birds, and in an area of 50 square yards, there must have been a hundred of them.

"They're not really egrets," Betty said. "One of the books down there says they're some kind of cowbird that emigrated from India on cattle boats a long while ago. They don't look it, but they like to eat ticks."

In addition to the egrets or cowbirds there were many white and blue cranes, some of them 4 feet tall. Disturbed from their stiltlike stance at the banks of the canals, they flew in circles around the boat, tucking up their legs like the wheels of an airplane, stretching out their long necks, instantly transforming themselves into long feathery arrows with wings.

It was the pelicans, however, which impressed Bob. He had never seen any before and spent hours studying them through the binoculars.

"I better not tell the people in Ireland about them," he said. "If I wrote that I saw some big bloody birds like geese with beaks a foot long, they would surer than hell think I had been on the bottle, and if I said they had great sacks hanging from those beaks in which to hold fish, they'd be calling the doctor for sure."

When he saw the pelicans collapse in midair and plummet beak downward after fish, he became convinced that they were highly dangerous.

"Regular dive bombers they are, with that great murderous weapon out in front of them! If they took a notion, they could come right down through these awnings, burying their bayonets in our heads. To think that our very existence depends on their tiny pealike brains and whatever good will they have in their chickenlike hearts!"

As we got into the Indian River, we saw mullet jumping all around us.

"Something must be after them," Bob said.

"Maybe," I replied. "People around here never can agree why mullet always jump so much. Out of fear sometimes, perhaps, but my father observed that they jump even in quiet pools, in clear water where one can see no larger fish are around. People always assume they are driven by fear, he said, but perhaps they jump for joy."

"Ah, they must lead a fine life," Bob said. "All the rivers and bays are their very own, with never a cent to pay for rent."

"But it isn't always a bed of roses," Betty said. "Look!"

Down the channel ahead of us a school of porpoises came swimming rapidly, flashing their polished backs in the sun and scattering the mullet in every direction. Wheeling to follow the *Pretty Betty,* three porpoises repeatedly crisscrossed our wake, and finally put on an extraordinary show, swimming right on the surface beside the boat and occasionally leaping as high as our rails. They were great glossy fellows, 7 to 8 feet long, with the peculiar eternal smile which porpoises present to the world, even when they die.

"Now there are the jolly fellows!" Bob said. "Do they always sport about like this?"

"I never saw them quite so frisky," I said, and it was true that in all my years on the river I had never seen the porpoises put on such a display.

Viewing the river through the eyes of Bob and Betty, neither of whom had seen it before, gave me a new appreciation of it. Orange groves with the fruit glowing in the sun, groves of palm trees silhouetted against the sky, and great white mansions with green lawns slanting down to the water's edge—all elicited their cries of admiration. Holding Jessie on his knee in the tall captain's chair, Bob said, "Child, it will be a great disappointment when you enter into heaven after a trip like this."

My sense of high exaltation received a sudden jolt just before dusk when I glanced at the temperature gauge of the port engine and saw that it was rising rapidly toward 200 degrees, the danger point.

"That damn compound hasn't worked!" I said to Betty. "She's leaking water again."

"Ah, that's a bad sign," Bob replied sagaciously. "When a steam engine runs out of water, she can blow sky high, and I suppose diesels are much the same."

"Almost," I replied nervously and slowed the engines down. "Betty, take the wheel, will you? Just keep her between those markers ahead."

Down in the engine room I crawled forward, trying not to burn myself on hot metal, and examined the heat exchanger, which looked much like a car's radiator. Sure enough, it was out of water. Carl had told me I could fill it even when it was hot if I kept the engine running, and there was a small hose handy, connected to our water pump. Soon after I started the job, I smelled burning rubber, and water spurted from a spot where the hose crossed sizzling iron. Cursing, I wrapped tape around the hole and held the hose in place until water overflowed.

When I got on deck, the temperature of the engine had already fallen.

"Why, you're a great mechanic to be able to do that!" Bob said.

"I'm afraid it won't last long."

"What does that mean?" Betty asked.

"The engine seems to be losing more water than it ever did. Maybe we'll have to have it pulled out of the boat."

"Is that an expensive job?" Bob asked.

"I don't know. If it has to be rebuilt. . . ."

The sun was sinking low in the sky by now, and the lights of a bridge began to sparkle like a necklace across the river far ahead. Suddenly feeling as depressed as I had been elated, I steered toward one of the small towns which line the Indian River and decided to moor for the night.

As we came alongside a wharf, Betty expertly tossed a bow line to a dock attendant, leaped ashore with a coil of rope in her hand and tossed one end of it to the stern, where Bob stood. Looking baffled, he wound it around and around a cleat, leaving much of it snarled about his feet in the cockpit. Jumping back aboard, Betty showed him how to take a half-hitch and coil the unused portion.

"If we don't take care, the boat will look like an explosion in a spaghetti factory," she said.

With a baffled expression on his face, Bob painstakingly took up another line and attempted to make it fast to a cleat.

"The hell with it," he said suddenly when the half-hitch didn't come out right. "That's why I joined the army, not the navy. Ropes always turn into snakes in my hand."

"It's easy, Dad! Try again!"

"It's no use. Jessie's father, God rest his soul, always said that the Irish are lubberly, and he was right. We are remembered at sea only by the Irish pennant, which is supposed to be some kind of a disgrace."

"It's ridiculous to think you can't learn!"

"No, it's a hopeless cause. It was the English that did this to us—for centuries they didn't let us have ships. Lubberly I am, and lubberly I'll be until the day I die—it's bred into my blood."

"But we need your help!"

"What did you do before I got here, and what will you do when I leave?"

"We can manage," I said. "Let's forget it. Betty, don't hurry with supper. Tonight I feel like a drink."

"Yes, today is a day we should be celebrating," Bob said, and perhaps I imagined that he gave me a sly glance as he drew from his inside coat pocket an envelope and gave it to Betty—not a letter for her to mail this time, I realized as she opened it, but a card to mark a birthday which in the excitement and worry of the cruise I had forgotten. Today was December the third.

"Oh, Dad, that's nice of you," Betty said and gave me a smile which was both forgiving and hurt. Always before, I had celebrated her birthday with presents on the breakfast table and an announcement of plans for dinner at a good restaurant.

Perhaps I was becoming paranoid, but I was furious at Bob for not reminding me in private and giving me a chance to hurry ashore and buy a gift. Suspecting that he had been waiting all day to prove himself more loving than I, my anger was increased by the fact that usually it was he who ignored such occasions and I who stepped forward with smug remembrance. Not content with stealing my roles as novelist and captain, he was now after my position of the thoughtful man.

"December third!" I said bitterly. "Betty, I didn't really forget."

She knew I was lying, and so did Bob. He was smiling, obviously enjoying his mean little triumph.

"I was going to surprise you by having a taxi come down and take us all out to dinner!" I said, improvising wildly. "If I'd only had a chance to go ashore. . . ."

"You can go now, lad," Bob said, gazing up at the sky as though asking God's forgiveness for me. "I'm sure you didn't need me to remind you."

"He *never* needs reminding," Betty said loyally.

Hastily I jumped ashore. To reach the shopping section, I had to walk several blocks despite my painful physical condition, and the only shop open was a drugstore. Seeking a gift that looked as though it had been planned far in advance, I examined large boxes of candy, showy cartons of perfume and a display of cheap watches revolving on a huge wheel. Finally I found an electric manicure set and concocted a fatuous tale of long seeking something which would do justice to the fact that Betty had, among other things, once been a successful hand model and always took unusually good care of her long fingernails, despite the rigors of the boat. By the time I had called a taxi, made dinner reservations at a nearby restaurant and got back to the wharf, I had half-convinced myself that I was following a carefully laid plan.

"Ah, it's great to have such ingenuity," Bob said as I gave Betty her package, which was miserably wrapped in drugstore paper. "Who would ever have thought that you could have found a gift so fast?"

"Why, I can go into the manicure business!" Betty said. "I've got more equipment than a dentist!"

"The taxi is waiting to take us all to dinner," I said, hoping I was giving the impression that somehow I had called well ahead of time to make all the arrangements. "I believe they may even have a cake."

That evening turned out to be a sample of many like it that were to follow. While we waited for steaks, Bob went to the bar for a drink. I have never quite understood how he does it, for he is much too well-mannered to strike up conversations with strangers in any obvious way, but somehow Bob knows everyone in a bar ten minutes after he enters unless other Irishmen are present, in which case his accent and appearance cause instant introductions. On that particular evening he returned to our table with half a dozen people who wanted to help Betty cele-brate her birthday, and by the time her cake arrived, oddly decorated with Fourth of July sparklers, almost everyone in the large dining room, including a dozen women of various ages, had gathered in a circle around us. No local celebrity could possibly have received a louder rendition of the birthday song, which Bob made into a virtuoso performance with his mel-lifluous tenor.

All this was fun and Betty enjoyed it, but she looked worried when Jessica began rubbing her eyes sleepily and it was ob-viously time to go back to the boat.

"We're never going to be able to get Dad out of here," she whispered to me.

"One of his friends will probably run him back if he can't get a taxi."

"I'm afraid he'll get into trouble."

"He seems to have taken pretty good care of himself for a number of years."

"How do they feel about fanny-patting in Florida?"

"It is not widely known as a Puritanical state."

"Well, we'll hope for the best," she said with a sigh. "Dad, we've got to get Jessie home to the boat."

"Run along, pet," he said with a wave of his hand. When he put his arm down, I saw that it rested across the shoulders of a thin, bespectacled woman who had moved her chair close beside his.

I was tired, and as soon as I got back to the boat I went to sleep. A little after two in the morning I heard Bob come aboard with a half-dozen people who did a great deal of laugh-ing and thumping around in the deckhouse, but after glancing at my watch, I turned over and tried to go back to sleep. Before long there was a heavy step at our companionway and Bob's voice shouted, "Betty? Are you asleep, pet?"

"Hush!" I called.

"What do you want, Dad?" Betty inquired groggily.

"How about a spot of tea and scrambled eggs? I have some fine new friends here."

"For Christ's sake!" I began. "Do you know—"

"Never mind," Betty hissed at me. "It's easier to get the eggs at a time like this."

"But if he gets away with—"

"I'll talk to him in the morning when he's sober. You go back to sleep."

I tried, but the sounds of revelry mounted in the deckhouse. Finally growing used to laughter and to songs, I dozed but awoke with a start at the sound of angry shouting. Hastily throwing on my bathrobe, I went on deck, just in time to see a throng of people retreating down the wharf.

"Crazy Irishman!" a woman shouted over her shoulder, and from the sound of her voice, she was almost in tears.

"I didn't do anything!" Bob shouted into the night. "May God be my witness and strike me dead if I lie, *I didn't do anything!*"

There was no answer but the slamming of a car door in the shadows at the head of the wharf and the sound of a car pulling away.

"I don't know why she got so upset," Bob said, throwing out his hands in a gesture of appeal to Betty. "I didn't do anything wrong at all!"

"Sure, Dad," Betty said with a yawn. "Come on. It's time for us all to go to bed."

Muttering sentences in which the phrase "innocent as Christ himself" occurred a great deal, Bob lay down, and Betty collapsed in her bunk across from mine.

"I guess we better sail early in the morning," she said, "some time before people generally get up around here. They might come back."

"All right."

There was a pause before she added, "I think Dad has finally found the perfect life—cruising."

"I'm glad he enjoys it," I replied grimly.

"It's beautiful," she said, "beautiful! Every night he can raise hell and be out of town even before he wakes up. This way of life was invented for him."

# 19

⚓

One of the great pleasures of living on a boat, I was discovering, is that no matter how often one learns better, motion still gives the illusion of progress, and the hope of leaving one's troubles behind never dies. The next morning Bob had a bad headache, but the town we had left was as much out of sight as though it had never existed, and the channel winding ahead was new as the day after tomorrow, miles and miles of bright water untinged by regret. Sitting in the sunlight by the wheel, I felt it would be absurd to give the old man lectures which would only elicit more pious denials of guilt. It was too nice a day for recriminations, and there was too much else to think about. Farther up the river was a boatyard I remembered from the days of my youth, and I decided to tie up there to have the engines examined once again, to get an estimate on the cost of removing the bulkhead which separated the galley from the forward stateroom and to see another doctor.

The physician was obviously a necessity, for the pain in my groin suddenly flared up far worse than anything I had experienced. This time it didn't subside when I sat very still in the captain's chair, and it was all I could do to maneuver the boat alongside a wharf when we finally reached the yard. It was high noon, and the sun beat so strongly on the awning over my head that sweat poured over my body, stinging the raw flesh.

"Betty," I said weakly, "I've got to have a shower. Please call a doctor and see if you can get him to come down to the boat."

"Poor lad," Bob said, wagging his head sympathetically. "Do you suppose it comes from drinking?"

Unable to comment, I waddled hastily to the shower. Scared by the fact that for the first time my clothes were badly stained with blood, I stepped under the water and recoiled—the spray on my raw skin felt like liquid fire.

"The doctor—" Betty began, coming to the open hatch. Seeing me leaning on the edge of the bunk with my eyes closed, she said, "Are you all right?"

"Not really."

"The doctor wants you to come up to his office. He can't make house calls until tomorrow."

"We better go," I said. "Until I get this thing fixed, we have to live right here. There's no point in trying to go any farther."

"I think you should find a cure, even if you have to fly back to New York and check in at a hospital."

The thought of leaving Betty, Bob and the baby on the boat in a small Florida town depressed me, but I was in too much pain to think about it. Like an old man I hobbled to a car the boatyard lent us, with Betty supporting one arm and Bob the other. My confidence in the ability of doctors to conquer my mysterious malady was at a low point, and I was grateful for the bottle Bob shoved at me as I sank into the back seat of the station wagon. After I had two good swallows the pain seemed to ebb, but Bob's question had excited the voices of my Puritan ancestors. *Was* the disappearance of my skin in crucial areas the result of years of too much drinking, and if so, why had it occurred now when I thought I was drinking so much less? Was I suffering some deep disturbance of my fundamental chemistry as a part of withdrawal symptoms?

It was absurd to think that my agony was some long-delayed punishment, but the thought persisted until I had two more drinks. Trying to walk normally, I entered a crowded waiting room.

"Are you in pain?" a crisply uniformed nurse asked.

"Yes."

"The doctor will see you right away."

A sign on his desk said that the doctor's name was Robert A. Nalley. He was a heavy, tall man with glossy black hair, and despite my cynicism concerning physicians, he soon convinced me that he was almost God.

"Wow, you must be in terrible pain," he said the instant he examined me. "I don't usually do this, but you've got to live while I cure you."

"What are you going to do?"

"Demerol," he said, preparing a needle. "Do you have any objections?"

"No."

The hypodermic hurt hardly at all. Almost immediately my anguish disappeared, and the world seemed a marvelous place.

"Sit down," the doctor said.

The chair felt unusually comfortable.

"You've got quite a serious condition there," Dr. Nalley said.

"I have been quite aware of that. What's it called?"

"The technical name is unpronounceable, and the others are unprintable."

"How is it caused?"

"The honest truth is no one has any idea. But I think I know how to cure it. I'm going to use a shotgun approach."

There were more injections, a prescription for drugs and a handful of pills he took from his sample drawer.

"Go home and lie down for a couple of days," he said. "Let me know how you're coming along."

I had lost my confidence in pills, but some of these contained Demerol, and I passed a blissful forty-eight hours.

"Maybe it's just the drug, but I think I'm cured," I said to Betty. "There's no more pain at all."

"I hope this guy Nalley knows what he's doing," she replied worriedly.

As it turned out, he did. When the pills were gone the pain

did not come back, and to my astonishment, I found that my skin had completely healed.

"How could such a terrible thing go away so fast?" I asked Dr. Nalley.

"The skin is mysterious. It can heal or deteriorate with astonishing speed."

"What was in those pills? I know the red ones were Demerol, but how about the white ones?"

"Cortisone. It works as an anti-inflammatory agent. Of course, if you ask *why* long enough, you'll find yourself backed out of medicine into philosophy."

There was a pause before he added, "Does it surprise you that the human body is such a mystery?"

"Yes."

"You mean you haven't settled for the basic fact that life is a mystery?"

"I'm beginning to," I said.

With the pain gone for the first time in weeks, I felt marvelously young, and instead of taking a taxi, I walked back to the boat, occasionally breaking into brief sprints. When I arrived, I was out of breath but still jubilant.

"I'm cured!" I announced to Betty. "For the first time, really, I can enjoy this boat without squirming in pain."

"Thank God," she said, "but I'm afraid we have bad news."

"What now?"

"It's just that the mechanic has finished looking at the engine, and he's like the man in Jacksonville—he says he doesn't really know what is wrong with it or what has caused the leak."

"That is not surprising."

"A guy from the yard also looked at the galley, and he says it's hard to give an estimate until he actually takes that bulkhead down and sees what is involved. The price is all based on time, and he says the bulkhead might come out easily or present all kinds of problems."

"That's the way it is," I said. "Nobody knows anything. Fundamentally, life itself is a mystery. Can you find a sitter in this town? Call your father! I'm a healthy man again, and I think it's time we all went out and had a drink."

"You know how that is likely to end up."

"Who cares? We can sail in the morning and find a place where we all are innocent again. For more than a month I have been dragging around like an old man. Let's go somewhere and dance!"

Nothing about our life was predictable, as I should have known. That night Bob didn't drink at all and sat staring at me with such stern disapproval that I soon gave up and took Betty back to the boat.

"That's the way he is," Betty said. "When Dad goes on the wagon, he drives everybody onto the wagon. Sober, he can't stand the sight of sin."

The next day I was glad I had a clear head, for a large package of mail arrived, and in it were letters from both my older daughters, confirming their plans to bring young men for the fast-approaching Christmas vacations, and there were also letters announcing that five other people planned to join us for the holidays. One of these was from a woman who had attended our "farewell party," where I had apparently broadcast invitations indiscriminately, and the other was from Mort Leavy, my lawyer and business manager, whom I had on many occasions begged to come down with his wife and two teen-age daughters.

"Why did you do it?" Betty asked incredulously.

"I don't know. When we first bought the boat, she seemed so enormous to me, and Mort has done so much to help. . . ."

"I like Mort fine, but what are we going to do with all these people? How many are there at the latest count?"

"Thirteen," I replied miserably. "Unless David comes, but he's been planning to stay with his mother."

"We'll sink, and that has nothing to do with its being an unlucky number."

"I told the kids they might have to use sleeping bags."

"Then everything will be fine when everybody is asleep, but

how am I going to feed them all on a three-burner stove? How am I going to clean up after them all in a sink no bigger than your hat?"

"We'll find a way."

"How?"

"I have an idea," I said with sudden inspiration. "I think my father has provided a solution."

"Are you off your head?"

"What would you think if we put our surplus guests up in a great estate with a private swimming pool and beach? We could use the boat for day trips then, taking a few out at a time."

"What great estate?"

"One that Otto Kahn built a long while ago in Palm Beach."

"Is it a hotel now? Anyway, it would be too expensive. We've invited all these people down as our guests, and we would have to pay their bills."

"They'd stay for free."

"Don't be maddening. What are you talking about?"

"When we first moved to Ormond Beach a long, long while ago, there wasn't any good school, public or private, so my father helped to start one. That school is now at Palm Beach on the Otto Kahn estate. During the Christmas holidays its dormitories will be empty. So. . . ."

"Will they let us?"

"It will be sponging a little, but they really do owe a lot to my father—he was chairman of their board of trustees for years. I don't think he would mind if we cashed in on an old debt."

"You didn't tell me that your father used to run a school."

Her voice was accusing, as though she thought I had been as unfair to my own father as I occasionally was to hers.

"He didn't really run it himself. After looking around, he found a piano teacher from the Midwest. Her name was Inez Graham."

The name Inez Graham brought back all kinds of memories centering on that tall, angular woman. Miss Inez, the colored servants used to call her in those curious days between the first two world wars. There was a pause, and the expression on my face made Betty's voice soft.

"What was she like?"

"As she used to say herself, she had a horse face and a nasal voice and not much formal education. During the Depression she was going from house to house in Daytona giving piano lessons. How Dad knew she could run a school I have no idea."

" 'She had the ambition and I had the academic degrees,' he used to say. In those days there were plenty of college graduates who needed work. With Dad's help she hired a couple and got permission to hold classes in the basement of a hotel. She had a half sister named Evelyn Eckes who did the secretarial work. I was never clear how it all worked out, but inside of about twenty years, Inez moved to Palm Beach and bought the Otto Kahn estate."

"I don't mean to be corny, but that's why I love America," Betty said. "In Ireland she'd still be rubbing her hands before a tiny electric fire in the basement of a hotel wondering where her next pupil was coming from."

"What's that?" Bob asked, coming down to see if the tea kettle was on the stove.

Briefly she told him the story.

"Now this Otto Kahn, who was he?"

"A great financier," I replied. "I have heard it said he was the only man in the world old J. P. Morgan considered an equal."

The idea of seeing a Palm Beach estate built by a multimillionaire appealed to Bob greatly.

"Can we take some pictures of me standing by some great swimming pool?" he asked. "I would love to send them home. After all, that's what the people in Ireland expect."

I guessed that he had done a little boasting about going to visit his daughter aboard a yacht and that he had been disappointed by the size of the *Pretty Betty*, which looked surprisingly small in photographs. His enthusiasm for visiting the Graham-Eckes School gave me an idea. Despite his abhorrence for living alone, perhaps he would consent to stay there during the holidays. Not only would that free a bunk for the new guests; it would remove the hazards of the snoring, the constant requests for tea when Betty was busy and the tension which kept building between us regardless of the best intentions on all sides.

"Do you think Bob would mind moving ashore for a couple of weeks?" I asked Betty that night. "I think they have quite a palatial guest suite."

"He would be terribly hurt," she replied, looking terribly hurt herself. "Couldn't we make a rule that relatives live aboard and friends sleep ashore? That might save a lot of feelings."

For a moment I did not reply.

"I know he's difficult!" she said passionately. "But haven't you noticed how much he's trying? Last night he did the dishes for me. Do you know what that means to him? In Dublin a man won't be seen pushing a baby carriage. He was brought up to think it a disgrace to do a woman's work. I don't think he ever before touched a dish in his life!"

"I know he's trying," I said miserably. "I'm sorry. He can stay aboard."

"No, he'd be murder when the boat got crowded—I admit that. I just can't stand hearing you criticize him."

"I didn't say anything. I just—"

"It's your tone of voice and the way you look at him. He knows you don't like him. He worries about it a lot."

"I love the man! It's just—"

"You don't have to tell me! I lived with him for twenty years! But try to be nice to him, please, if you love me. Your eyes blaze so when you look at him sometimes."

"His eyes blaze too."

"I know, but he can't help it. He's old and sick and worried about his factory. There's been trouble with the union. He says if they keep telling him what to do, he's going to shut down."

"Somebody should welcome him to the twentieth century."

"It's too late for that, but he's trying. He asked me yesterday if he could contribute to the food bill, and I know he doesn't have any money."

"I thought his factory was going marvelously."

"He had to borrow money to build it, and now if he has to shut down. . . ."

"I understand that he's under tension," I said.

"I didn't say you weren't under tension too! You don't have to tell me about taxes and college bills and all the rest."

"I didn't say anything!"

"You sound like him. The trouble is I know both of you so well that neither of you has to say anything. I'm always standing in the middle of this great Goddamn silent argument."

"I'm sorry," I said, meaning it.

"You can't help it—neither of you can. But you're younger and healthier than he is. It should be easier for you to give in."

"I'll try my damnedest."

"So will I. Let me try to suggest that he move ashore. He's not a stupid man, and when he thinks it over, he'll see that will be best."

# 20

⚓

During the next two days the boatyard opened up the galley and added a big hinged shelf which increased the counter space. Bob supervised the job carefully, making sure all the original molding was saved, and gave useful suggestions about the design.

"It's better, but it's still no place to cook for a crowd," he said, studying the final result. "How many people did you say were coming aboard?"

"There'll be thirteen of us," Betty said. "I hate that unlucky number. We'll have to pick at least one fortunate soul and put him in the Otto Kahn estate. I understand that they put guests in the great man's bedroom itself."

"*Do* they, now?"

"I visited it once, and they have a lot of gold-colored furniture," I said. "The living room is about eighty feet long with a huge window looking out on the Gulf Stream."

"Eighty feet long! A man would feel like a king living in a place like that."

"Would you like to go?" Betty said. "It would only be for a few days."

"I would consider it an honor," Bob said and, getting up with dignity, walked to the after cabin.

"He knows we're trying to get rid of him," Betty said, her voice trembling.

"Maybe he'll feel better if we put Becky and Lisa ashore too. He likes them, and he'll know that if we don't have room for my own daughters—"

"Won't they mind that?"

"I've been worried about how we'll separate them and their young men. Sleeping accommodations will be tough enough aboard here without worrying about chaperonage."

"Oh, my God, you really are a Puritan!"

"Well, we can't put them all in a double stateroom together! I'm not liberated enough for that."

"How could they be safer? It would be like making love on the subway during rush hour."

"The girls will want to be spotlessly dressed and made up all the time. They'd go crazy in our tiny heads."

There was a moment of silence.

"You really are good at improvising to make up for our complete lack of planning," she said. "Maybe this whole Christmas fiasco actually will turn out to be fun."

Two days later we anchored in Lake Worth near the school, whose property bisected the entire island of Palm Beach. A crusty old man who did not seem in the least impressed by the fact that my father had helped to start the school refused to let us moor at the old Otto Kahn dock, and I had a sudden fear that by returning here I was being pretentiously ridiculous. Nevertheless, we all took the dinghy ashore and walked toward the main office. Near the lake were a big new dormitory and several other modern buildings. Not only had Miss Graham and Miss Eckes acquired the Otto Kahn estate; they had obviously added to it. Not a person was to be seen on the elaborate tennis courts or in the carefully tended gardens, and the only sound was the chirping of birds.

"Where is everybody?" Betty asked.

"I guess the Christmas vacation has started. We may have the place all to ourselves."

In an office I met a nice old lady who remembered that I had attended the school when it was started in the basement of that old hotel in Daytona, and she obviously revered my father.

"Dr. Graham always admired Professor Wilson so much," she said. "She has always put him at the head of the list of founders. I'm sure you can stay till the students come back."

The two titles surprised me—Inez had been innocent of even a bachelor's degree, as far as I remembered, and my father had rarely used the title of Professor even when he was teaching journalism at N.Y.U. Apparently time and the success of the school had conferred these honors, and I guessed that my father would be amused at our welcome.

And he would be astonished at the luxury of these new quarters, which to his New England mind would seem a strange setting for anything so austere as education, I thought. The main body of the Otto Kahn estate and the surrounding terraces had been preserved like a museum, and much of the furniture retained its original elegance.

"Ah, this is the real thing, all right," Bob said, taking a Napoleonic stance at the head of the huge swimming pool. "To think that the man who built all this is in his grave, God rest his soul, while I, who never built anything in my life but a few cinder block walls am standing here in the sunshine enjoying it!"

The atmosphere of the vast deserted estate was to me oppressive. The only people we met were old caretakers and resident teachers who seemed completely cowed by the lingering solemnity of Big Money coupled with Academic Dignity. For the first time I wondered whether it was wise to leave Bob here. The walls of the great estate, which time had cracked a little, looked as though they would come tumbling down if anyone threw back his head and laughed or let out even a chuckle of bawdy humor. This school was dedicated to training Ladies and Gentlemen. The class pictures of unsmiling girls in long dresses and boys in white dinner jackets fostered the notion that in these surroundings even the very young became sedate. The housekeeper who showed us the rooms we could use was friendly, but there was a look in her eye that made me dread the thought of what she would do if there was any carousing in these stately corridors.

The guest suite assigned to Bob turned out to be almost as grand as we had predicted, though obviously it was not the main chamber of the great house. Sitting on the edge of a four-poster bed, Bob took off his shoes and lay down.

"Now if you can only get a picture of me reclining like this," he said. "Do you mind if I take a little nap?"

Leaving him there, we walked back to the dinghy.

"I hope Dad doesn't meet a lot of people in some bar and bring them all back to his place at three in the morning," Betty said suddenly.

"There isn't any bar nearby, and he doesn't have a car."

"Never underestimate his ingenuity."

She looked worried as she placed Jessica in the stern of the small boat.

As things turned out, the impact of the crew of the *Pretty Betty* upon the Graham-Eckes School was sharp, but it did not come in quite the way we had expected. It was my daughter Becky who first upset the tradition of gracious living.

A freshman at Boston University, Becky was beautiful and Becky was blond. Usually Becky dressed and acted with far more dignity than is associated with her age, but in an attempt to save me money, she took a bus from Boston to Palm Beach and, quite sensibly, dressed for that rigorous trip in a sweatshirt and blue jeans. Because the friend who was to join her headed a rock and roll band at his college and liked to practice, she brought along her guitar. I had written her that I would meet her at the bus station in West Palm Beach, a foolish gesture born of ignorance of the fact that buses nowadays rarely finish long journeys on any predicted schedule. She was due at the terminal at 11 P.M. I waited there reading until two in the morning and then decided I better go back to the boat to warn Betty that something had gone wrong.

Arriving in my absence, Becky took a taxi to the school,

dismissed it and wandered around the ghostly campus, her guitar and a box of clothes under her arms. Finding her way to Lake Worth, she turned to the nearest building where a hall light gleamed. No one answered when she knocked, but a door proved unlocked. Seeing no reason to be afraid of what obviously was a dormitory, Becky went in, found a room with a bed and collapsed into immediate sleep.

The only trouble was it turned out to be the bed of a resident teacher, a middle-aged bachelor who had been out visiting late with friends. Returning at about four in the morning, he was dumbfounded to find a guitar in the middle of his floor and a shapely blonde in dungarees on his bed. A little hysterically, according to Becky, he awoke her and demanded to know who she was.

"Rebecca Wilson," she said. "My father is an alumnus."

"Who is he? What's his name?"

"Sloan Wilson. I was supposed to meet him tonight."

"At what time?" the teacher asked suspiciously.

"Whenever my bus got in."

"You're his *daughter?*" The teacher glanced at her closely, noting, no doubt, that Becky in many ways looks unusually mature.

"Yes, I'm his daughter!" Becky retorted, sensing a slur, and remembering some of my reminiscences, added, by way of identification, "*His* father helped to start this school in Daytona a long while ago."

"Professor Wilson?" the teacher asked. "You're the granddaughter of Professor Wilson, the Founder?"

"Exactly," Becky said with satisfaction. "I'm here to join my father on his yacht."

This proved the wrong thing to say. I had warned Becky that we had no place to store suitcases on the boat, and she had packed her clothes in a cardboard box. Her dungarees, sweatshirt and usually immaculate hair had grown rumpled on the bus and on the bed while she slept. Her guitar case was a battered secondhand model handed down to her by her sister, and the general impression smacked little of the Palm Beach yachting set.

"I don't believe you," the teacher said firmly. "Please get out of my room or I will call the police!"

That proved unnecessary, for at that moment a police car turned into the driveway of the school, its red light flashing. As we learned later, Bob had grown desperate in his solitary surroundings and had borrowed a car. In a local bar there had been the usual chain of developments. The police had arrived, possibly when Bob had had difficulty making some distinction between the horn and the starting button of the unfamiliar automobile. At any rate, they were Irish, as by an act of some Irish saint so many policemen are, and instead of taking Bob to a cell to sober up, they were affably driving him home.

The teacher who had discovered Becky in his bed was so excited that he didn't stop to wonder why the police car was there.

"Officer!" he said as the patrol wagon drew to a halt. "I want to report a strange girl in my room."

"Where?" a cop asked as he helped Bob from the back seat.

"There!" the teacher retorted triumphantly and pointed to Becky, who had followed him, still trying to explain.

"I was supposed to meet my *father* here!" Becky said, blinking desperately in the bright glare of the officer's flashlight.

"Who's *he?*"

"Sloan Wilson. He's an alumnus of this school, and he's a writer. He wrote *The Man in the Gray Flannel Suit* and—"

"Sloan Wilson?" Bob bellowed, shaking off the other policeman's arm. "Why, he's the bastard who married my daughter and marooned me in this godforsaken place!"

"Bob!" Becky exclaimed in astonishment.

"Who are you?" Bob demanded belligerently.

"Becky! Don't you remember?"

"Becky, my pet, thank God I've found you! In this garden of ghosts I need a friendly face!"

Completely confused, the policemen and the teacher went to

the school's office, pounded on the door and woke up a great many people. Finally they reached the housekeeper, who recognized Bob, dismissed the cops and, after questioning them both closely, gave Becky a room and helped Bob to his.

School people are generally more tolerant than they appear, and this proved to be the case the next morning when I arrived and was told the whole story, including the fact that Becky's friend, who arrived a few hours after she did, had insisted on staying in the guest house with her instead of coming to his pipe berth in the forecastle of our boat.

"Don't worry," Betty said. "Dad will chaperone them."

"That does not comfort me."

"They're both very responsible young people!"

"The housekeeper will still think the situation most irregular."

"Then *she* will chaperone them."

"They won't like that boy there. I saw him prowling about the piano in the music room. If he gets going with Becky and her guitar and your father's Irish tenor. . . . It will be terrible, even if Bob doesn't bring in all his friends."

"You *said* they had the whole place for themselves!"

"Not for making all that noise! Such a thing has never happened before."

"If that's true, it's about time."

"I don't know what Otto Kahn was like, but the ghosts of Miss Graham and my father will smite them."

"That's ridiculous. Come on back to the boat. The Leavys will be coming any minute, and we should be showing them aboard."

As we discovered in the next few days, Mort Leavy, whose clients consisted mostly of writers and actors, accepted the chaos aboard our boat with perfect aplomb.

"My family can all stay in one cabin," he said cheerfully. "The girls can sleep on the floor."

They had just finished unpacking and stowing their suitcases at the school when a telegram arrived there from my oldest daughter, Lisa, who had suddenly come down with a bad case of bronchitis. She and her young man had decided not to come.

The brevity of her message worried me as much as its contents. In many ways Lisa and I were much alike, and during my own youth I had often got bronchitis when I was violently unhappy.

In the fancy office of the old Otto Kahn estate I tried to telephone her. It took several minutes for the call to go through, and while I waited, I paced back and forth, thinking of my oldest daughter. Like me, Lisa loved travel. On a trip to Ireland with Betty and me, she had liked Dublin so much that she had decided to leave the University of Pennsylvania to take her junior year at Trinity College there. But like me, Lisa fell in love hard. Just before leaving Philadelphia, she had met Peter Strick and had missed him so much that she had dropped out of Trinity after only a few months, much to my consternation. Since I had had no choice in the matter, I had tried to console myself by thinking that she seemed mature enough to know what was best for her own happiness. Back in Philadelphia, she had busied herself with editing a small magazine and had promised me she would resume her studies at the University of Pennsylvania.

When the operator finally got her on the wire, Lisa sounded so hoarse that I couldn't tell much about her emotional state. Between coughs she kept repeating that she was fine, really fine, and Peter was fine too, except that he also had acute bronchitis.

"They're both miserable," I said to Betty, "and there's nothing at all we can do about it except pay medical bills."

"And make sure we have room for them during their Easter vacation," she replied. "I don't think they'd be happy aboard now even if they were well."

There was a moment of silence.

"We've got to worry about the problems at hand," Betty continued. "We could really fit everybody aboard now, if only that bitch you invited at that horrible party wouldn't come. She ought to have had more sense than to believe you anyhow when everyone was drinking like that."

"Maybe I can call and tell her to come later," I said. "I really feel we ought to get that whole crowd out of that school."

Trying to shove worries about Lisa out of my mind, I telephoned our friend in New York. She sounded miffed, but she became understanding when I explained how I had overestimated the size of our boat. Bob was delighted when he found he could move back aboard, and both Becky and her friend liked the idea of starting immediately on a cruise to the Florida Keys. The resident teachers at the school and the old caretakers did not make any great objection as I helped Becky carry out her guitar and cardboard box. Gripping a bottle of Scotch, with which he had prepared to arm himself against the loneliness of his exile, Bob stuffed his dirty laundry into a purloined pillowcase and bid the suddenly smiling housekeeper a fond farewell.

"Nobody can say you don't have a nice place here," he said gallantly. "The only reason I'm leaving is that, on the whole, I prefer life aboard the yacht."

Apparently he did not regret these words even when he saw the arrangements Betty had made to please me. Dislodged from his usual bunk in the deckhouse, Bob was wedged into the tiny crew's quarters with Becky's long-haired musician. Jessica, Betty and I filled the forward stateroom, while Rebecca ruled the deckhouse in solitary splendor and Mort Leavy's family of four huddled in the after cabin.

"For the next week you've all got a choice of hamburgers or hot dogs," Betty called from the galley. She was greeted by loud cheers.

The tide was fair again and so was the wind as we sped down Lake Worth, leaving all the great mansions of Palm Beach behind. Mort, who had steered me through so many financial hazards, stood at the wheel by my side, a short, stocky man whom I had rarely seen smile before. When we came to the first bridge, I showed him how to blow three blasts on the big air horn.

"That's great," he said as the traffic came to a halt and the massive span opened. "Now I see why people get hung up on boats. All you have to do is make a loud noise, and the whole world stops to let you through."

Finding that Mort learned the channel markers quickly, I went below to see how all the passengers were making out in their crowded quarters. Bob, I discovered, was in the galley, forking frankfurters from a big pot and handing them to Betty, who was buttering rolls. Mort's wife, Fay, and Rebecca were setting up a card table in the deckhouse, and the musician was bent over the ship's piano, playing it just loud enough to be heard over the engines. On a seat up in the bow Mort's two teen-age daughters were busy mixing a salad in several of our small bowls and cleaning up after Jessie, who was trying to help.

"You know, it's true what they say—people always have more fun in third class," Betty called to me. "Go on back to the bridge, captain. It will be another hour before we start to dance and sing."

Although I had dreaded having Bob aboard an overcrowded boat, the rigors of that cruise brought out the best in him, as well as in everyone else. Obviously we were all jammed so closely together that the slightest lack of consideration would be miserably magnified. Realizing this, Bob didn't ask for tea once and drank very little, even when the rest of us were enjoying Christmas cocktails. The trip to the Keys proved to be more pleasant than I had dared to hope, with no mechanical break-downs and no personal flare-ups. High up on the bow Becky and her musician sat most of the time communing with each other, hardly noticing that they were at sea. Mort and his family appeared to love the ceaseless activity of the fish and birds which made the sea and sky appear even more bursting with life than the boat itself. Moored alongside a low key near Jewfish Creek, we could see no land either east or west of us, despite the fact that we were protected from the open ocean by many reefs and shoals. The unobscured sunsets and sunrises were so brilliant that Mort said he would like to get an option on them and put them on in Radio City. The only difficulty lay in preparing meals for so many people, but the women cooperated well, and almost every other night we found a place where we could go ashore for dinner.

My pleasure in the cruise was increased by having such a large audience to witness my incredible skill in handling the boat. Actually, the job of mooring a 54-foot motor boat is so simple that the Navy and Coast Guard can train farm boys to do it in a few weeks, but one of the joys of owning a boat lies in the fact that many passengers feel tempted to clap when one comes alongside a wharf without smashing in the bow. The props for giving a virtuoso performance at the helm are superb on most yachts, for the designers understand the dramatic instincts of their clients. The wheel of the *Pretty Betty*, like that of most boats, was larger and more ornate than it had to be, and the many dials and levers on the instrument panel seemed deliberately arranged to make them appear as complicated as possible. The tall captain's chair, the polished chart table at my left side and the big air horns with which yachts commonly give each other signals without the slightest practical need were all superb for self-dramatization. Since I had reached an age and girth which placed athletic feats of skill and daring beyond my reach, the opportunity to stand up high on the open bridge of the *Pretty Betty* and command the attention of a small throng was especially satisfactory. Fay, Mort and their daughters were an especially good audience. Once when I backed the boat into a slip they congratulated me as though I had hit a home run in the World Series.

Usually Bob felt compelled to squelch me on such occasions by making a funny joke that directed attention to him or by making caustic remarks about my tendency to run a small yacht as though it were a battleship, but during this Christmas vacation he concentrated on learning how to handle the stern lines and even told Mort that I was "a fine lad when it came to handling a boat." If I interpreted his inflections to mean that I was good for only this highly specialized form of activity, that undoubtedly was a problem all my own.

Bob and I had no trouble until the vacation was over and we returned our guests to Palm Beach to catch their planes. Exhausted, he lay down on the bunk in the deckhouse and fanned his face with an old copy of *Yachting Magazine*.

"Well, lad," he said, "what's next?"

"Finally the Bahamas, I hope," Betty said, sticking her head up a hatch from the galley.

"We have a month before we're supposed to take my mother on a cruise of the canals," I said. "That would give us plenty of time to see quite a few of the islands and come back."

"But that involves going right out in the open ocean, doesn't it, lad?" Bob asked.

"Yes, but we'd always be close enough to a port to run for shelter."

He looked glum.

"Will she rock around much?" he asked.

"She might."

Was there a barely suppressed note of satisfaction in my voice? Betty shot me a warning glance.

"Isn't there somewhere else we could go? Somewhere nice and quiet?"

"We haven't seen Key West yet," Betty said.

"But the *whole point* is to see the Bahamas, as you often said. We chose a boat for that and—"

"Well, I'm not going to be with you forever," Bob said, leaving me in doubt whether he was threatening imminent death or a return to Ireland.

"You don't seem to mind the idea of sticking to the canals for the sake of your own mother," Betty said acidly.

"She's eighty years old!"

"Well, I'm not feeling so young myself."

Bob thumped his chest over his heart, and perhaps it was because I remembered that my own father's health had forbidden us from venturing farther than the Florida Keys that I felt so absurdly trapped.

"They say Key West is nice," Betty said. "We could try the Bahamas later, after your mother goes home."

"I think that would be a good idea," Bob said gravely, as though the matter had already been decided.

"There are plenty of doctors in the Bahamas. Christ, half the doctors in America apparently own a yacht, and the place will be swarming with them this time of the year."

"I don't think it's wise, lad," Bob said. "It's not only my ticker, it's your engines."

His voice seemed to me to betray the triumph of a trump card played.

"The engines are plenty good enough!"

"No, it's not normal for them to lose water like that, as you well know. You should run them for a while to see if it's going to get better or worse before you head out into the Great Unknown."

"It's not the Great Unknown. It's just—"

"But we really should have the engines in top shape, even if we do have to have them rebuilt," Betty added. "All the books say that before you go to the Bahamas—"

"How are you going to run for shelter, lad, if your engines give out?"

The infuriating thing was that he was obviously right. Limping around with engines that constantly needed fresh water was permissible for the canals and the keys, but if there was some worsening fault which couldn't be seen without hauling the engines out, we could easily find ourselves in real trouble if we were far from land and farther from mechanics. The expense of opening the decks and lifting the engines ashore would be bad enough in the States, but in the Bahamas it could be much worse.

"All right, we'll go to Key West and see how things work out," I said.

"That's a sensible lad," Bob concluded. "Betty, how about a cup of tea?"

There was no hint of apology in his request. Obviously, I thought with unwilling resentment, the man who made the important decisions deserved a few prerogatives. On a boat, as on land, a woman should jump to please the head of the family.

I am being petty, I told myself, insecure and absurd, but that didn't help. On the way down the inland route to Miami I found myself compiling a great list of Bob's faults, as though I were preparing a case for the prosecution.

No matter how many times I tried to instruct him, he wouldn't learn how to steer the boat, and I never got any relief from the wheel. He just said he was lubberly, and that was that.

Would I like it if he took over my job of piloting?

No, but he at least should learn to spell me once in a while.

Also, Bob never scrubbed the decks or did anything else to help me keep the boat shipshape. All day he just lay on the bunk in the deckhouse in his undershirt, gassing away about Ireland endlessly with his daughter.

Despite his Great Mechanical Ability, he never went into the engine room, even once.

He seemed to me to be getting our personal accounts all mixed up. Of course, it was hard to get money out of Ireland, but it was equally hard for me to keep money from my own government. Still, why did I get so upset about petty cash?

He was an old man with a bad heart and a failing business, Betty said, and we were in the prime of life, when we should be taking care of the generations on either side of us. True enough, but was the situation really that simple? Perhaps I could reconcile myself to the care of a sick old man, but how about one who at the stroke of eight every evening we were in port suddenly transformed himself into a gay young blade apparently intent upon seducing every woman in town? How did one handle a father-in-law who could wear a suit I had regrettably grown out of and who never stayed aboard to sit with Jessica while Betty and I went ashore because he was too intent on his own revels?

Not that Betty and I had the strength for many revels. After a day of navigating tricky channels, I was often ready for bed before the sun went down, and caring for Jessica, in addition to acting as cook and deckhand, was already making Betty look drawn despite her suntan. In the evening it was only Bob who, having rested all day, had the vigor to change his clothes, slick down his hair, polish his shoes and jump jauntily to even the highest pier. In addition to my suit and my yachting cap, he often took along ten dollars of my money to finance his play. I didn't have a sick old father-in-law; I had a wayward son at night and a demanding boss by day. If this kept up, Betty and I might as well go into the charter business and get paid for our labors.

All this was childish, of course, but I couldn't help my resentment. It boiled over in Miami when I got up at seven in the morning to sail for Key West. There was a stiff wind blowing, and I needed help with the dock lines. Going to the deckhouse, where Bob was still asleep, I said, "Hey, can you lend me a hand? I'd like to sail in about twenty minutes."

"What?" he grunted.

"We're going to sail in twenty minutes. Betty shouldn't have to handle all the lines alone."

"We're going to sail in twenty minutes," he said, mimicking me, and rose out of his bunk so suddenly that I thought he was going to charge like a rhinoceros. Instead, he stopped not more than a foot from me and shouted, "What is this, the bloody navy? I'm not going to sail in twenty minutes. I'm going to stay right here until noon!"

"You'll stay on the dock then. Get your clothes if you want, and get off."

"What is this?" Betty asked, appearing in the companionway, her face as pale as though her worst nightmare had suddenly come true.

"This big captain here gives me ten minutes to get up and

put my clothes on!" Bob retorted. "What the hell is the hurry—
is the entire Japanese fleet out there waiting to be sunk? Why
can't we stay here like civilized people and have our breakfast in
our own sweet time?"

"Well, why?" Betty demanded, her eyes shooting fire at me.

I had a good answer, so good that I began to suspect I had laid
a kind of trap.

"Listen, Bob," I said softly and reasonably. "The channel
leads from here west. That's why they call it Key West—it's west
as well as south of Miami."

"So?" Bob demanded belligerently.

"The channel is rather tricky, but the water is clear. An
experienced pilot can judge the depth of it accurately—so long
as he has the sun at his back. After about one o'clock in the
afternoon the sun will be in my eyes, and since I'm the only one
who can steer this boat, I'd like to tie up soon after. If we get a
late start, we won't be able to make Marathon, which is my
destination. If you can't get up in the morning to help your
daughter with the lines, we'll just have to anchor out, and you
won't like that. There will be no women and no bars."

"You see, Dad," Betty said, desperately trying to ignore my
sarcasm. "He really does know what he's doing. He has a
reason."

"No man is going to roust me out of bed like a bloody
private!"

"And no man is going to stand there and tell me when I can
and when I cannot sail my own boat anywhere I damn please!"

"I didn't tell you you couldn't sail."

"You said you were going to stay here until noon. That's up
to you. That wharf up there belongs to the city of Miami."

"Please!" Betty said. "You're being so Goddamn childish!"

"Never mind!" Bob retorted. "I'll go. I know when I'm not
wanted."

Rather helplessly he looked around, trying to locate his
personal effects, which were scattered all over the boat.

"Sit down, Dad," Betty said. "You're not going anywhere."

Bewildered, he sat down on the bunk and scratched his chin.

"Say you're sorry," Betty said to me.

"I'm sorry!"

Unable to quell my fury, which stemmed partly from the fact that I suspected she would have accompanied her father ashore if she had had to make a choice, I marched out on deck like a small boy, slamming the deckhouse door behind me. Finding release in intense activity, I started the diesels, cast the dock lines off by myself, and with a great roar of the engines managed to twist the boat away from the wharf in the face of the wind. Within five minutes we were slicing through the water at full speed, bound for Marathon.

It was half an hour before Betty appeared on deck, and by that time I was even more disgusted at myself than I was at her father, but for some reason I was still angry at her.

"Do you want to know why he got so mad?" she asked.

"Why?"

"He had a date at eleven to see a woman he met last night. She's just a friend, but he thought it might be nice if she made the trip with us."

"Why didn't he tell me?"

"He thought you'd disapprove. He wanted to discuss it with me first and have me ask you. The woman is a nice person who could help with the cooking and the baby, he said, and I might be able to get a rest."

"He can call her from Marathon, or he can use the radio telephone if he likes."

"All right."

There was a pause.

"Sloan, why do you get so terribly angry?"

"Why does he?"

"I don't know, I never did. I thought in that way you would be different."

"You always said we were a lot alike."

"I didn't know it ran that deep."

"It's childish, I know, but I'm angry in part because you always seem to side with him."

"I'm just trying to keep the peace. I can't stand to see either of you torn apart."

"I'm not being torn apart. It takes more than one old Irishman. . . ."

"That's why I always seem to side with him."

"I'll try my best not to let it happen again," I said gruffly.

"You won't have to worry about him for long. He says he's leaving when we get to Key West."

"And that's my fault," I groaned. "I suppose I've been driving him to it."

"He's been driving at you, too. He knows he can't stay here with us forever. For one thing, his business is calling him back. Maybe for some reason he wanted an explosion as much as you did. I hope it clears the air."

Bob didn't come on deck all day, but that night he was affable, although a little distant. After dinner he went ashore and called his friend in Miami, and she drove down to join us the next day. As he had promised Betty, she was a nice woman who knew a lot about both children and boats, as well as wild old Irishmen, and having her aboard was like a vacation for all of us.

The next week was extremely pleasant. After his friend left, Bob busied himself with fishing in Key West. Dissatisfied with the Spanish mackerel he caught, he stood beside a huge tarpon another man had brought to the wharf and had Betty take a picture to be shown to all his friends in Ireland. While she waited for the Polaroid to develop the shot, he did a little soft-shoe dance, as he often did when his exuberance got the better of his patience. That night he helped to do the dishes and was so charming that in my heart I accused him of inflicting a final torture upon me by behaving so well that I hated to see him leave as much as I had dreaded to see him arrive. On the

morning of his departure he corrected that, however, by order-
ing me about like a male secretary.

"Now, find out when the planes leave, will you, lad? And
while you're at it, get me a timetable for the buses and the
trains from Miami."

As soon as I returned from this errand, he said, "I'm going to
have to ship my heavy suitcase direct to the Cunard Line. Will
you call Railway Express and take care of it?"

"Oh, Lord, I do hate to see him go," I said to Betty, "but why
can't he take care of these little chores himself?"

"If you can't do it with love, don't do it," Betty said. "How
many times do I have to tell you that he's old and in a strange
country? Little things get him all confused."

In the end, Bob decided to take a bus to Miami, there to
catch a train, for he said he hated air travel. We accompanied
him in a taxi to the terminal in Key West. Just before he got on
the bus, he clapped me hard on the shoulder and said, "See you
soon in Ireland, I hope, lad. I do appreciate all you've done for
me, and as heaven is my witness, you're a great lad when it
comes to handling a boat."

With Jessie standing beside her, Betty clung to him hard
until the driver motioned him impatiently to get on the bus.
Giving Jessie a quick kiss, Bob ran. As the door slammed
behind him, Betty stood watching the stalwart, silver-haired
figure walking down the aisle of the bus past the windows, his
image flickering like an old-fashioned movie run too slow.
When the bus pulled out, she collapsed in tears on my shoulder.

"I'm afraid I'll never see him alive again," she said, digging
her nails into my flesh. Jessie, who was hugging our legs, began
to cry.

"We'll go to Ireland. Soon."

"I think his heart is worse than he told me. That's why he
shipped that big bag."

"You'll see him again," I said, but my assurance sounded
patently false.

"I know he's sometimes an awful bastard," she said, straightening up and reaching into her bag for Kleenex, "but you've got to admit one thing: I've got the most beautiful, beautiful father that any girl ever had."

When we got back to the boat, Betty played the piano for a long time, as she often does when she is deeply troubled.

"Damn," she said finally, slamming down the lid.

"What's the trouble?"

"I think I may have made an awful mistake."

"What?"

"Dad said he planned to be in New York for a few days, and he asked me for the addresses of some of our friends—you know how he hates to be alone."

"So?"

"I gave him some telephone numbers, and now I think I should have said I had forgotten them."

"Why?"

"You know how he is when he gets lonely, and on his last night in America he always raises hell. I just hope he doesn't get into trouble. Nobody in New York knows how to handle him."

"He'll be all right," I said, but my reassurance again sounded patently false.

# 21

⚓

My antidote to depression has always been movement of one form or another, and though it has rarely enabled me to leave my troubles behind, it has often been successful at taking my mind off them. That night while Betty was still mourning the departure of her father I went to the after cabin and unrolled a lot of charts. There the South Atlantic lay before me with Florida's long peninsula dribbling away into a chain of islands at the last of which we were. To the west was the Gulf of Mexico and to the east the Grand Bank of the Bahamas with more than 700 islands not far below the horizon. Here was a feast indeed for a hungry sailor. I was lucky enough to have the time and the boat to go almost anywhere here, if I could only solve the riddle of the engines.

The Dry Tortugas—the words seemed to leap at me from the chart, where they labeled a dot in the ocean about 75 miles west of Key West. The Dry Tortugas! In my youth I had always wanted to visit them, for there had seemed a special music in the name, despite the fact that the books said it meant only that the old Spanish explorers had found no water there but plenty of turtles, which were their chief source of meat. Because of his health, my father had never wanted to go beyond Key West, and later, when I had my charter schooner, I had secretly concluded that my navigational skills, which at the time were almost entirely self-taught, were too modest to permit a search for small islands that couldn't be found by coasting along some large body of land. Still, the Dry Tortugas had remained in my mind as a sort of ultimate, one of the many goals in life I had been unable to reach.

Well, why not go there now? The engines were still leaking water, but they showed no signs of having damaged themselves in all the hundreds of miles we had already sailed. Unlike the Bahamas, the Dry Tortugas were United States territory, which meant that they were still under the protection of our Coast Guard. One of the things that had secretly bothered me about going to the Bahamas was the knowledge that the Coast Guard did not operate there. Besides, great beds of shrimp had recently been discovered around the Dry Tortugas, and many trawlers would be near. Going there really would not be dangerous, and the voyage would have the advantage of getting us out of narrow channels, letting us see how we and the *Pretty Betty* behaved in the open sea. If the weather was good, they were only a day away, and within a week we could return to Key West to meet my mother. Then what?

To keep her in the sheltered waters an eighty-year-old woman had a right to demand, we could head back for Miami and the canals. Or, if we didn't want to retrace our steps, we could pick a calm day and cross the upper part of the Gulf of Mexico to reach the west coast of Florida. Perhaps we could inspect the Everglades, which I and my mother had always wanted to see. Then we could take the canal from Fort Myers to Lake Okee-chobee in the center part of the state. That canal continued back to the east coast, coming out at Stuart, which is not far from Palm Beach. There I could review the performance of the engines and make some definite decision about hauling them out of the boat for major repairs. Mother would go back to New York, perhaps having been nicked for a big loan by her oldest son, the big success of the family, and one way or another we would press on to the Bahamas at last.

"Betty!" I said. "I have a plan," and with a tobacco-stained finger I traced out the journey for her on the charts.

"Good," she said. "I know it isn't the fault of Key West or anyone, yet somehow this place is full of the sadness of my father. Let's sail at dawn."

But it wasn't that easy. The wind the next day was strong enough to make the shrimp boats stay at Key West, where they lay jostling restlessly at their moorings with the ice in their holds melting away like their money. When the brawny trawlers won't work, I concluded, the open sea is no place for the *Pretty Betty*.

For several days the "front," as modern sailors have taken to calling storms, moved through, and we decided to enjoy Key West as much as possible.

It is, we found, a curious town, where the king of Florida business, the tourist industry, plays second fiddle to the Navy and the fishing fleet. Poets and painters come there, making the settlement into a kind of Southern Provincetown, but the real action comes from the sailors swaggering down the streets looking for the pretty Cuban girls who fled Havana seeking a new kind of life.

Living on the waterfront, as we were, we met many of the Navy boys, who seemed to me to be a sort of reincarnation of my wartime self, and we also met some of the shrimpers, who are said to be a clannish and sometimes dangerous set.

"Don't get mixed up with the shrimpers," a haggard bare-footed poet who somehow wandered aboard our boat said. "They drink the whole time they're in port. If you anchor in one of their favorite places, they'll drive you crazy with their wake, and if that doesn't work, they'll jostle you out—the shrimpers don't worry about a few scratches on their paint. Never ask a shrimper to come aboard your boat. He'll drink your booze, insult your wife and scare your daughters. Worse than that, he's likely to come back later with his friends, smash his way into your boat and steal you blind. They run out of money when they're stormbound, and nothing stands in the way of more booze."

Studying large-scale charts of the area while we waited for a calm spell, I tried to make a plan that would introduce Betty and the baby to the open ocean in a way that would not disprove my old boasts about sailing without spilling a cup of tea.

Almost halfway to the Dry Tortugas was another tiny group of islands, the Marquesas Keys; they were often used as a target area for Navy bombers, but no maneuvers were currently under way. If we got a quiet morning we could anchor near a beach there and sail at three the following morning for the Tortugas. Doing it that way, I could probably see the tall lighthouse on Loggerhead Key, one of the Tortuga group, long before dawn, and when Betty and Jessie woke up in the morning, our anchor would already be down at Garden Key, the biggest of those small islands.

Aside from the threat of my leaky engines, there would be only one real danger in venturing to sea aboard the *Pretty Betty*. This was a peril about which I sometimes had nightmares, the chance of my taking a bad fall on a rolling deck, becoming incapacitated in some other way, or worst of all, falling overboard, leaving Betty and the baby to cope with the situation alone. To guard against that eventuality, I had taught her the essentials of maneuvering the boat and of using the radio telephone, but still the possibility of leaving Betty and the baby alone on the high seas was not a pleasant one and would not be a comforting last thought for a drowning man.

Of course, I exaggerated the hazards of going to sea, but it might be wise to get someone to go with us on this trip, our first venture into the open ocean. Then the idea came to me: why not ask the Perfect Man?

The Perfect Man was a fellow we had met at the marina in Key West, and we had given him that title because he did, indeed, seem to be curiously without flaws. Although he was about my age, he was slender as a stripling, and he smilingly limited himself to one cocktail before dinner and one highball before bed. Naturally, the Perfect Man didn't smoke, but to avoid the impression of being a goody-goody, he told an occasional off-color joke, invariably choosing really witty ones. Although he lived on a tiny motor cruiser he had brought from Kansas on a trailer behind his Lincoln, the Perfect Man was always as spotlessly dressed as though he had an enormous collection of white ducks, pale blue sport shirts and unstained sneakers. We gave him the title of the Perfect Man when we noticed the curious fact that he could go trolling out in the Gulf Stream, repair his engines, come back to the marina and clean the enormous fish he always caught, all without getting a spot of grease or blood on his clothes and without ruffling his neatly parted black hair. When Betty coined his title, I hated him, but part of the man's perfection was that one couldn't dislike him for long—he was far too easygoing and courteous.

Naturally, his companion on his dinky cruiser was the Perfect Wife, a tall, thin woman whose white dresses were always immaculate and whose red hair was always set in elaborate fashion. Even his little boat was perfect for prudent people who could cheerfully spend vacations in quarters that made those aboard the *Pretty Betty* look enormous. The Perfect Man owned a huge real estate business, but he didn't buy large yachts because he was saving his money to buy separate companies for each of his children. The reason he was spending two months on his pocket cruiser was that he wanted his sons to learn how to run his business while he was away. The Perfect Man was very good at delegating responsibility, and when one of his sons telephoned to say that he had made a mistake which caused a loss of $10,000, the Perfect Man laughed tolerantly and said he would simply count that as tuition to the practical school of business.

The Perfect Man and his wife had talked to me about going to the Dry Tortugas, where the fishing was supposed to be about the best in the world at the time, but they feared their 24-

foot craft was too small for the voyage. Why not ask them to go with us?

"Betty!" I said. "For the next few days, how would you like to have the Perfect Crew?"

"No," she said when I explained my idea.

"Why not?"

"We'll find out that something terrible is the matter with them. People that good on the surface must have some dreadful hidden vice, and I don't want to find out about it when we're way out there in the middle of the ocean."

"That's ridiculous. There *are* good people in the world, you know. It's some flaw in us that's been attracting so many kooks."

"Take a chance if you want," she said, slamming down a frying pan. "I think they're dangerous."

And so the Perfect Couple moved aboard the *Pretty Betty* carrying one tiny seabag because they always traveled light, and immediately they offered to pay half the food, fuel and liquor bills. Apparently for their benefit, the weather immediately moderated, and we sailed for the Marquesas Keys.

This was a delightful journey. Standing at the wheel with his trim, bronzed body in spotless white bathing trunks, the Perfect Man was cautious without being in the least nervous, a fact which astonished me because he had never before been more than a few miles from shore. While I took my turn at the wheel, he asked for tools and repaired some fittings that had been loose for weeks. When we dropped anchor off a beach that would have been a good setting for a movie about the South Seas, he dove overboard and went running up the sand with the energy of a boy of nineteen. All the while, his Perfect Wife sat in the deckhouse serenely knitting and beaming benignly at everyone.

"I hate them both," Betty said as I rowed her and Jessie ashore in the dinghy. "I bet he's a necrophiliac or something really dreadful like that."

I was in my usual state of bewildered semiexhaustion by the time I pulled the dinghy up on the beach, but the Perfect Man skipped about gathering shells for my baby and teaching her how to swim. He said to Betty, "You're one of the few women who look really good in a bikini," but there was not a suggestion of improper motive in his tone or manner.

Hoping that a swim would revive my energy, I waded waist-deep into the water.

"There are sea urchins here," I called to the Perfect Man. "Watch out for them. They can give you an awful—"

My sentence ended in a sharp screech as I launched myself in the water, and brought my knee down hard on a sea urchin. The spines broke off in the wound as they always do, and when I washed the blood away I saw that my skin was tattooed with the creature's purple dye.

Cursing, I went back to the boat, where the Perfect Man's wife said that she would be glad to treat the wound because she had just completed a first aid course in preparation for their cruise. That night my knee ached painfully, but the sky was so clear as the orange sun sank into the purple sea that I couldn't help but be cheerful. Immediately after steaks, which the Perfect Man's wife tastefully prepared, I told Betty that I wanted to sail at three in the morning and went to bed.

At about midnight I awoke when Betty joined me.

"Well, I talked to the Perfect Couple all evening, and I found out what's wrong with them," she said with satisfaction.

"Is it ghastly?"

"Yes—they have the worst vice of all. They are boring. They are unutterable bores."

"I always found them amusing."

"You wait until you talk to them for six straight hours. They have no gossip—they say nothing but good about anyone. They have no funny stories to tell about themselves, for there's nothing particularly funny about an unending series of triumphs. They won't talk about money, religion, politics or sex because that's bad taste. What, for Christ's sake, is left?"

"What *did* you talk about?"

"The Perfect Wife doesn't talk at all. She just sews and smiles."

"What did he talk about?"

"Almost nothing—he's a Good Listener. For God's sake, I found myself putting on a regular monologue up there. It was either that or sit listening to the radio, which is apparently their usual diversion."

"But they're still the salt of the earth."

"Give me some pepper. Lord, I miss Dad. Do you?"

"Yes," I said, and was glad to discover that I was only half-lying.

When my alarm clock awoke me at two-thirty, a quarter-moon was shining on an almost motionless sea, and although there was a line of gray clouds on the eastern horizon, it looked like a grand morning to start for the Dry Tortugas. Our electric windlass brought the anchor up smartly, and a single touch of the starting buttons was enough to bring the diesels to life. The Perfect Man took the wheel while I studied the chart. Maybe he was a bore, I reflected, but his habit of silence and his calm air of competence were a comfort when we were under way.

This was the first time I had really headed out to sea at night since the war, and I had forgotten how far a man can see with only a hint of a moon. Astern, the sandy beach where we had swum glowed a pale yellow, and almost against the horizon I could see the outline of a big tanker at least 10 miles away. A reflection from our port running light glowed ruby on our chart, and for hundreds of yards astern our wake stirred up the phosphorescence of the sea, creating a dimly lit path.

Taking the wheel while my friend went down to prepare coffee, I glanced at a card I had prepared giving the courses and the time we should see each light we were to pass. In eighteen minutes a buoy with a white flasher should appear over the horizon dead ahead. When the Perfect Man brought me coffee, I told him this and he smiled with gentle tolerance, for as he said, he couldn't understand why people made a Big Deal out of navigation and all that. With his little boat, which went almost

40 miles an hour, he just set a course and barreled gaily ahead till he got there.

"With a boat this size it's different," I said. "I have to learn how fast she goes under all different kinds of conditions for each engine speed."

"Can't you get a speedometer?"

"Yes," I said, unwilling to admit that in many ways I was stuck in the days of my youth, when such gadgets were rarely employed.

Still, the Perfect Man acted impressed when each light showed up precisely on schedule, and like me, he began to enjoy the game of attempting to be the Perfect Navigator.

"There's only one thing wrong," I said two hours later. "We should have seen that big light on Loggerhead Key twenty minutes ago."

"That's funny," the Perfect Man said, picking up the binoculars. "There isn't even a glow on the horizon."

Another ten minutes went by.

"How high is that light?" he asked.

"A hundred feet—it's a big lighthouse."

"We should see it by now," he said imperturbably. "Do you suppose the Coast Guard let it go out?"

"That *never* happens."

"There's always a first time," he said casually.

When anything unexplained happens at sea, my insides always start churning like a Mixmaster, and my imagination tries to conquer my common sense. Perhaps there were swift currents here which had swept us far off course since we had passed the last buoy. Perhaps our compass had suddenly gone wrong, spinning us around to head for the nearest reef.

But the current tables carried no warnings for this part of the ocean. Neither did the chart or the pilot book, and the spare compass I kept in the deckhouse matched the steering compass precisely. For another half hour we sliced along, but still no light appeared ahead.

"It's funny, because the visibility looks good," my friend said quietly, pointing toward the lights of a shrimp boat about 10 miles away.

"Maybe there's a local rain squall blanketing the light," I replied.

That explanation sounded farfetched, but my mind told me it was by far the most logical one, even though my imagination kept conjuring up horrors.

"Anyway, we'll know pretty soon," he said mildly. "Hell, we should be there in a couple of hours."

I had timed our arrival for eight o'clock in the morning, hoping to pick up the light while it was still dark and then to give the morning mists time to evaporate, but as the darkness faded, we still saw no flashing beam on the horizon ahead. It was a gray, unimpressive dawn with low-hanging clouds obscuring the sun.

"Hell, we couldn't see a light now anyhow," he said as the day brightened. "We'll have to wait until we're right on top of it."

The fear which arose in me now I knew to be completely unreasonable. After all, there was no war on locally, and we were still only about 60 miles from Key West. If something had gone wrong and we were to arrive at the theoretical position of the Dry Tortugas only to find empty sea, we could turn around and go back. Surely I could manage to stumble upon some part of the entire North American Continent!

But why had I been so foolish as to save money by not buying a sextant and chronometer? Why hadn't I been boning up on my celestial navigation instead of sitting around gassing with all my relatives and friends? The ocean has a way of reckoning with a man's weaknesses. Was a long, bewildering time of blundering around without knowing my position going to be my punishment?

Nonsense, nonsense—that was only my Puritan expectation of retribution. Hardly anyone used celestial navigation on short runs to the Bahamas and the Tortugas. It wasn't necessary. I had been wise to bring a piano instead of a sextant.

But where was the lighthouse? Ahead were only banks of gray clouds.

"What kind of land are we looking for?" my friend asked cheerfully.

"Low, sandy islands. Garden Key has an old fort on it."

"That's where they imprisoned Dr. Mudd after he treated the man who shot Lincoln."

"Yes," I said, completely uninterested in history at the moment. "I think those clouds ahead are thick enough to have obscured the light."

"Must be. We sure didn't see it."

Another half hour ticked by. The clouds thickened, and gradually it began to rain.

"With the visibility like this, we can damn near run into that fort without seeing it," the Perfect Man said with perfect equanimity.

"Yep."

"Can you tell anything from the depth of the water?"

"It's too deep for soundings until you get right on top of the keys."

"What time are we due there?"

"Another thirty-five minutes."

As the seconds ticked by, I found myself growing so tense that I longed for a drink, but I had taken a solemn vow to myself not to start that when we were under way. Staring into the rain clouds ahead, I began to imagine mountains coming down to the sea, great liners headed straight for us, anything.

Christ, if you can work up this kind of sweat over a 70-mile sail you really are due for the loony bin, I told myself.

Steering error—why hadn't I thought of that most obvious cause of trouble? I had stayed on course, but was the Perfect Man really reliable? Leaning over the compass, I checked and found that he was making no error.

"Have you been right on course all along?" I asked.

"Far as I know," he replied with a chuckle.

Somehow a feeling arose in me that we were far to the left of where we should be. There was an enormous temptation to bring the boat 20 degrees to the right, but I could think of no real reason for the change.

"Remember that the compass is always more reliable than blind instinct."

That I remembered from some textbook, and I was glad I did, because a few minutes later I felt virtually certain that we should change course drastically to go left.

"How much time before we're supposed to be there?" my friend asked.

"About twenty minutes. I think I better slow down. This visibility is really closing in."

With the speed cut, the engines were quiet, and we could hear the rain beating on the awnings. I turned on the Fathometer, but the water was still much too deep for it to give us a reading.

"The sun seems to be trying to burn through," the Perfect Man said.

And then, about five minutes later, it happened. The *Pretty Betty* steamed through the curtain of rain which had obscured the lighthouse, and there close ahead were the Dry Tortugas, their white beaches sparkling in a shaft of sunshine coming down like the beam of a giant spotlight between two low-lying clouds. The scene was so breathtaking that it seemed contrived, as though a set designer had overdone it. To our left was Fort Jefferson, a massive, brooding pile of red brick walls, and to our right was a fleet of shrimp boats, their white, rain-washed hulls sparkling like yachts. Overhead was a clearly defined rainbow with one end of its arc just above the tall white lighthouse of Loggerhead Key.

"Golly Jehosafats!" the Perfect Man said in awe.

It was the nearest I had heard him come to swearing.

I shoved the throttles down, and the *Pretty Betty* romped ahead, tossing her bow up as though she were proud of a job

well done. In the deckhouse below, the ship's clock rang eight
bells.

That was the time Betty usually got up, and she was right on
schedule. Sticking her head through the deckhouse door sleepily, she gazed out over our stern at the gray sea and rubbing her
eyes said, "Where are we?"

"Shut your eyes and come here," I said.

"What do you mean?"

"Do as I say!"

When she closed her eyes, I gave the helm to my friend and
helped her to the bridge, turning her face toward the bow, just
ahead of which the rainbow now seemed to connect the great
brick fortress and the lighthouse.

"Open your eyes," I said in a theatrical tone which seemed to
suit the vision ahead. "Betty, I give you the Dry Tortugas!"

"Wow!"

Betty sucked in her breath sharply.

"That's some present!" she added. "Why didn't you tell me
they are so beautiful?"

"This is my first visit too."

"It's wonderful how all those little charts and things work for
you. Here we can go wandering around the world as though
we'd been everywhere and still have the thrill of seeing each
new place for the first time."

"That's why I love boats," I said softly. "When I pay all the
bills, this is the kind of thing I remember."

# 22

⚓

That morning, which had dawned with such ridiculously intensified worry, had another spectacular sight to give us. Seeing that the government wharf on Garden Key was empty, I decided to moor there. Edging alongside in a swift current, we were so busy getting the dock lines out that we were all moored before I chanced to glance down. The water between the wharf and the boat was so clear that the *Pretty Betty* seemed somehow to be suspended in slightly bluish light, and there, lying layer on layer, were so many huge fish that I thought I was staring into an overstocked aquarium.

"Jumping Jehosafats!" the Perfect Man yelled and ran to tell his wife, who was getting breakfast. Standing by the rail, he pointed down for her.

"*Yippee!*" she yelled, sounding exactly like the cowboys on television rodeos.

"That did it," Betty whispered to me softly.

"Did what?"

"She just got an orgasm. I bet it's her first in twenty years."

"Hush. He was a great help to me last night."

"I know, I'm awful, but those people make me *want* to be wicked."

Although we had, in all fact, concluded only a brief trip which any shrimper or mariner of any description would consider perfectly routine, the strains of the voyage and the excitement of the landfall had left me exhausted. While the Perfect Man and his wife rushed around preparing fishing gear and lowering the dinghy, I went below and slept soundly for nine hours. When I awoke, the rain clouds had shut down again and a strong wind was whipping the tall grass that grew in clumps on the ramparts of the old fort. Eight shrimpers had anchored on the other side of the channel, nesting together companionably, and a big Coast Guard buoy tender had moored at the wharf ahead of us.

"Quite a storm must be coming up," I said to Betty. "Those shrimpers don't nest up like that in here unless they expect real trouble."

"Is there any danger?"

"The only thing to fear is maybe a long wait with nothing much to do. We're safe as can be here, and we won't sail until this blows over."

That night the wind piped up to about 40 knots, sending the surf smashing across the reefs on both ends of our island, but nestled snugly in the lee of the old fort, the *Pretty Betty* didn't even tremble. After listening to the weather reports, I said to Betty, "It looks as though we might be here for about a week. I hope you're not going to be bored to death, because there's nothing ashore but that crumbling fort."

As it turned out, there was nothing boring about the Dry Tortugas, and we spent one of the best weeks of our lives stormbound there. For entertainment there were the shrimpers —great, bawdy, laughing men who rowed over to exchange tubs of fresh shrimp for a six-pack of beer and who often stayed to eat the shrimp and drink the beer with us. For serious study there was the history of the fort and the nearby breeding grounds of the sooty tern, both of which were described in literature supplied by the caretaker of the fort. And for hard work there were our engines, which the Perfect Man said we should take completely apart in order to locate the source of the freshwater leaks.

*"Take completely apart?"* I asked incredulously. "What are you, some kind of diesel specialist?"

"No, but I know a little, and I bet they've got plenty of diesel specialists over on that buoy tender. I bet they also have plenty of tools and parts. Didn't you used to be in the Coast Guard?"

"Long enough to know you don't ask them for help unless there's an emergency."

"I bet those men are bored to death sitting over there with nothing to do."

"Coast Guardsmen always have something to do. If their skipper doesn't see to that, they have dice and cards."

"Will you let me start to take a look inside those engines?" the Perfect Man asked. "Then if I get in trouble, you'll have a real emergency, and the Coast Guard will have to help."

"You better let him," Betty said in private to me while I thought the matter over. "That man has never failed at anything in his life."

The Dry Tortugas did not prove to be a place for him to break his record. After he got into the engines, the Perfect Man strolled over to the Coast Guard cutter to borrow a wrench. There he struck up a conversation with the engineering officer, whom he invited back to the *Pretty Betty* for a drink. The engineering officer agreed to stay for dinner and to ask his commanding officer to join us. That gentleman proved to be a lieutenant who had once served aboard the United States Coast Guard cutter *Buttonwood*, on which I had briefly been the navigator in the South Pacific during World War II. That bond and a week of weather that kept the buoy tender from its work proved to be enough, and almost the entire "black gang" of the cutter was soon crowded into our engine room with the Perfect Man, apparently tearing our diesels down to scrap iron and building them up from scratch.

Sitting in the tall captain's chair with a can of beer in my hand, I supervised the operation. What could be sweeter than to watch experts fix one's engines for free?

"Why are you doing this?" I asked a chief machinist as he

emerged from my engine room covered with grease. "Surely I can't pretend that this is line of duty."

"It's sort of a challenge," he said with a shrug. "I never knew diesels to lose water like that before, two of them at the same time without any known reason. I want to find why."

"All up and down the inland route, no one could tell."

"I'm going to put some yellow dye in there under pressure. Then, by God, I'll see where it comes out."

"*Semper paratus,*" I sang in the shower that night.

"What's that?" Betty asked.

"It's the Coast Guard anthem. I don't know why in hell I never learned all the words. When we leave here I think we'll finally be free of worry about those diesels."

During the long days of rain Betty spent a lot of time reading aloud to Jessie.

"I've given up on children's books," she said to me. "How can I read a thing well if I myself hate it? Jessie likes lots of things that also interest me."

"Like what?"

"Her favorite now is the pamphlet on sooty terns. It's fantastic. Do you know that sooty tern parents take turns standing by their egg to shield it from the sun? It's the reverse of all the rest of the bird world. Instead of keeping their eggs warm, they lay them out there in the open sun and have to keep them cool. Jessie has been practicing with an egg on the foredeck."

One night, shortly before we left, I couldn't sleep and came on deck. Ragged clouds were blowing over a quarter-moon, and turning, I saw the Perfect Man, who was sitting in a deck chair abaft the wheel.

There was a clinking sound, and to my astonishment, I realized that he had a glass in one hand and a bottle of vodka on the seat beside him.

"Want a shot?" he asked.

"Sure."

"Usually I get by on two drinks a day, but tonight I got to

thinking about my boys. The younger one may be called up for Vietnam."

"I'm worried about my son too. He's seventeen."

A deep sigh emanated from the Perfect Man.

Close at our side there was the sound of oars, and a dory with two shrimpers appeared from the darkness on the other side of the channel.

"You guys want to trade some beer for shrimp?" a man in an orange slicker called.

"We don't have beer, but we got vodka!" the Perfect Man replied. "Come aboard!"

Within a half hour we were having quite a party, with shrimpers rowing in from the entire stormbound fleet. There is not a great deal I remember about it, but I recall the Perfect Man standing up and giving a very dignified lecture on the follies of the military mind while all the shrimpers cheered.

Betty, I noticed, had been watching this from the open door of the deckhouse, where she had been sitting with the Perfect Man's wife, who simply continued to smile and sew throughout the entire wild night. When the Perfect Man finally staggered to his bunk and all the shrimpers went back to their ships, Betty climbed up on the tall captain's chair and sat staring at the sullen outline of the great hexagonal fort.

"I wish the Perfect Man would run for President," she said.

That party served us as a real introduction to the shrimpers, and they took to rowing over to visit our boat, bringing their own liquor, which is the biggest compliment a shrimper can pay you. They were wild fellows, many of them from backwoods settlements in Georgia and both Carolinas, where many of their boats had been built of longleaf yellow pine and cypress felled in the great swamps and mule-dragged to the sea. There were several Negroes among them, and though they were all Southerners, there didn't seem to be any racial friction, perhaps because the shrimpers, who have to haul great nets at night, often in heavy seas, have one of the most brutal jobs in the world, and the only thing which seems to integrate the races really well, other than sex, is extreme hardship. Many of the men wore the red wool hats of the Georgia cracker even in the heat of the Dry Tortugas, and their deep Southern voices were full of explosive laughter.

One of the reasons the shrimpers liked to visit us was that their own boats were full of the indescribable smell of rotting fish, and they were forbidden to go ashore at Garden Key.

"Why?" I asked a lean, rather saturnine man from St. Augustine who had been the skipper of a shrimper for ten years, despite the fact that he was only twenty-eight.

"It's a government park," he said.

"Aren't parks supposed to be for public recreation?"

He shrugged.

"The government guys who run it have wives," he said. "Some of our boys raised a little hell. . . ."

There was, I learned, a running war of long standing between the shrimpers and all government forces. My friends on the Coast Guard cutter were appalled that I allowed the shrimpers aboard.

"They're the scum of the ocean," a pink-faced lieutenant junior-grade told us. "Of course they don't allow them ashore! They'd tear up the whole place in no time."

"How could they tear up that fort?" Betty asked innocently.

"I would blush to tell you," the lieutenant junior-grade replied.

"Come on, sonny," Betty said. "From the sound of your voice I'd say you come from Brooklyn. Have they started to blush easy there?"

"They fight with knives when they get to drinking," the lieutenant junior-grade said with dignity, "and they seem to take special delight in urinating in public, sometimes whole crews of them at a time up there on those high ramparts."

"That's pretty bad," Betty said with exaggerated solemnity.

"They also are terrible seamen," the lieutenant junior-grade continued. "Usually we let them take care of each other. If the

Coast Guard answered every shrimper distress call, we wouldn't have time for anything else."

"How can they be terrible seamen and work out there day and night?" I asked.

He shrugged.

"They spend their money on booze, not on their boats, and what little equipment they have is rotten. A lot of them can't even navigate. Some of those fleets come out of the Georgia swamps with sharecroppers as skippers."

"How do they find the Dry Tortugas?" Betty asked.

"They have a lead boat, sometimes the only one who even has a chart. When they get separated from him, they panic and call us on the distress frequencies."

"Do they make much money?" the Perfect Man asked.

"They work on shares, the way most fisherman do. Sometimes they'll tie into a good bed of shrimp and make fifteen hundred dollars a week, but more often they'll stay out a month and come back owing for the ice and groceries."

"They're gambling men," Betty said. "Like actors and writers."

"And when their luck is out, watch out for them. God knows what they bring in and out of Cuba—we can't stop and search them all. Every once in a while a plush yacht disappears out here. I'm not sure we've seen the last of the pirates."

Despite these dire descriptions, the shrimpers who sat around our deckhouse listening to Betty play the piano and jouncing Jessie on their knees seemed benign enough—until, that is, the subject of the Coast Guard and Navy came up.

"Those bastards!" a barrel-chested man in a red shirt said. "They call us lousy seamen. Well, you give me five million bucks of equipment, a trained crew of thirty men, and no fish to catch. Then I'll show you how to stay out of trouble."

A thin man in a cap that looked as though it had been made for skiing spat delicately into an open beer can.

"Hell!" he said. "They're little boys tied to their Uncle Sam. Coasties just live for their pension."

"You know why they're really out for us?" the man in the wool cap continued. "We take their girls, that's why. Liberty for a Coasty ends at midnight, and after that the town is ours. If we get a good week we have money like even an admiral never saw, and besides that, we can take girls back to the ships with us. All the Navy and Coasty boys get is the culls a shrimper wouldn't look at."

This man talked most of the night with us and the next day brought a Cuban girl who was living on his trawler with him over to meet Betty. She was a shy beauty who knew little English, but her eyes lit up when she saw Betty's sewing machine. For an entire afternoon the two women, helped by the Perfect Man's wife, cut out dress patterns on a bunk in the after cabin.

The shrimpers almost made me disloyal to my old love, the Coast Guard. It was the Coast Guardsmen who found the trouble in our engines and wouldn't accept even a bottle of Scotch in payment.

"Your port engine has a pinhole in the block, and your starboard engine is leaking through the freeze plug," the cutter's engineer said. "Even if I didn't have to pay the bills myself, I wouldn't have them hauled out of the boat for that. The water is shooting out without doing a bit of harm. If you get sick of pouring more in, try some more compounds in bigger doses. The brown kind that has a metal base is best."

I thanked him, unable fully to express my relief from the constant worry about the engines. Now the whole feast of the Bahamas for which our charts provided an elaborate menu was waiting for us, and the seas outside our snug harbor in the Dry Tortugas were already flattening out.

"You going over to the islands now?" the shrimper in the wool hat asked as he helped Betty cast our lines off the wharf.

"No. I'm going back to Florida."

"What the hell for? It's the Bahamas where the real action is this time of the year. That's where I'd go if I didn't have to fish."

Somehow I didn't have the heart to tell this swashbuckling shrimper that I had to go back to Key West to meet my mother and take her for a cruise of the canals. Doubtless he thought me a tamed enough spirit without that.

"We have to pick up supplies," I said.

"You got enough shrimp?"

"Our freezer is full."

With a wave, he dropped the loops of our lines into the water, and Betty hauled them in.

The trip back to Key West went so smoothly that I became convinced we were finally getting used to the boat, a feeling which before long turned out to be overly optimistic but which was pleasant while it lasted.

As the sharp bow of the *Pretty Betty* serenely parted a mirrorlike sea, I sat at the wheel forming plans to make my mother's visit as pleasant as possible for all of us. Just as I had greeted her father aboard with considerable apprehension, I sensed that much as Betty loved my mother, she was worried about the problems she might present during a long visit on a small boat. The obvious difficulties one might expect in taking an eighty-year-old woman on a cruise did not bother me—Mother was still spry enough to get aboard, even when the pier was very high or low, and although she had lost a lot of weight recently, her health was robust. She would not be frightened or seasick if we stuck to the canals, and there were enough books aboard to occupy her when she got bored. Still, there was a problem, for just as Bob and I often drank too much, my mother had a serious vice which she had difficulty in controlling: she was a talker, a nonstop talker, day and night.

"I know it and I hate it, but I can't stop it," she had often said to me. "I think it's because I have lived alone so much. When I get near people. . . ."

Her weakness was one I could easily understand because I shared it, as most of my family did. My brother's wife once observed that all people who married into our family should be required to take vows of silence, because they never got a chance to talk anyway. Betty had been too loyal to agree openly, but one summer when Mother had visited us in a house we rented in Ireland, I had seen Betty grow more and more pale and wild-eyed as Mother amiably followed her from room to room, declaiming in a loud voice about books she had read, adventures she had had on her many travels, and dead relatives she wished Betty could have known.

"I love her, but I can't do my housework," Betty had said to me, collapsing into tears one night and holding her hands over her ears. "I have to have thoughts of my own sometimes, and it's getting so I can't hear myself think!"

"She's a little deaf," I had said. "She doesn't realize how loud. . . ."

"I don't want to hurt her feelings, but the baby is all upset—I haven't been able to pay a bit of attention to her."

"I'll try to have a talk with my mother."

"No! Can't you tell her I'm sick and have to be alone in my room for a few hours every afternoon?"

"That would worry her terribly. She's a perfectly reasonable person, and she never hesitates to tell me I should cut down on the booze."

That night I had as tactfully as possible suggested to Mother that Betty was a very quiet person, a gentle, serene soul who needed long intervals of silence and who got rattled badly when she got involved in too much conversation.

"I know. I talk too much," Mother had said briefly, but her eyes had looked stricken, and for several hours she had stayed in her room. During the first part of the next day she had sat reading in a corner, but then one of the characters in the book had reminded her of her grandfather, and she had got started on Oswego, New York, the little town where she had grown up.

That house in Ireland had been big, and her visit short. Betty had submitted patiently, but how would she stand up to two weeks of a verbal barrage on a small boat?

Obviously it wouldn't help to warn Mother about talking any more than it would to warn Bob against raising hell ashore, but perhaps there was another solution. Born at the Naval Academy and both the daughter and the sister of regular naval officers, Mother had a special feeling about ships. Ashore she was a feminist who ever since her days at Vassar had been dedicated to the proposition that women could do anything men could do, usually better. In any house or apartment where she lived her word was law, or had been ever since the death of my father, and I had never understood quite how he had worked out his situation with her. On horseback she had, until well into her sixties, proved that even cavalry officers had difficulty keeping up with her. In automobiles she had been an incurable backseat driver, even with my father, who never had an accident during his entire life. But aboard boats, I had discovered with wonder early in my youth, Mother was entirely different. Aboard boats she felt unable to cope with the elements and showed real respect for the strength and knowledge of a man.

With what some of my psychiatrist friends would call a sudden insight, a real breakthrough, I found myself suspecting that this was why I had always loved boats and the sea, and also why many women hated them. The sea, after all, is a man's domain that often requires the strength of male muscles, regardless of what they decide at Vassar. The authority of a captain in time of emergency supersedes all talk about the equality of the sexes. Life afloat is simply an intensification of life ashore, requiring men to be more dominant and women to be more feminine. This didn't seem to constitute much of a problem for Betty, but it posed a real difficulty for most of the women I had ever met, many of whom had solved it by getting seasick the moment they set foot on a boat, even at a dock, and demanding to be taken ashore.

But my mother had never done that. Sure, she had got seasick when it was rough, but she had liked to take cruises in the canals, and I had never heard her give my father directions when the wheel he held in his hand had nautical spokes.

Still, I dreaded the thought of having another heart-to-heart with Mother about her talking—there would be no way at all to keep the hurt from her eyes. Would it be possible to put up some kind of a sign?

SILENCE ON THE BRIDGE!

One of the Coast Guard cutters aboard which I had served had boasted such a sign, as did many vessels, and that was usually a standing order in the Merchant Marine. Although I was sensitive about Bob's charge that I tried to run a small yacht like a battleship, there seemed to be justification for emergency measures now. After considerable thought, I bought a stenciling set and on a bulkhead near the wheel painted in official-appearing red letters: SILENCE ON THE BRIDGE. Because I thought it would please my mother, I added under it: NO DRINKING UNDER WAY!

"That will protect you," Betty said wryly when she saw the sign and I explained it. "How about me down below?"

"Mother always stays on deck while we're under way—she never wants to miss anything. And at night she'll usually be tired enough to go to bed early."

"She'll probably spend most of her time right there," Betty said, gesturing toward a small deck just abaft the wheel where we had set up two comfortable chairs.

"That's part of the bridge," I said quickly. "After all, the helmsman can hear people talking there, and all this isn't complete nonsense. It really does take concentration to navigate these tricky channels."

"Will she know that's part of the bridge?"

"I'll make sure," I said, and on the deck by the chairs I stenciled: NO TALKING HERE ON THE BRIDGE! NO DRINKING UNDER WAY!

"I doubt if it will work," Betty said, "but if it doesn't, let's be nice about it. She's eighty years old. I hate to think what I'll be like then."

But it did work beautifully. The first thing Mother noticed when she hopped spryly aboard in Key West, holding a black hat on her head with one hand, was the signs, which I had deliberately sanded a little so they wouldn't look brand-new.

"That's a good idea," she said dryly. "I hope you've been under way most of the time."

"We've covered a good many miles."

"Are we going to get under way right now?"

"In the morning if the weather is right. I'm waiting for a good day to cross Florida Bay. After that it will be all canals."

"Fine," she said, and as Betty helped her unpack in the after cabin, she gave her a full biography of the many interesting people she had met on her flight from New York.

The weather predictions were good that night, and the sea looked like green linoleum at dawn the next day as we steamed out of Key West. The thought that I was crossing the upper part of the Gulf of Mexico with only Betty, an eighty-year-old woman and a small child as crew made me a little nervous at first, but the steady beat of the diesels, into which I had poured a new compound, was reassuring. In one of the chairs astern of me Mother sat looking with admiration at the pelicans swooping around us, but she didn't say a word, and she contented herself with a pleasant nod when Betty came to sit in the other chair with the baby on her lap.

"What's that?" Jessie suddenly called shrilly, pointing at a log floating in the water. "Is that an alligator?"

"No, child," Mother said sternly. "You must be absolutely quiet. You are aboard a ship, and there must be silence on the bridge!"

# 23

⚓

"For such a screwed-up country, the United States is a beautiful land," Betty said that night as we lay at anchor in the Little Shark River, which runs deep into the Everglades. Around the banks of the still black water were unusually tall cypress and mangrove trees, each of them decorated with a variety of birds. Almost at our feet the reflection of a three-quarters moon was dimpled by the ripples of mullet.

I was feeling particularly good that night, for we had crossed Florida Bay, the upper part of the Gulf, without incident. Afraid that I would miss the concealed mouth of the river, which was marked only by an inconspicuous beacon half-obscured by trees, and that I would not know which way to turn to find it, I had kept several miles to the north and had then followed the coast, which had looked much like that of New Guinea, lush, impenetrable and wild. Now the sudden squawks of alarm we heard from the mangroves around us sounded like jungle cries.

"The raccoons and owls must be after the birds," Mother said. "They hunt at night."

"The book says this river is a famous place for fish," Betty said. "It seems a shame to anchor here and not try it."

"That would be fun," Mother said, and Jessie set up a great hue and cry, demanding a line.

Despite my love for the water, I have always hated fishing. Snarled lines infuriate me, hooks near the eyes of children scare me, and the mess of bleeding fish sinking into teak decks can cause a stain it takes days to eradicate. Grumbling, I got out lines and thawed some frozen shrimp. Almost immediately Jessie caught a catfish.

"Let me land it," I shouted, grabbing the line from her. "They call these fish Oscar the Terrible down here. They have a poisonous spine on their back, and they're very clever at— OUCH!"

"You don't have to keep teaching us by example," Betty said irritably. "Did he really get you?"

"Yes," I said, sucking the wound in my hand. "He stuck that thing right through the landing net."

"Will you die?" Jessie asked.

"It's not a fatal poison," Mother said serenely. "It just stings like a bee. I remember when that happened to you in Ormond."

My whole arm began to throb, and I was furious at my womenfolk for giving me so little sympathy. Going to the deckhouse, I poured myself a stiff drink.

"Isn't a vessel at anchor legally considered under way?" my mother asked when I came out, glass in hand.

"No," I replied sourly. "Anyway, you people are talking, aren't you?"

"We aren't on the bridge," Mother said from the after cockpit. "If a storm came up, we would all have to rely on your judgment. This would be a terrible place to drag ashore."

I took one more gulp of the whiskey and threw the rest away.

Everyone aboard appeared to enjoy the sights and sounds of the Little Shark River so much that the next morning I decided to explore it a little more, pressing farther into the swamp. Usually I kept the *Pretty Betty* in deep channels, but the Perfect Man, who with his wife had gone back aboard their pocket cruiser in Key West, had made me feel self-conscious about being overanxious and so morbidly cautious that I lost a lot of the fun of cruising. The chart showed that there was a minimum of 7 feet of water in the river as it wound in a circle around an island where tall dead oaks stood like skeletons with their branches bleached white in the sun, and our Fathometer, pulsing away on the bridge beside me, showed 9 feet, which would be about right for that stage of the tide.

"After we go around that island we'll head back," I said. "The current shifts the mud in these rivers unpredictably, and it would be easy to get lost farther up."

At slow speed, the *Pretty Betty* passed so close to the island that a tall blue heron fishing by a fallen tree started up with alarm, the tips of its wings, as it took off, leaving little circles in the still water like the wake of a small boat being rowed hard. Suddenly the *Pretty Betty* began to steer in a peculiar way, her bow weaving back and forth as, feeling the suction close against her bottom, she began to seek deeper water. Immediately I shoved both engines into reverse. The Fathometer flickered indecisively near the point which showed no water under the keel.

"I guess the mud has built up here more than the chart shows," I said.

"Are we aground?" Betty asked.

Keeping quiet, Mother glared at her.

"Maybe the bow touched soft mud. She's pulling out now."

Beneath us the propellers sent up great swirls of tawny mud and dead leaves as the *Pretty Betty,* gracefully acknowledging an error, backed to a bend in the river where the Fathometer again showed 10 feet under her. There I shoved the clutches ahead and spun the wheel, and we headed back to the Gulf.

"That was a fairly close shave," I said. "There wouldn't be any real danger, but if we got stuck there on a falling tide, I'd have to radio for the Coast Guard, and it might take them awhile to haul us out."

"A miss is as good as a mile," Betty said, and Mother nodded silent agreement.

We congratulated ourselves too soon. Glancing at the instrument panel, I saw that the temperature gauges of both engines were soaring past 200 degrees, the danger point. Quickly cutting off the engines, I ran forward and hurriedly anchored before we drifted ashore.

"Engines are heating up," I called over my shoulder.

"I thought the Coast Guard fixed them!" Betty said.

"She must have sucked mud into her intakes."

"Are we under way now?" Mother asked.

"We're anchored."

"That happened once when we were cruising in the *Kia Ora*. Your father fixed it when the captain couldn't. He was always very clever with engines."

There was a pause during which the great swamp seemed to hum with silence.

"Do you think you can fix it?" Betty asked.

In my heart I knew I couldn't—engines always make me feel completely defeated even before I pick up a wrench. That's why I had twin engines—the theory was that they could never fail you, not both at the same time. Still, it was wrong to feel so helpless. I wasn't a child anymore.

"In theory it's perfectly simple," I said. "These engines are cooled by fresh water in a radiator, just like a car. But in a car the rush of air keeps the water from overheating. In our engine room there's no wind, so the engines suck in salt water and circulate it around the baffle plates. Somewhere in the system there must be strainers that can be cleaned."

It was strange how memory worked. Suddenly in my mind there was a picture of my father—who usually sat in the cockpit of our little schooner while the professional captain and I did the work—climbing out of the hatch over the little auxiliary engine and handing me a glass cup about the size of my fist with a screen in it firmly packed with mud.

"Here's your trouble," he said. "Get a bucket and wash this out."

"I remember," I said to my mother, and going down to the engine room of the *Pretty Betty*, I examined every inch of machinery, looking for similar glass cups or metal bulges that could house them. There weren't any. Cursing, I went to the deckhouse and got down a manual about the size of the New York telephone book. Several sections were devoted to the cooling system, but manuals of that sort are written for people who know a lot about engines, and I couldn't make head or tail of either the text or the diagrams, which looked vaguely medical.

Remembering that we had had the saltwater pumps rebuilt, I examined them closely, for it seemed logical that they would be near the strainers, yet I could find no little glass cups anywhere near them. Overhead hung a row of shiny new wrenches I had bought for emergencies, but there didn't seem to be much sense in indiscriminately unscrewing things, creating a greater mess than I already had.

"What are we going to do?" Betty asked as I climbed out of the engine room looking puzzled.

"We can always radio the Coast Guard," Mother said.

"I doubt if they would think this a real emergency. We're safely anchored. They have to be careful not to take business from the commercial tugs."

"Could they fly a mechanic in from Fort Myers or Key West?" Betty asked.

"Sure. It's just a question of money. The plane alone would probably cost several hundred bucks."

"If it's a real emergency, I'll be glad to help," Mother said, nervously fingering her purse.

"Hell, let's wait awhile before we call anybody," I said. "When the engines cool down, I'll start them up again. Maybe they'll work some of the stuff out."

After considerable experimentation, I found that the port engine began to emit a small stream from the pipe in our side where cooling salt water was supposed to gush out, and its temperature remained at 180 degrees if I kept it at slow speed. No water emitted from the starboard engine, and its temperature immediately soared. Shutting it down, I glanced at my watch.

"I think I'll try to make Naples," I said. "If the weather holds, we ought to be able to crawl in there just about dark."

Making about 3 knots with only one engine barely turning over, we tied up at Naples shortly after sunset. Immediately I called a mechanic, and an obliging young man said he'd stop in on his way home from work.

"Well, it's simple," he said as soon as he climbed into our engine room. "Your strainers are next to the water intakes, up forward in the bilge."

Crawling between the engines, he reached down and soon showed me two cylinders about the size of a large box of oatmeal. They were packed with soggy dead leaves and mud.

"I saw those big things," I said. "I thought the strainers were about the size of a small coffee cup."

"They are in a small gas engine," the mechanic said pityingly. "You know, you ought to learn something about these diesels before you start to operate them."

"Yes," I said, feeling a rush of remorse for not learning such an obvious thing as how to clean the strainers before I had ever started. "On a boat there are so many details."

"The engines ain't a detail, mister. I wish more skippers realized that."

"I know," I said humbly to this stern critic I was employing. "I won't give myself liberty tonight."

He laughed, but I still felt incurably lax and stupid as I went aft for dinner.

"You're just like your father," my mother said. "He was always at his best in emergencies. I think it's wonderful how you got us out of that swamp despite engine trouble."

"I never have a worry with him in charge," Betty said. "He really knows *everything* about the ocean and boats."

"You're a good daddy," Jessie said, adding her bit to the praise.

"Thank you, kind ladies," I said, glad that the stern mechanic had gone ashore. "We're not under way now. Will anyone join me for a drink?"

The rest of that serenely silent cruise with my mother was sheer delight. Spinning up the Caloosahatchee River on a morning when both the water and the sky were a sparkling blue, we entered the long straight canal that leads to Lake Okeechobee. Gone were the richly manicured estates of Palm Beach and Naples. This was Indian country, where the proud Seminoles, who had never been defeated in any war except economic ones, now lived in pathetic shacks and puttered about the canals in dugout canoes incongruously powered by shiny outboard engines. This was also cow country, where great hump-backed Brahman bulls stood neck-deep in the water of the canals, gazing at us morosely until our wake sent them lumbering up the steep banks to their grazing land. Buzzards and hawks circled overhead, and twice Betty was able to show Jessie an alligator.

That night we tied up at La Belle, a sleepy town nestling in the shade of moss-hung oaks. Half-hidden in a bend of the river the Army engineers had cut off from the main channel, we saw an extraordinary sight: an incredibly narrow, tall-stacked, old-fashioned steam yacht more than 100 feet long, with the paint and varnish peeling off its once fancy superstructure. Upon inquiry, I learned that a lady poet lived there surrounded by lily pads and printed her own verse on a small handpress she kept in the forecastle. On further inquiry, I discovered that this extraordinary craft, which was only 14 feet wide, had been built by old J. P. Morgan to whisk him at high speeds from his Long Island estate to Wall Street. How it got in the hands of a lady poet who owned her own printing press, I never found out.

Frustrated because I told her she couldn't visit the steam yacht without an introduction or an invitation, Mother curled up in the deckhouse with a copy of Mr. Blanchard's *Cruising Guide to the Southern Coast.*

"Do you know that Lake Okeechobee is the second-largest

lake wholly in the United States?" she asked, and then she blanched.

"What's the matter?" Betty asked.

"Are we going to cross this lake tomorrow?"

"Yes," I said.

"Listen to this: 'Lake Okeechobee has a bad reputation. . . . It is large and it is shallow. Storms raise an enormous sea, and before it was so carefully embanked and canal-drained, they periodically used to blow almost all the water out of it over the low-lying land around.' "

"Don't worry about it," Betty said. "He wrote the same kind of thing about Albemarle Sound, and that turned out to be a snap."

"Why does he scare people?"

"He's a darn good cruise writer," I said. "It's just his job to warn inexperienced yachtsmen that any fairly large body of water can kick up, especially shallow ones."

"I hope Lake Okeechobee will be all right," Mother said, returning to the book.

A moment later she added, "Great heavens! Do you know that a hurricane killed two thousand people here in nineteen twenty-six? Why did we come to this place?"

"It's not the hurricane season," I said.

"There's something about the water that makes almost everybody even more cautious than they have to be," Betty said. "I like it—it makes me feel safe. Wouldn't it be a good idea if people read a book like this before they drove on the Merritt Parkway? Think what old Mr. Blanchard could do with the death rate on that over the last twenty years! He'd make it sound like a regular battle."

"Perhaps," Mother said. "I'll not worry, because I know you know how to handle it."

Giving Betty and me each a hasty kiss, she went to bed.

There was a quick thunderstorm while we crossed the lake the next day, and for a moment I thought Mr. Blanchard's dire forebodings were going to be justified, but the *Pretty Betty* rolled just enough to send streams of silver water cascading from her awnings, and scurried into the shelter of the canals at the other side.

"You certainly can bring a boat through anything!" Mother said, and it amused me to reflect that I could never remember her giving me such heartfelt compliments ashore, even when I did such fairly difficult things as making a living for several people with a typewriter. The only person I had ever met who made me think this was something of a feat was Betty, who commonly congratulated me with awe every time I brought home a bag of groceries.

That afternoon we moored at Indiantown, where there was a delightful place for Jessica to play under the live oaks. Holding a scrap of Spanish moss to her chin, she said, "Do I look like an old man?"

"You had a great-uncle who wore a beard occasionally," Mother said. "He had quite a good record in the Spanish-American War. I wish you could have met him, Betty. . . ."

Loitering lazily in every river and bay, we took more than a week to sail the few miles back to Palm Beach. There Mother set off to visit the school she and my father had helped to found. I was afraid the authorities there might alarm her with tales of the Christmas visit Bob and Becky had paid them, but those understanding educators kept quiet and greeted my mother as though she were Otto Kahn's wife.

The slip where we moored at West Palm Beach was exposed to the wake of many elaborate fishing cruisers which pounded through Lake Worth without the slightest concern for the discomfort caused by their wash.

"This is where the rich people live, all right," Betty said as she grimly lunged after a flying pot. "They're bastards, every one!"

"How do you know they're rich?" Mother asked, clinging valiantly to a table.

"Because those Goddamn fish boats they build here cost about one hundred and twenty-five thousand dollars," I said.

"That much?" Mother said sadly. "I know people who have lived a lifetime on that."

As the rolling of our boat subsided, she sat down on a bunk.

"Your great-grandfather had two yachts," she said to me. "On Lake Ontario he kept a steam yacht, and then he had a barge yacht which horses used to pull through the Erie Canal to New York. It was great fun when I was Jessie's age, because when I got tired of the boat they let me ride the horses."

"Did he do all that on one hundred and twenty-five thousand?" I asked.

Mother flinched.

"He was in the railroad business, and he never talked about money," she said. "People didn't do that in those days, and they didn't swear, and even on the boats, people served us our dinner on silver trays. I suppose it wasn't at all good for the servants, but when I was Jessie's age, it seemed a lovely kind of life."

That night we rented a car and took Mother to the airport. As she hugged me good-bye, she said, "I had a beautiful cruise, and I liked those signs you painted. I was pretty good, wasn't I? I didn't talk *once* on the bridge."

"You were marvelous," Betty said, and I saw that as when her father left, she was holding back the tears with difficulty.

"I hope you keep under way a great deal," Mother said to me. "Diesel oil is a lot cheaper than alcohol, I expect."

"A lot cheaper."

"You all look well. I don't worry about you. Everybody else seems to, but I don't. Visit me next summer."

Turning abruptly, Mother walked away, a stocky, determined woman carrying a light seabag because she knew there is no place to store suitcases aboard small yachts.

Once more the departure of a member of our crew caused a terrible letdown, and again the cure for that proved to be our

charts of the Bahamas, which still offered the promise
new world.

"In a curious way, this cruise with your father and
has been an expedition into the past," I said to Betty a~
over the chart table. "Especially for me, because most of the
time I've been in the waters of my youth. But now we will be
entering what for me has always been a world of dreams. Grand
Bahama, the Berry Islands, New Providence, Eleuthera—and
best of all, the Exumas. I have always heard that the colors of
the water there are more beautiful than anywhere else in the
world."

"Are you still really thinking of making our home there—I
mean *permanently?*"

"Only madmen make their home in dreams. Tomorrow at
dawn let's crank up these old diesels and see what's really beyond the horizon over there."

# 24

⚓

Always before, the weather had treated us well, but now the prevailing southeasterly winds blew steadily over the Gulf Stream at 20 knots night and day for more than a week. Seas were reported at 8 to 12 feet high.

"It wouldn't be dangerous, but it sure as hell would disprove my theory that I can take you cruising without spilling a teacup," I said to Betty.

For three days we remained at a boatyard in Lake Worth, rolling viciously each time one of the big fishing cruisers rushed by.

"Hell, let's go to the Bahamas," Betty said finally. "The Gulf Stream can't be much worse than it is right here, and if I sit around cussing the rich people much more I'm going to turn into a Communist."

"I don't know," I said worriedly. "Those seas will be hitting us right on the starboard bow. Jessie is almost sure to be sick, and when you clean it up. . . ."

"Why don't you try it and let us see what it's like? If we hate it, we can turn around and come in."

"All right," I replied. "We begin by lashing down everything that can move belowdecks."

An hour later we cast off and headed for the Lake Worth inlet. The little pennant we flew from a staff on the bow to show that we were members of the Northern Lake George Yacht Club, which my father had helped to start many years ago in the Adirondacks, stood out straight in the wind and made an angry crackling sound, as though it thought members of an inland sailing club had no right to be steering toward the open sea on a day like that. Turning near the old Otto Kahn estate, we headed out between the big stone breakwaters guarding the opening between Lake Worth and the ocean. A fast current was funneling in and there were a few groundswells humping their backs where they had got in between the jetties. Tossing her bow up suddenly, the *Pretty Betty* reared like a startled horse. Holding Jessie tightly in both arms, Betty lay down on a seat just abaft the wheel.

"How long will it be like this?" she asked.

"We're not even out in the open yet. If we can maintain ten knots, we can get over to Grand Bahama in six hours."

"What's happening?" Jessie asked in alarm. "What's the boat *doing?*"

"Riding the waves," Betty said determinedly. "It's *fun.*"

The big bell buoy just beyond the inlet was bent low before the wind and current. Seas were breaking over it, and as though in mourning for all dead sailors, its bell tolled dismally. As we came abeam it, the *Pretty Betty* began to roll heavily in addition to her pitching. Getting from my tall captain's chair to brace myself against the wheel, I glanced at Betty and saw that she was embracing Jessie with one arm and a stanchion with the other. Both she and the child looked pale, but they said nothing. Rising to the top of a white-maned comber, the *Pretty Betty* plunged down the other side and at the same time rolled so steeply that the aluminum captain's chair capsized, banging against the rail.

"It won't be so bad farther out," I said, deliberately keeping my voice calm. "These seas are just feeling shoal water."

"I hate it!" Betty replied. "We both hate it!"

"Then let's go back in."

"Will it always be like this out here?"

"It's just a question of time before we get a calm day. It may take patience to wait."

"Take us in! I love Palm Beach. Those rich people were bothering me hardly at all."

I spun the wheel, and ingloriously the *Pretty Betty* presented her shapely stern to the seas and scooted back to the safety of the breakwaters. Within fifteen minutes we were serenely riding the placid waters of Lake Worth, heading back to the boatyard.

Days passed, with the southeast winds still blowing, and often there was heavy rain. The sport cruisers kept dashing back and forth, making us cling to our dishes as we ate, and the mail brought news which was deeply depressing. Several of our friends in New York wrote to say that Bob had indeed got in trouble during his last night in America. None of the people who took it upon themselves to send us lurid accounts of his debacle had actually witnessed it, but that whole group of old acquaintances was obviously titillated.

"Maybe the devil did get into him," Betty said sadly, "but those great friends seem to rush to their typewriters with such relish to tell me about it. If they've got complaints, why don't they get in touch with him?"

"It's part of his genius," I said bitterly. "When he goes lecturing with me or sits on the bridge of this boat, he takes the bows, but when he gets in trouble, we get the complaints."

"Now are you mad at him too?" Betty asked.

"I guess we might as well get angry at the Gulf Stream."

"Our old friends apparently expect me to disown him," Betty said. "Most of them are always bitching against their fathers—it's the whole big modern thing to do. I know he's terrible sometimes, but I still love him, and if we have to choose between him and your literary friends. . . ."

"We'll choose your old man, no matter what the hell happened."

"Thanks," Betty said. "I'll send him some of these letters. I'm sure he'll say he didn't do anything at all, but he should learn the kind of hornet's nest he stirred up."

For a long while she puzzled over a letter to her father, biting the end of her pen.

"Mommy," Jessica said, interrupting suddenly. "Puhee has gone. She hasn't been aboard all day."

As it turned out, the cat had disappeared—perhaps it had fallen overboard when there was no one to rescue it, or perhaps it had strayed and got lost in the city streets. Going ashore with Jessica, Betty wandered around the docks for hours calling, "Puhee, Puhee," which was the way the baby pronounced the only name to which the cat had ever answered. Even when it started to rain again, Betty and Jessie continued the search. Betty looked exhausted when she finally gave up, and late that night I awoke to find her crying, holding the baby in her arms and sobbing inconsolably.

"Poor Puhee," she said. "She was such a beautiful, beautiful cat. . . ."

As though the mailman hadn't done enough to Betty, he brought, only a few days later, a letter from an aunt saying that her beloved Scotch grandmother, the widow of the sailor, was seriously ill in Brooklyn.

"She's eighty-four," Betty said sadly and reached for Jessie, hugging her tight to her bosom, as though the child's youth were an antidote to old age and death. After a few minutes she got up and furiously started to clean the deckhouse.

Although I had seen "Grammy," as Betty's family called her, only a few times, I had liked the old lady. More than that, she had fascinated me, and I had asked Betty many questions about her. Mary Margaret Thompson had been born in a hamlet in Scotland called Kirkcudbright. The town's name, she had explained to her grandchildren, was three words run together: church-cow-hill, a perfect word picture.

Grammy's father had been a London bobby often away from home, and her mother died when she was two years old. Mary Margaret was raised by an aunt in Kirkcudbright, and when she was just "a slip of a young girl," she fell in love with the local jeweler's son, Alfred McSkimming. The trouble was that Alfred

McSkimming wanted to be a sailor and had already apprenticed himself to the captain of a great sailing ship. He never talked of love or marriage, and when he left Kirkcudbright for a voyage to South America, Mary Thompson felt she had no reason to hope she would ever see him again.

For two years no letters came from Alfred McSkimming, and the only way she could get any news from him was to trace the voyages of his vessel through the shipping columns of the newspapers. She was a pretty girl who attracted plenty of suitors, and her aunt felt she was "daft" to sit alone dreaming of a distant sailor. Yet after more than two years of no communication, and despite the fact that he had made or received no promises, a brief note came to Mary Thompson from him, enclosing a steamship ticket and a request that she meet him in Brooklyn to get married.

"You mean, you had never even talked about it before he left?" Betty had often asked her grandmother.

"No, Grampy was never much of a talker," the old lady had answered. "But from the time we were wee bairn, we always understood each other."

In Brooklyn, Alfred McSkimming married his girl the day she stepped from the boat, and he gave up the sea to seek work in the nearby shipyards. A rigger and a painter, he didn't make much money back in those days before the First World War, and he had too mild a nature, Grammy said, ever to get rich in New York. Nevertheless, they reared seven children and bought a neat little house near the waterfront. When there wasn't much work in the shipyards during depressions, Grampy worked as a construction man on skyscrapers—his training on sailing vessels had left him without fear of height.

There were times when they faced the most grinding kind of poverty, and Grammy had grim tales of carrying a sick son from crowded clinic to crowded clinic until he finally died on the charity table of a medical school where, Grammy claimed, the operation had been delayed to let the students assemble for a lesson. Yet bad times were always followed by good ones. Her surviving children got responsible jobs while they were still in their teens, and Grampy went on working until his mid-seventies, when he caught a fatal case of pneumonia while lying on his back and painting the bottom of a yacht much like the *Pretty Betty*—a fact my wife occasionally reminded me of when I complained too much about boatyard bills.

When I first met Grammy, she was living with two of her middle-aged children who, at the time, were unmarried. After more than sixty years in Brooklyn, she retained her soft Scottish burr, and somehow her neat little house crowded with flowerpots looked like a country cottage, no matter how close the city of Brooklyn crowded around it. And there Grammy, who was physically powerful even in her eighties, ruled with as much imperious poise as any ancient queen of the Scots. It was clear that if by chance the President of the United States should call on Grammy, she would not be in the least ruffled but would ask him to sit down, offer him a cup of tea and deplore with him the difficulties of raising children in the modern world. To all her children and grandchildren she had given a curious air of classlessness which enabled them, like Betty, to go anywhere and talk to anyone with a kind of naturalness and modest self-assurance I had always associated with very old and big wealth.

Now, when Betty finally turned off the vacuum cleaner in the deckhouse, I said, "Do you want to fly back to Brooklyn?"

"That would worry Grammy terribly," she said, brushing her forehead. "No, she wouldn't want that unless she knew she was at death's door."

There was a moment of silence.

"She would want us to go on to the Bahamas and have a good time. 'I like to think of Betty and wee Jessie swimming in the warm winter sun'—that's what she said when I visited her last and a neighbor asked her what she thought of my going to live it up in Palm Beach with the yachting set."

Living it up in Palm Beach did not prove very gay for us, however, while we waited for the weather to moderate. As a matter of fact, we had nothing at all to do. Our impact on the Graham-Eckes School had been such that I didn't feel like renewing that connection, and in any case, our social life was hampered by the lack of reliable sitters who didn't panic at the thought of being left alone with a child on a boat. Once a lady who lived on a nearby houseboat volunteered for the job, and I took Betty ashore to see the sights before going to a meeting of the Navy League, which a friend insisted we attend because, he said, there would be a lot of reserve officers with their wives, people who might make our stay in Palm Beach less lonely.

Our trip ashore was not a success. At a bar where we stopped to have dinner, we heard a tough young man who said he had just returned from Vietnam tell some friends that he had brought back as a souvenir a necklace of dried human ears.

"Do they really do things like that?" Betty asked me in a shocked voice.

"Some of the boys on my ship collected teeth when we went ashore in Manila shortly after a battle. Fear doesn't always make Christians. . . ."

"It's strange to think they're fighting over there while we make such a big deal of the hardships of living on a yacht."

"Yes," I said and had another drink. Our appetite gone, Betty and I went on to the meeting of the Navy League.

It was the wrong night for us to be there. By some curious coincidence, another man freshly back from the war in Vietnam was the speaker. This time it was no bloodthirsty sergeant but a scholarly-appearing Marine general, who with obvious sincerity said we were winning magnificent victories to hold back Communism in the East. Most of the audience stood and clapped.

"Why didn't you stand up?" a sweet-faced middle-aged woman next to me asked accusingly.

"I don't agree with him."

"Why not?"

"I don't think we're defeating Communism over there."

Then the whole debate started, with all my arguments, as well as those of my opponents, sounding weary, futile and stereotyped. When we had all tired ourselves someone suggested drinks.

"I don't know," my sweet-faced opponent said to me. "That's where these debates always end—with a drink."

"So it seems."

For a moment she looked lost.

"I have two sons over there," she said. "I simply can't allow myself to think that our government doesn't know what it is doing. All those brilliant, distinguished men. . . ."

There was a long pause.

"I haven't been able to believe in any religion for a long time," the sweet-faced woman continued. "Now maybe I can't believe in my own government. It's too much. I can't allow myself to begin to doubt like that. . . ."

Getting hastily to her feet, she went over and joined the admiring throng that was asking questions of the general.

"Yes," I heard him say, turning to her with courtly charm. "Yes, I think we're winning. You'll see real progress in another year. . . ."

Thoroughly depressed, Betty and I went back to the boat. There we found a message to telephone my mother, who had stopped off in Daytona to see friends.

"They're going to drive me down to Delray Beach," Mother said. "We have some distant cousins living there. If the weather is still keeping you away from the Bahamas, how about bringing the boat and helping me to celebrate my birthday?"

Delray Beach was only a few miles down the canal, and we were suddenly eager to see my mother again for a birthday celebration. The next day at about five in the afternoon, we met her and with our relatives went for dinner to the Delray Yacht Club, which had rented us a slip. There a small thing happened which would not have annoyed me so much if we hadn't already been discouraged. A waitress seated us at a nice table, took our order for drinks and a moment later reappeared.

"Are you people members of this club?" she asked.

"No," one of our relatives said. "We don't go in for boats much."

"We're members of the Northern Lake George Yacht Club, which is registered," I said quickly. "I'm sure you know that registered yacht clubs usually exchange privileges."

"The Northern Lake George Yacht Club?" the waitress asked, sounding puzzled.

"It's in the Adirondacks," my mother said. "My husband helped to start it. He was the commodore there for years. It all began when there was no real place for the children to sail. . . ."

"Just a moment," the waitress said and disappeared.

A moment later a stuffy man came to say that we definitely could not be served at the Delray Yacht Club.

"Damn!" Betty said as we walked out, trying to ignore the curious stares of other diners. "Sloan and I don't mind, Mother, but you're not used to getting kicked out of places."

"I don't understand it," Mother said. "Up there at Lake George, we really have some very distinguished members. I shall tell them what to do if anyone from this yacht club happens to show up!"

This possibility seemed a rather remote hope for revenge. On the way back to the boat, Mother seemed to brood about this, but she didn't say anything as long as our Delray Beach relatives were with us. All through dinner at a local restaurant she was unusually quiet, and she didn't explode until her Daytona friends started to drive her home.

"Good-bye, son," she then said to me. "Don't you worry about that Delray Yacht Club. They say Delray is just a place for people who can't get into the Everglades Club in Palm Beach. People who are socially insecure rarely are able to be courteous."

Giving Betty a kiss on the forehead, she jumped into the car, waved a white-gloved hand and drove away.

"Do we have to go back to Palm Beach?" Betty asked when we returned to the boat. "Somehow I feel that like the people in this town, we're not really making it there."

"That southeaster is still pretty strong," I said, noting that our brave little Northern Lake George pennant was still standing straight out in the wind.

"Hell, you say you can make it in six hours," Betty replied. "I know, it was awful when we tried last time, but if Jessie and I took Dramamine and stayed below in our bunks, we could hang on for half a day."

"You might want to go ashore for good."

"You've got to quit worrying about that. I'm dying to get over to the Bahamas. All those gambling casinos may be wicked, but they sound glamorous, and I'm sure we'd meet all kinds of interesting people over there."

"The beaches will be good too, and the skin diving. It should be considerably warmer."

"What the hell," she said. "I feel reckless. Apparently there's nothing out there that the fishing boats can't take. Let's just batten down the hatches and barrel through."

"How about dawn tomorrow?"

"All right. If I do any bitching just remind me that I was the one who said, 'Let's batten down the hatches and barrel through.' "

"Just where did you pick up that phrase, anyway?"

"It was one of my grandfather's favorites. He used to tell me sea stories all the time. When he described a storm, he usually used to end by saying, 'But we had a good ship. We just battened down the hatches and barreled through.' "

There was a pause.

"Can we call Grammy from Grand Bahama, or will we be completely out of touch?"

"We can call her."

"Then what's keeping us?"

The next morning Betty and the baby stayed in their bunks while I got under way. Figuring that the wind and the Gulf Stream would shove us well north, I charted a course to a point 15 miles to the south of West End, a large resort on the nearest tip of the island of Grand Bahama, just about 56 miles across the Gulf Stream. The weather hadn't changed since our first try at the crossing, but no complaints came from the cabin, and my own restless desire finally to accomplish my lifelong ambition to cruise the Bahamas made the discomfort of the plunging boat easy to bear. The hull of the *Pretty Betty* didn't drift as much as I thought it would. The only anxious moments came when the island didn't show up on time, but finally I saw a few clumps of palm trees dotting the horizon well to our left.

"Land ho!" I called down the hatch to Betty.

"Ugh," she answered weakly. "Call me when all this rolling around is going to stop."

Within half an hour we came under the lee of a yellow beach. The *Pretty Betty* cut serenely through blue water which suddenly became as calm as Lake George. Before I had a chance to call her, Betty came on deck holding Jessica. They both looked pale and bedraggled, but they broke into smiles as soon as they saw the nearby shore.

After a long pause, Betty took a deep breath and, putting Jessie down, held her arms out to the sun.

"The Bahamas!" she said. "Maybe we will stay here forever. By God, they look as good as they sound!"

# 25

⚓

In the excitement of crossing the Gulf Stream, we entirely forgot Wilson's Law 63A: Any event which is long looked forward to and is supposed to be marvelous is apt to end up miserably. For years I had longed to sail my own boat to the Bahamas, and for months I had worked to achieve that goal, but what I found when I first got there was simply a large second-class resort hotel. Charter planes were bringing in virtually the entire membership of some Midwestern country club. When, wearing an old sword fisherman's cap, I went up to the bar seeking God knows what kind of Bahamian flavor, a group of ancient golfers surrounded me, and I discovered that as a "yachtsman" I represented to them the same dream of adventure I was seeking. For an hour I found myself telling sea stories, desperately acting out for myself the whole fantasy we all had come to find. Several of my newfound friends were so intrigued by the idea of a man sailing the islands alone with his wife and a small daughter that they insisted on following me back to the boat, where Betty and Jessie were sleeping off the effects of seasickness. Hearing voices in the deckhouse, Betty got up and found herself surrounded by fat men in sport shirts who wanted her to pose by the wheel for souvenir snapshots.

"Damn it, you lead them on!" she said to me when the crowd finally left for the bridge rooms and the shuffleboard courts. "You don't want to see tourist attractions—you want to be one!"

Before I could think of an adequate reply, she went back to sleep, and I was left on deck to stare out over the moonlit harbor. The restlessness I had felt all winter was getting much worse, I discovered. There was a temptation to cast off the dock lines immediately and plunge on through the Bahamas in a desperate search for some island which approximated the visions of unspoiled beauty I had carried in my head for so long. What would I do if the Bahamas turned out to be only another kind of Florida playground, one endless resort where old people nodded in the sun and vacationing youngsters leaped in endless pursuit of each other from swimming pool to bar and back again? Ever since we had bought the boat I had been intent on getting to the Bahamas without once ever trying to explain to myself what exactly I hoped to find there except beaches and pretty-colored water. For a long while the Bahamas had served to give our cruise, and to a large extent my whole life, an immediate, tangible goal. What would I do if in getting here at last, I discovered that I had somehow lost much more than I had found?

It was certainly too early to give up on the Bahamas, I told myself. West End was known to be only a part of Miami that had somehow come adrift, and people who had cruised these waters were quick to point out that Grand Bahama itself was anything but typical of the whole chain of islands. After seeing Freeport, which had become famous for its gambling, we would push on to the out islands, where everything would be different.

The voyage from West End to Freeport was only about 35 miles, and we undertook it in good humor, for the seas had subsided and the ocean was like a great glistening pond. Almost as soon as the radio towers of West End had faded astern, we saw the tall white buildings of Freeport and Lucayan Beach growing out of the misty horizon. As we came abeam, we could see a reef rising in the clear water beneath us. Just outside the breakwater leading to the marina of the Lucayan Beach Hotel, a glass-bottomed barge with a thatch-roofed hut on it circled lazily while a pretty girl in a pink bikini posed on the bow for old people with cameras.

"This is going to be just another tourist trap," Betty said.

"But a really gaudy one."

"Do you think you can find a sitter?"

"They might have some sort of service at the hotel. As soon as we get in, I'll walk up and find out."

We moored at a marina where there were a lot of fancy yachts and one huge houseboat with a terrace and outdoor cooking fireplace on its bow. A magazine article I had read claimed that the gambling here was run by the Mafia and that the casino was frequented by call girls, and perhaps because of this, the many handsome men and women lounging on the beach nearby looked to me to be raffishly sinister. Still, I was not prepared for the exchange that took place while I waited for a water taxi to take me to the hotel. On the wharf a tired-appearing blonde in a yellow beach coat came up to me, smiled and said, "Are you looking for something?"

"Is this where you get the boat to the hotel?" I asked.

"Yes. What are you looking for there?"

"A sitter," I replied simply.

"A sitter?" she asked, sounding puzzled. "What the hell is that, some kind of position I never heard of? Well, I tell you what, baby—you show me and I'll try."

With a high, raucous laugh at my look of astonishment, she threw a cigarette at my feet and waddled off on high-heeled beach shoes, her dumpy figure and weary gait giving her a curious air of pathos.

The Lucayan Beach Hotel proved to be an ostentatious hostelry with a large interior garden, fountains and several elaborate restaurants, in addition to the much-advertised gambling casino. The air of gaiety for which the establishment obviously strived so hard was somewhat impaired by the guests, most of whom looked as though they had been imported directly from an old people's home, but the waitresses, assistant managers and other hired help were handsome young people much like the paragons in the posters used to portray Grand Bahama as the Riviera of the New World. One of the assistant managers agreed to send a housekeeper down to our boat to serve as a sitter. On the way back to the marina I passed many real estate offices where sales were obviously being pushed with all the fervor of the old Florida land boom. The idea of settling on this flat, ugly island had never occurred to me, but when I was accosted by a brash salesman who assured me that people were making their fortunes there virtually overnight, the temptation to fleece a fleecer became overpowering.

"I'd like to see the island and learn as much as I can about it," I said. "I'm not sure that this is the place for me to make major investments. I'd need a lot of information to make up my mind."

By this probably immoral stratagem, I found myself immediately supplied with a free car, a driver and a guide. At the marina these gentlemen waited for me impatiently while I went to get Betty and Jessica.

"They're going to drive us all over the island," I said to Betty. "They even want to buy us dinner."

This kind of legal larceny usually appeals to my wife's fundamental sense of justice, but now she obviously lacked enthusiasm.

"In a minute," she said. "I got the mail."

"Anything important?"

"Good and bad news. David is coming down. . . ."

I had given up hope that my son would join us, for I knew he had taken a leave of absence from school to work as a ski patrolman in Vermont. By going to Summer School, he had assured me, he would still be ready for college in the fall. The school and his mother had approved this plan, but still it seemed odd to me. This further change in his plans made me wonder whether he was in some sort of trouble he had left out of his letters.

"Did he say why he was leaving his job?" I asked.

"No. I also heard from Aunt Jean about Grammy. She thinks she's dying."

"Do you want to fly home?"

"With David coming, you're going to want to see *all* the islands. We can't just welcome him here and take off."

"We could make a brief trip back to New York."

"Maybe Grammy will be sick a long time. I don't know what to do. I hate to leave here and go places where we will be completely out of touch."

"For the time being, we'll just stay put and see what happens," I said. "Come on. Right now we're going to take a free drive around the island."

The trip took several hours. In the back of the car Betty sat almost expressionless and stared at the wonders proudly pointed out by the salesmen. In the bleak interior of the island we saw small suburbs which looked as though they had been transported intact from Long Island or New Rochelle. The promoters were building an international shopping center, where each of many nations was represented by a restaurant or a store. There was an English pub with authentic British beer and a huge brand-new gambling casino for people who tired of the one in the Lucayan Beach Hotel, and transportation was available in authentic London two-decker buses which contributed to the "foreign atmosphere" by driving on the left-hand side of the new roads being bulldozed through the endless acres of scrub pine.

Everywhere an almost hysterical attempt was being made to entertain the tired old tourists who were being shuttled over from Florida by a whole fleet of airplanes. Grand Bahama was obviously trying its best to earn its wicked reputation. It was entirely possible, a salesman assured me when Betty was taking Jessica to a rest room, to meet really beautiful women in any of the many island bars or in the casinos, where they presumably went to the winners like a stack of blue chips. Food in some of the hotels was prepared by chefs flown directly from Paris. "If a guy isn't thrilled enough by gambling, screwing and eating," one happy salesman said to me, "we'll even take him down to the beach, strap him to a big kite, and fly him one hundred feet up in the air."

Apparently this final, drastic thrill was popular with the tourists, for the young athletes who dragged the big man-carrying kite behind a motor boat near the beach of the Lucayan Hotel were kept busy. The potbellied men in bright swimming trunks looked terrified as they were being strapped to the crossbars of the kite, where, Betty said, they looked like a grotesque caricature of a crucifixion scene, but the screams that came when the whole crazy contraption went aloft were usually taken for delight.

That night Betty and I dutifully lost $20 to the blackjack and roulette wheel operators in one of the gambling casinos. The price seemed small in view of the fact that we had the opportunity to watch a yellow-faced bald man in a white dinner coat lose $30,000 at dice in an hour, a spectacle which furnished us with food for speculation for a long time. How had he earned the $30,000 in the first place? Did the loss ruin him, or did he shrug it off? How could a man intelligent enough to make that kind of money be stupid enough to get drunk and roll it away with professional gamblers? Obviously there was no answer to these questions. The strange, sallow little man just ordered another drink and stumbled out the door of the gambling casino as though nothing had happened.

The croupiers and dealers on Grand Bahama had none of the silky courtesy one associates with professionals at the great casinos of the world. Gruff and surly, they seemed to me to have been recruited from back-room crap games in third-rate nightclubs the world over. Still, fat ladies in elaborate evening gowns and furs made bearable by the air conditioning lined up to put their money down on the roulette tables.

Soon tired of this spectacle, we went to an ornate dining room and ordered roast duck. Although it was surprisingly good, Betty did not seem interested in either the food on her plate or the raucous conversation of a thin woman with orange hair at a nearby table who kept twisting the diamond rings on her gnarled old fingers as she discussed the tax exemptions of Freeport with an eager young salesman we had met earlier that day.

"I'm sorry to be such bad company," Betty said, suddenly putting her fork down. "I can't get my mind off Grammy. With everybody throwing money around this place, I keep wondering if she's got enough for her medical bills."

"Maybe you better call up and find out."

Together we went to a telephone in the lobby. It took several minutes for the call to go through, and while we waited in that strange atmosphere of indoor gardens and refrigerated minks, some dam of words seemed to break in Betty and she talked compulsively about her grandmother, as though it were necessary for her to review her whole life immediately.

The telephone rang.

"Your call to Brooklyn is going through now," the operator said.

While Betty talked to her aunt I stared at some cut-rate French perfumes in a fancy display case. You could buy lots of things cheap in Grand Bahama—cameras from Germany, simulated pearls from Japan. In a surprisingly short time, Betty was back beside me.

"Jean says they don't need money, but Grammy would like to see me," she said breathlessly.

"We'll fly back tomorrow."

"How about David?"

"He won't mind being aboard the boat alone for a few days. Grand Bahama isn't such a boring place for a very young man."

"Will he be all right?"

"I'm sure."

All the way back to the boat Betty didn't say anything. After seeing that the baby was all right and paying off the sitter, she got herself a cup of tea and sat down at the table.

"Thanks for being willing to help if she had needed money," she said. "I want to tell you something strange."

"What?"

"Well, you know Grampy never made much money. In his day the people who worked in boatyards didn't get paid so much, and they raised seven kids, right through the Depression. I don't understand it. I mean, even for the Scotch. . . ."

She paused and then continued.

"You tell me how she did it. Jean laughed when I asked if she needed money for Grammy. She says Grammy has several savings accounts set aside for illness. The mortgage on her house is all paid up. She's going to leave all her surviving children and grandchildren a couple of thousand dollars each."

The next few days were extremely confusing. My seventeen-year-old son, David, arrived from Vermont with a suitcase full of ski clothes, two cameras and little else. Obviously he was anxious to talk to me about something, but almost as soon as he stepped aboard the boat, we had to leave for Brooklyn. As the plane took off and I saw the island of Grand Bahama suddenly made beautiful by distance, I sank back in my seat with a feeling of intense depression.

An old lady was dying, an old lady I didn't know very well but whom I had come to admire and who obviously meant a great deal to my wife. Beside me, Betty, her tanned face gone curiously pale, tried to sleep with Jessie on her lap.

But it was more than the approaching death of my wife's grandmother which was bothering me. My son, so tall yet so childlike, posed a thousand questions which neither of us was able to put into words. He had come down to talk to me more than to visit new places, but as so often had happened to us in the past, circumstances had conspired against us, and we had practically passed each other at the airport.

How long would I be forced to leave him alone on the boat? Perhaps the old lady's illness would drag on for weeks or even months, and Betty would feel obligated to stay with her. What a curious place Grand Bahama was to leave a seventeen-year-old boy!

Or would he regard it as a kind of heaven? Plenty of the

young men on the boats at the pier where we lay did. The people on a nearby houseboat ran a kind of nonstop party, serving Bloody Marys to anyone who wanted to stop in at ten in the morning. Elevenses, a custom of the island, usually consisted of bullshots, a horrid mixture of bouillon and vodka, and they soon led to cocktails before luncheon. Reclining on the decks of the yachts, the young men had their pick of the girls who strolled down from the hotel.

"A fresh crop of girls comes in with every plane," a tall, rather saturnine man who had quit a business career in New York to look after other people's yachts had told me. "Some are professionals, but many are nice working girls who have saved all year to fly to the islands and find romance. It's marvelous. Here they invariably find it."

How curious to reflect that after years of criticizing my own father for being a Puritan, I was now hugely concerned with the chastity of my son! Liberal though I was toward myself and my friends, the idea of my son lolling about a yacht with itinerant secretaries in search of romance appalled me, and I made up my mind to get back to Grand Bahama in a few days if Betty could possibly spare me. With this resolution I slept, but when I awoke I felt even worse.

Of course I'm depressed, I thought with sinking heart. Hadn't I been becoming aware for a long time that my idea of buying a boat and getting away from it all was turning into a fiasco? At first I had been sick and the boat had kept breaking down. For weeks we had been enmeshed with relatives, and when we finally had accomplished our goal of reaching the Bahamas, we had found only a dreary gambling resort. Deep in me was the conviction that I wasn't going to find any place I liked, that there was something the matter with me, some profound discontent which always made me happy to leave places and never happy to stay. Was our whole life aboard the boat going to develop into an endless flight from everything we found? How long could Betty survive life aboard a boat which seemed under a curse like that of the *Flying Dutchman*, doomed endlessly to sail the seas without ever finding a home port?

This sense of being involved in a headlong flight which might go on forever increased during the next week. Brooklyn, its crowded streets covered with grimy snow, appalled me. Regardless of the discomforts of the boat, it almost always was in beautiful surroundings, and I had forgotten how ugly a city in winter can be. The friends and relatives of the old lady who was dying all appeared to me as heroes and heroines of some great endless tragedy. Where did they find the courage to keep shuttling to and from their jobs on the subway day after day, year in and year out, raising children, tending the sick, paying their bills while the gray snow came down and turned to mud at their feet? The only person I seemed really able to understand was the old Scotch lady we found propped up on pillows in a house she had cleaned for something like fifty years. Ill as she was, she smiled when she saw Betty, but with a note of apology she explained that she was terribly tired and didn't really know how long she wanted to go on. A few hours later she lapsed into unconsciousness, and the next night she let her head fall back and quietly died.

During the preparations for the funeral, Betty was unusually calm, but there was a look of shock on her face which led me to believe that, like me, she was somehow mourning not only her grandmother but all of us. It was not until we were aboard the plane flying back to Grand Bahama that she could bring herself to talk.

"There goes New York," she said as the big jet roared into the sky. "Now Grammy's gone, it really isn't home anymore anyway. Grammy's house is where everyone in the family ran when things went wrong."

There was a long pause during which she stared at the city, now disappearing into the clouds.

"It's up to us to make a place like that now for ourselves and the kids," she said.

"Do you want to sell the boat and buy a house somewhere?"

"I don't know yet. We were looking for something we haven't found. Maybe not a house, but a home port at least. All of a sudden I don't even know what to say when people ask where I'm from."

"Yes, we need a home port. Let's take a look at more of the Bahamas and make up our mind where to make our base."

"And you've got to get some work done," she continued. "I've seen how restless you are. You can't keep cruising all the time—it's not your nature."

"When we find a place we like, we'll tie up for a year maybe. That will give me a chance to work and you a chance to see if we've found a place where we want to settle permanently."

"I can see it in my mind," she said. "A little town with a good school and a beach and a grocery store. Some place very quiet and beautiful. I know what we're looking for, at least."

"Yes."

"I want to get on the boat and just keep going until we find it."

"That's what we'll do."

"Good." She smiled for the first time in days and went to sleep while Jessica still stared out the window at the sea of clouds beneath.

When we got back to the marina, I found to my relief that our old boat still had the power to lift my heart. During our absence David had busied himself with cleaning and polishing. At the end of the pier the *Pretty Betty* waited, her machinery all in working order after months of repairs. If my main desire in life was flight and discovery, here was the ideal tool for us. The weather was perfect, and David had already got out the charts for the Berry Islands.

# 26

⚓

At dawn the next morning we cast off the lines. As David coiled them down I realized that one reason for my sudden attack of good spirits was that finally I had a crew suitable for the open sea. The joys of privacy and independence are great, but it is never really prudent to voyage far from land with only a woman and a small child as crew. Knowing that David was capable of taking over if anything happened to me, I did not feel the fear that usually robbed adventure of much of its joy.

As we left the breakwater of the Lucayan Beach Hotel, we saw the speedboat that towed the big, red man-carrying kite dashing along the shore, its airborne passenger hanging limp in his harness as he swung back and forth. The sea was so smooth that we could see the coral reef beneath us clearly enough to scare us, but our Fathometer told us there were 5 feet under our keel. In a few minutes the coral disappeared. With no wind at all, the water was deep blue, its polished surface speckled with dust.

At the wheel David stood in his swimming trunks, his tall, lean body glistening with suntan oil. Staring at the compass, he said nothing. For about half an hour I stood beside him at the chart table. Aft Betty was hanging up some clothes on a line she had rigged across the cockpit while Jessie handed her pins from

a yellow plastic bucket. The pins, I saw, were the old-fashioned
kind, weatherbeaten as driftwood. Just before leaving her grandmother's home Betty had taken a bag of them from the basement. As a child she had often played with those clothespins,
she said—somehow they reminded her of her grandmother more
than anything else in the house.

"How far to the islands?" David asked.

"About sixty miles. You'll see a white lighthouse with a big
red stripe."

"Will it be this calm all the way?"

"If we're lucky."

For another hour he steered without talking. Sometimes he
glanced at me, swallowed and wet his lips as though he were
about to speak but then looked back to the compass. There
were many questions I wanted to ask him, for there had been
few words between us in many months, but there seemed to be a
kind of danger in breaking the calm of the day. As we drew
farther from shore, the surface of the sea became clean enough
to mirror the fluffy white clouds in the sky overhead.

"Do you want me to take the wheel for a while?" I asked.

"Am I doing it wrong?"

"You've been right on course. I thought you might be tired."

"It's not difficult. Is she much harder to steer when it's
rough?"

"A little."

"What would you do if we ran our sixty miles and the lighthouse wasn't there?"

"I'd recheck my figures."

"And if you couldn't find what had gone wrong?"

"I'd panic."

He laughed.

"Seriously. What would you do?"

"I'd control the panic. I've had that happen often."

"But how would you find out where we were?"

"There are lots of ways, but if they all failed we could turn back and find Grand Bahama again. Or Florida. They are big targets."

"Then why can't we be totally confident?"

"That would be more dangerous than panic."

"Do you ever feel panic ashore?"

"Often."

"What about?"

"Failing at whatever I'm trying to do. Going broke. It's a long list."

"Does everybody feel that way?"

"I don't know."

He lit a cigarette, glancing at me to see if I would object. Beneath our feet the engines rumbled along steadily, healed completely by the latest elixir I had given them to stop their freshwater leaks.

"Look!" Betty said. "I think we're going to have a passenger."

A small land bird with a yellow breast was fluttering in circles around the boat, dipping and rising erratically. Almost falling into the sea, it darted upward and landed on our mast, where it stood preening its ruffled feathers.

"That's good luck," I said.

"Can we catch it?" Jessie asked.

"No," Betty said. "It just wants a ride to shore. We mustn't bother it."

"I want to catch it," Jessie said, and her mother had to hold her back.

As the day wore on, David began to glance around the horizon more and more nervously. He had never been out of sight of land in a small boat before, and the sensation of being entirely dependent upon our own skills obviously was bothering him.

"If the engines broke down, could you get anybody on the radio telephone?" he asked.

"Probably."

"I think I see a reef up ahead. Is there supposed to be a reef here?"

"No. That's a bank of seaweed."

"How can you be sure?"

"I know where we are and I know what seaweed looks like."

Perhaps I was overdefensive, but I began to suspect that his nervousness stemmed from a basic lack of confidence in me. Had he grown up to think of his father as some sort of a stout bumbler sitting around the house with a drink in his hand and doing nothing useful except disappearing into a room once in a while to make disconcerting noises on a typewriter? The things David did well and had done well since the age of ten or eleven, I couldn't do at all or didn't want to do. Perhaps because I had been brought up in Florida, skiing had always filled me with horror. Chess, one of his loves, had always bored me, as did fishing, hiking and team sports of any kind. The concept of his father as an idiot had perhaps penetrated so deeply that the boy felt in terror of his life here on the limitless sea with no one but me to show him the way home. Filled with desire to prove my competence, I consulted tables about the height of the tower we were seeking and announced, "We will see the lighthouse at precisely twelve fifty-three."

"You're kidding."

"It's a game I play. You wait and see—I won't be far off. The visibility is perfect, and there is a table which tells you how far you can see all objects of a given height."

At twelve thirty Betty appeared with a tray of ham sandwiches and cold milk. After eating mine, I took the wheel and tried to appear nonchalant as I glanced at my watch. Leaving his sandwich on its paper plate, David studied the horizon ahead with the binoculars. A muscle on his cheek twitched, and I guessed that for reasons neither of us understood he half hoped I would be wrong and half wanted me to be right.

"I don't see anything yet," he said.

"You've still got six more minutes."

"How can you be so sure of your speed?"

"I've timed the boat over a measured mile at different engine revolutions, and I always keep track of our rate from buoy to buoy. That way you learn what a boat will do under various conditions."

"How about currents?"

"There aren't any here."

"You've only got five more minutes."

There was an interval of silence during which he lit another cigarette. It was absurd to feel such tension, but my mouth was dry, and I asked Betty to bring me a glass of iced tea.

"It's twelve fifty-three," David said quietly as I took the first sip. "I still don't see anything."

"Give me the binoculars."

Expressionless, he handed them to me and took the wheel. Raising them to my eyes I studied the white clouds on the horizon ahead. Mirrored in the sea, they shimmered confusingly. Without saying anything, I climbed on top of the deckhouse, and bracing myself against our tiny ornamental mast in a way that made our exhausted bird flutter his wings nervously, I made out a tiny blur.

"There it is," I said before I was quite sure. "It's there, all right."

"Come down and take the wheel. I want to see it."

"Just a second. I want to straighten out some lines up here first."

For about five minutes I stalled, fussing about the foredeck. Then I looked through the binoculars again, and sure enough, there was the lighthouse and the dim outline of land bisecting the clouds beneath it. Going aft, I handed the binoculars to my son with great nonchalance. At that moment the bird took off and darted toward shore.

"It takes experience to sort land from clouds," I said.

He grinned.

"By God, we've made it. But you were five minutes late!"

Something about his manner angered me and also angered me for being angered. Leaving my son at the wheel, I went forward to get the anchor ready. By the time I had a new nylon line out of its box, my irritation had died. The lighthouse was looming up like a great stick of candy now, its broad red stripe gleaming in the sunshine.

An hour later we rounded a point and saw a cove with fairly big bluffs leading down to a sandy beach. Here were the Bahamas in all their glory exactly as advertised—pale green water so clear that the coral bottom looked close while it was still 30 feet deep. The anchor left a trail of bubbles as it went spiraling down. Simultaneously there was a second splash as David dove from the wheel, clutching a snorkel and face mask. For about three minutes he swam toward the lighthouse. A hundred yards from the beach he paused, adjusted his mask and disappeared beneath the surface. Almost immediately he surfaced.

"Hey, come here!" he shouted. "It's fantastic!"

"What do you see?" Betty asked.

"Billions and billions of little fish, a whole blizzard of them!"

Grabbing face masks, Betty and I put a life preserver on Jessie and jumped into the dinghy with her. When we got to the beach near David, we waded out, looked under the water and found ourselves standing in the middle of a school of fish so thick it seemed a miracle that no tail or fin ever touched us. As far as we could see underwater, millions of silvery minnows about three inches long sparkled in the sun. They swam so close together that they appeared to be a great river of fish which parted briefly when a swimmer's leg appeared and then closed around it. Out where David was swimming there was suddenly a swirl of white water and several splashes.

"Jesus!" David called excitedly. "Some great big fish are swooping in. I'm going back to get a spear."

Lying with my face in the water, I  saw a school of jack dashing in for a raid. As though it were one great beast, the school of small fish shivered, spun and headed for the crescent-shaped beach. Trapped against the shore, the small fish started beating the surface of the water to a froth while the jack darted back and forth with open jaws. Then there was another splash and David appeared with a long fish spear, chasing the jack. Around and around they all went through the white-whipped water. Twice David speared jack about three feet long, but the steel shaft he used didn't have much of a barb, and the muscular fish twisted off and scooted away to deep water while the rest of the hunt became even more frantic.

For almost an hour this continued. Finally exhausted, David walked ashore and threw himself full length on the beach. In a few minutes the jack too disappeared, and the vast school of small fish quieted down. Regaining his breath, David sat up.

"I wonder why all those small fish are here," he said.

"So the big fish can eat them," Jessie replied.

"But they must be eating something too. Let's take some samples."

Scooping up handfuls of sand and seaweed, David filled the dinghy's bailing bucket, and we went back to the boat. From his seabag he took a microscope about the size of a fountain pen and found that the seaweed was crawling with tiny, almost invisible shrimplike creatures.

"Why are those things there?" Jessie asked.

"I guess they eat the seaweed."

"Why is that there?"

"The currents must bring it in."

"Why?" Jessie asked innocently.

"I don't know," David said and, apparently annoyed by the necessity of that admission, got up and packed his microscope away.

That night a half-moon climbed above the lighthouse, causing the water and the beaches to glow with astonishing brilliance. After dinner we sat on deck sipping coffee.

"I've been terribly depressed," David said suddenly, throwing his cigarette overboard. "Did you know that?"

"Maybe I guessed."

"I don't understand anything," he said. "I don't want to

study hard and then go kill people in Vietnam. I don't seem to give a damn about learning any kind of business."

He shrugged his thin shoulders.

"I lost interest in studying," he continued. "Mom said I could take a leave of absence and make it up in the summer. But then I even got fed up with skiing."

"Have you liked it down here?"

"A little. It's been interesting. All those guys at Grand Bahama don't really do any work."

"Is that what you want?"

"I don't know. It just interests me that life can be so easy. Most of those guys who work on the yachts just sit around all day in the sun."

I didn't say anything, and Betty got up silently to put Jessie to bed.

"At school they keep telling us how hard we have to work to get into a good college," David continued. "Then you've got to work day and night to make a good graduate school. They keep telling us how tough the competition is nowadays. And then there's the Army. Or jail. A lot of the guys I know say they would rather go to jail."

There was a moment of silence.

"What would you do?" he asked.

"I was lucky. I believed in the war they handed me."

"What would you do now?"

"I think I might find myself a new country. Eight generations of our people have loved America, but I think we'd have to be pretty sick to love a country that forced a man to kill in defiance of his conscience or sent him to jail."

"If we think our country is wrong, shouldn't we stay at home and try to steer it right?"

"Up to the point of going to jail. I don't think that would serve any useful purpose."

"Are you thinking of the Bahamas?"

"It's just one possibility. We could, after all, make a home here. I don't think we're driven to it yet."

"I hate the thought. I can't help it. I never thought of myself as much of a patriot, but I hate it."

"So do I. And I hate jail for young men, and I hate killing when you don't think it's right. I also hate the possibility of your being killed uselessly. We are going to have a lot of thinking to do."

"This is too much for me all at once. I think I'll see if I can catch a fish."

Going up on the bow, he sat with a fishing pole on a deck box, a thin young man with long hair, hunching his shoulders against the cool evening breeze.

After a restless night I started the engines at dawn, and without being told, David went forward and got the anchor up, folding the stock and stowing it with an air of expertness I had never before seen him display anywhere but on a ski slope. Just as the sun broke out of a bank of purple clouds on the horizon, we started down the chain of Berry Islands and headed toward Chub Key, where we would jump off for Nassau. Standing at the chart table, David studied the desolate islands we passed as intently as though he were about to buy them.

"A few millionaires have big estates along here, and there is a native settlement in shallow water over on the other side, but there isn't any place we can go ashore until we get to some of the fishing clubs about fifty miles ahead," I said.

"You learn all that from the pilot book?"

"That's right."

Taking the pilot book from its shelf, David sat under an awning for the rest of the day, his face as intent on the printed pages as though he were studying for a final examination.

Chub Key turned out to be a rich man's fishing club in the process of noisy expansion. Bulldozers raised clouds of sand around a dredged basin for yachts.

"I want to see the real Bahamas," David said. "How long do we have to stay here?"

"We can leave in the morning if the weather's right. The sky looks a little funny to me."

"Do you really expect trouble?"

David's voice sounded skeptical.

"The sea isn't always as calm as you've seen it. There's a thirty-five-mile stretch of open water between us and Nassau."

"I'd like to feel the *Pretty Betty* kick up her heels a little, and I want to see as much of the Bahamas as I can before I have to go back."

"We'll try," I said.

At seven the next morning the weather reports were good, but the sky had a curious yellow tinge, and I felt uneasy.

"Can I start the engines?" David asked after listening to a second prediction of light southeasterly winds.

"We're not going," I said flatly.

"Why not?"

"I have a feeling in my bones that we're going to get a blow. The weather reports aren't always right."

"Your bones . . . ," David grumbled. "What are you so afraid of?"

"Have you ever heard of a rage over the Nassau bar?"

"No."

"When the wind blows up the surf breaks at the entrance to the harbor. It can look like the Niagara River just above the falls."

"But the weather report. . . ."

"I don't want to go," Betty said. "I trust your father's bones."

I was glad she backed me up, because I was on the verge of giving in to my son's impatience. About three hours later a real storm blasted through the Berry Islands. In the protected marina we suffered only from stinging sand and heavy rain, but the radio told us that a 100-foot excursion boat was wrecked trying to get into the Nassau harbor. Two people were lost aboard a small yacht there at the same time.

"I guess you knew what you were talking about," David said, unable to keep a note of astonishment from his voice.

The next morning we sailed to Nassau without incident. The tall towers of the city grew up out of the calm sea ahead of us, and the only reminder of the storm was the small yacht which lay with its side smashed in near the entrance to the harbor. Five big cruise ships were moored nearby, and native sloops were anchored on each side of the channel.

"I didn't have any idea that this was such a beautiful city," David said.

His enthusiasm was short-lived. The cruise ships had disgorged thousands of vacationers, and as soon as we stepped ashore we found Nassau to be even more of a frantic tourist center than Grand Bahama.

"I couldn't live here," David said in bewilderment as we tried to make our way down a narrow street crowded with shrill middle-aged ladies carrying huge straw shopping bags. "I'd rather go in the Army and kill people."

"Wait till we get to the out islands. I think you'll like them better."

But we couldn't go right away, for the wind started to blow and we were pinned down in a fancy marina for more than a week. For David it was a strange kind of incarceration. It was the time of the spring vacations in the United States, and hundreds of airplanes, as well as cruise ships, brought in hordes of students. The swimming pool near our boat and the surrounding terraces were full of sun maidens in bikinis. Apparently there were several girls to every boy. Night and day parties went full blast in many of the nearby hotel rooms, and all a young man had to do to get an invitation was to stroll down the street alone. When he went for a swim, David was immediately surrounded.

"I'm sort of worried about David," I confided to Betty. "Maybe we never should have brought him here."

"And you criticize your father for being a Puritan?"

"I don't think you have to be a Puritan to wonder what so much easy sex at such an early age does to people."

"Do you know where your son is now?"

"Don't tell me. Maybe I shouldn't know."

"He's back in the after cabin reading. He sort of sneaked in an hour ago. I think he has an idea you believe he should be out raising hell."

"Did he talk to you about it?"

"Yes. He's very disapproving of this place. He says there are just a lot of crazy girls out there looking for meaningless sex."

"Now I'm mad at him for being a Puritan. What's the matter with him?"

"He's in love with a girl sixteen years old back in Vermont. He's being faithful to her. He's very sweet, and he's terribly worried about you."

"Why?"

"He's afraid you're going to settle down here for life. He says the only thing he could do if he lived here would be to go into the hotel business, and he thinks he isn't the type."

"I just said there was a possibility we might move to the Bahamas. We were talking about the best way for an honest man to handle the draft."

"I'm keeping an open mind," Betty said, "but please don't ask me to bring Jessie up in this town. I can't imagine anything more horrible than that."

More and more Betty had been thinking about the question of where we would eventually settle down to put Jessie in school, and our disillusionment with what we had seen of the Bahamas increased her concern. Since the child had just turned three, we had plenty of time, but it was confusing not to have any idea at all where we might end up. In the months since we had left New York, Jessie seemed to me to have matured astonishingly, and it was no longer possible to think of her as a baby. Perhaps the constant contact with adults was making her more and more precocious, or maybe it was simply that I had never before so closely observed the development of a three-year-old. Although I had not attempted to teach her new words, she had picked up a surprisingly accurate nautical vocabulary, and she usually spoke in full sentences.

"Can I help put out the spring line?" she asked me when we came alongside a wharf one afternoon. "I know just the cleat where it goes on the stern."

While we waited for calm seas in Nassau, we took the dinghy over to Paradise Beach and tried to escape the crowd there by taking long walks along the shore. In some ways Jessie at three seemed to me to be far more aware than most adults. Stones of peculiar texture, bits of pretty-colored glass and oddly shaped chunks of driftwood interested her as much as the shells we sought, and she wanted to know the names of so many plants and birds that Betty bought a little nature handbook.

"I hope we never have to put her in some lousy school where some tired teacher just tries to keep all the kids quiet," Betty said to me that afternoon. "It would be like stepping on her face."

"I don't know where to look for a really good school," I replied. "The ones I sent my other kids to didn't seem to be Utopian, even though they were supposed to be the best."

"Promise me we'll never send her to boarding school!" she said as though struck by a sudden fear.

"That's an easy promise, as long as we can offer a happy home, either ashore or afloat."

There was a moment of silence, during which Betty rubbed her eyes nervously.

"I know this is crazy," she said suddenly, "but what would happen if we never sent her to school at all? The truant officers couldn't get us if we were living on a boat, could they?"

"I doubt if they would be our worst worry."

"I don't really see why girls have to get diplomas and credits anyway," Betty continued rebelliously. "We can teach her to read and to keep a checkbook. If we were traveling, she might pick up a lot of languages a hell of a lot better than kids do in classrooms."

"Maybe."

"She's going to be pretty—anyone can see that. You could give her a reading program. What man would ask for diplomas if he met a beautiful, well-read young woman who had spent her youth roaming the world?"

"Not many."

"What's the catch then? Why can't we do it?"

"You know as well as I do."

"Other kids," she said with a tone of defeat. "She has to grow up with other kids."

"That's what she already wants, I'm afraid. Do you notice how she always goes up to other children on the beach?"

"Anyway, she's not afraid of them," Betty said. "She doesn't even know how horrible kids can be."

We both laughed, but there was sadness in Betty's eyes, and that night she told Jessie stories even longer than usual when she put her to bed.

# 27

⚓

We had hoped that Lisa and Peter would join us for the spring vacations, but she wrote that her job as an editor would make that impossible and that Peter too had part-time work now which would rule out traveling. By the time the wind let up, David had only another three weeks with us before he was supposed to go back to school, and we decided to go to the town of Current on Eleuthera because Betty and I had visited it once three years before and had loved it. Somehow it seemed important now to go to a place we liked.

"It's just a sleepy little hamlet with a beautiful beach," I said to David. "If the weather pins us down again, we can rent a car and drive all over the island. I want to be sure you really see something of the Bahamas before you leave."

The ocean was less calm than I had thought it would be as we passed the end of the breakwater, but Betty and Jessie were growing used to the motion of the boat and sat on the bow admiring the flying fish which sprang from the crests of the waves and went skimming ahead of us. When we got a short distance away from it, Nassau, with its white towers surrounded by jade water, seemed beautiful again. Lost in thought, David stood poring over the charts while I spun the wheel back and forth, keeping the boat driving before a quartering sea. Ahead of us we saw a squat workboat throwing up cascades of spray as she butted her bow into the swells.

"That's the mail boat from Current," Betty said. "She's called the *Ego*, remember?"

"That's a funny name for a boat," David said.

"Maybe they all should be called that," Betty replied with a laugh.

"When were you on Eleuthera?" David asked me.

"Shortly after Jessie was born. We had just done some lecturing with Betty's father along, and we were all tired."

Three hours later, when we tied up at the dock in Current, the settlement looked just as I remembered it, like an old painting of the South Seas, with small houses nestled beside a wharf. The glittering colors of the shoals, ranging through every pastel shade of green, blue, yellow and lavender, were even more brilliant than I had recalled.

"God, it is unbelievably beautiful," David said. "What kind of people live here?"

"Lovely, simple people who go to church every Sunday and Wednesday," Betty said. "Go ashore and see for yourself."

This David did with a thoroughness that surprised me. For the next two weeks he roamed the island, asking questions and taking notes as though he were preparing a sociological document. Often I went with him. The houses of Current are small, weather-beaten cottages for the most part, strung along narrow roads which turn into footpaths unpredictably. Renting a car, we drove a few miles up the coast to Bogue, where the houses were even smaller and shabbier.

"When I was here last time, a teacher asked me to lecture in the school," I said to David. "The children didn't want to talk about books. They asked me to describe mountains and rivers and snow—all things they have never seen."

"Why are all the people in Bogue black and all the people in Current light-colored?" he asked.

"Obviously there is some sort of segregation. The people here claim it is voluntary."

David said nothing. That afternoon we got in the dinghy and went out to Current Island, a narrow strip of coral and sand with only a path leading between rows of shacks so small that they looked as though they were built as playhouses. There was no shade, and the sun was so hot that it took effort to brush away flies. Paralyzed by the heat, even the children sat listlessly staring about them, as though in a trance.

"How do people make a living here?" David asked.

"They weave baskets and catch fish. I suppose they don't need much cash."

He was silent until we got back to the dinghy. Just before I started the engine, he said, "Do you know what I think of the Bahamas so far?"

"What?"

"The beaches and the colors of the water are more beautiful than anything I had imagined, and the heat is the damnedest tranquilizer that was ever invented. This ought to be vacation headquarters for the whole world."

"They're trying to make it that."

"So there are a lot of fancy resorts and a lot of desperately poor villages on the out islands. I would think that after two months we'd all go out of our minds either from living in the middle of a carnival or from boredom. If only because of the heat, I don't think any of us would ever get any work done if we settled here."

"At least it would be peaceful," I said. "With air conditioning, we could work."

"I'm not sure how peaceful it would be. From what they say up in the general store, the black people are taking over the government and don't want to give work permits to outsiders. They have just about as much racial tension here as they do at home, except here the whites are the minority group."

Unable to think of an answer I started the outboard motor, and we went back to the boat.

That night I was restless. At about three in the morning I got up, went on deck and to my surprise found David sitting in the tall captain's chair at the wheel, smoking a cigarette.

"Can't you sleep either?" he asked with a grin.

"It's crazy, but I'd love to cast off the lines right now and sail.

Maybe it's some disease, but I love arriving and I love leaving every place we visit. I'm never very happy while we're there."

He threw his cigarette overboard, perhaps in deference to me because he knew I hated to see him smoke.

"I want to leave too," he said. "I want to go home."

"Right away?"

My voice sounded hurt, because he still had five more days to spend with us.

"I want to get back to my books," he said. "I've been goofing around much too long. It's funny, but the sight of all these people down here just sitting in the sun makes me crazy to get back to work."

"Have you had any more thoughts about the Army?"

"I can't give up the United States," he said, his voice making the statement sound like a confession of weakness. "I never realized before how American I am."

"In what way?"

"I like activity!" he said with passion. "I like things that move. These islands haven't changed in centuries. Everyone keeps saying that as though it were a great virtue."

"We really haven't seen much of the islands yet. There are more than seven hundred of them."

"But they don't have big universities. They don't have people working day and night to get things done. There's no place a guy like me can have a real career except at home."

"Is that what you want?"

"Maybe. Your restlessness makes you want to keep moving around from place to place. Mine makes me want to do things. I admit I don't know what yet, but there must be something for me to do. I go crazy when I'm idle. That's one thing this vacation taught me. At first I thought I was just tired of skiing, and then I thought it was all those crazy vacationers in Nassau. It's not that. I need work to do. And I'd like to make money someday. I want to learn how to be on my own."

"I need work too," I said. "That's one of the things that's

been bugging me. I need to tie up somewhere and get back to my typewriter."

"You can do that here, but I've got to get trained in something. You know how I feel about the war in Vietnam?"

"How?"

"I feel as though my country is crazy in some ways, but I can't help that because I'm part of it. I'm like a small child with a crazy father—I can't run away because I need him and I love him. So I have to stay home and work things out with him as best I can. Or maybe I'm like a small fish that knows big fish are trying to eat him, but he can't leave the water. Even the flying fish can stay up only a very short time."

"Yes," I said.

"Maybe they won't put me into the Army. Maybe the country will get better before then."

"I hope so."

"If not, I may have to go to jail for a couple of years. A kid with a crazy father has to take a beating sometimes if he can't reform the old man."

The next day we went back to Nassau, and David packed.

"Is it your books you want to get back to or your girl?" Betty asked him.

"Both. But it sounds better to say books."

With a grin he snapped his suitcase shut, and we drove to the airport. There were quick, embarrassed hugs, and suddenly he had gone. Somehow I had been afraid to ask when we were going to see him again.

All the way back to the boat we drove in silence, and during dinner I felt glum.

"Where do we go now?" Betty asked as she filled my coffee cup. "What's the next stop?"

It seemed to me that her voice was full of the most determined kind of heartiness.

"Where would you like to go?" I asked.

She shrugged.

"Anywhere. Andros, the Exumas. . . . I have a feeling that the Bahamas are going to turn out to be all pretty much the same."

"Do you like it here?"

"The water has very pretty colors, and the beaches are marvelous."

"But you hate it. The Bahamas are nothing like what we dreamed, not as a place to settle down."

"I don't know what we dreamed," she said with a curious tone of confusion.

"That it would be some place marvelous, the end of the rainbow, the answer to all problems, the Ponderosa Ranch."

"Were we really foolish enough to dream that?"

"I don't know about you. Maybe me a little."

"Do you want to go back to the States?"

"I don't know," I said in complete bewilderment. "I don't want to go back and buy a house in the suburbs—I tried that for twenty years and I hated it. I don't want to rent an apartment in New York—that didn't suit us either. My destiny seems to be to keep blundering through life finding places which disappoint me. I'm an idiot."

There was a moment of silence.

"I don't think we have to be idiots just because we don't want to settle in the Bahamas," she said. "We've never liked resorts for long, or very primitive places. At heart we're city people."

"But it is terrifying to think I may never find any place where I want to settle down."

"Let's figure out what we do like," she said.

"I like getting to new places and leaving the next day, preferably at dawn."

"And you like planning great projects, like this trip to the Bahamas. I never saw you happier than when you were looking for a boat."

"Yes, I love dreaming of change and working to make the dream come true."

"Is there any kind of change you would like to dream of now?"

"It's crazy," I replied. "I have secret dreams of getting a bigger boat, something that could take us to new places I've always wanted to see."

"Like where?"

"The West Indies. The canals of Europe, maybe. The Greek isles—I've always wanted to visit them. Is there any place you've always wished to go?"

"I always want to visit familiar places more than new ones. I'd like to sail right up the River Liffey in Dublin and stay for a whole summer near Dad, and I'd like to visit Scotland again to show you Kirkcudbright. I'd love to spend a year in London and a year in Paris. Is it possible that we could ever get a boat that could go to Europe?"

"I'd want a big trawler like the one I had in Greenland during the war. She would cost an impossible amount of money."

"Not to dream about. Could you and I sail such a boat if we were able to get her?"

"We'd have to get all the friends and relatives we could round up to help us on long voyages. On short hops I think you and I could handle a seventy-footer as well as we can the *Pretty Betty*."

"How much would a boat like that cost?"

"Fifty thousand dollars at the very least, and she would be more expensive to run, too."

"Well, it's a goal," she said. "It's something for you to work toward. I think you have real need of that."

"An impossible goal isn't much help. With the tax mess I'm in, I have no right even to think of buying a great yacht and sailing around the world."

"Couldn't you write travel books or something that would make the boat in part a business expense?"

"Travel books rarely make much money," I said gloomily.

"I don't mean you'd do nothing but travel books. You could

try all sorts of things. If you had a clear goal you'd have a lot more energy. After all, you have had great successes before."

"It might take me years, and we'd have to tie up someplace more or less permanently. One thing I've learned is that there just isn't time to work and to keep this boat moving."

"I've always wanted a home port," she said. "I don't think I really like traveling all the time. I'm tired of walking around trying to find where the nearest laundry is."

"Maybe we should just buy a house near a laundry."

"No, I still love the idea of living on a boat and moving around the world, if we could just stay in places we really liked for six or more months at a time. My ideal would be to tie up year after next in Dublin for the winter and let Jessie go to the school where I went. In the summer the older kids could join us with their girl and boy friends and help you sail the boat to the Greek isles. I think David would like that. He just hates the idea of living uselessly."

"The Ponderosa Ranch at sea!" I exclaimed half-bitterly, for the dream did seem impossible.

"Maybe you could get a shrimp boat and fix it up for a lot less than fifty thousand dollars. If we had enough room, she wouldn't have to be fancy. Dad could get a lot of the work done cheaply in Ireland, and I bet he could help you do a good travel book there too. Nobody knows more about Ireland than he does."

"We'd just end up fighting all the time."

"Not in Ireland—you know he's an entirely different person there. Now that he's back at work, his business is going fine again. He might even chip in for a bigger boat—in his last letter he sounded more enthusiastic than ever about the yachting life."

There was a pause while I tried to imagine what would happen if Bob and I found ourselves joint owners of a big trawler.

"And that school in Dublin is the reason why you always ask

.o spell words you can't find in the little dictionary,"
ntinued. "Jessie would get such lovely diction there."

ll, if we didn't like Ireland, we could always move on if
d the right boat. Maybe we could find some schoolteacher
would like to come along and tutor Jessie."

"Do you know what I think we should do?"

"Start looking at big shrimp boats?" I asked with a smile.

"We ought to see more of the Bahamas, not just as tourists but to do a magazine article."

"I'll need a lot of time to think about it," I said. "Right now, I better get out some new charts. If we want to see more of the Bahamas, we might as well start for the Exumas at dawn."

Suiting my actions to my words, I got out the charts and studied the pilot book.

"I think we better hire a native guide," I said.

"Won't that cost a lot?"

"If I'm going to be some kind of a travel writer, I've got to learn to be an expert. Unless I have a guide, I'll never get into some of those native settlements."

After inquiring around the docks, I employed Daniel Wright, a tall black man who had spent much of his life fishing in the Exumas. The next morning we set off across the Yellow Banks, where the chart showed clusters of dangerous coral heads. For two hours I watched our compass and the depth recorder to make sure Daniel knew what he was doing. Before lunch it became obvious that he knew far more about these waters than the makers of the ancient charts did, and I happily left the job of piloting to him.

The Exumas turned out to be a chain of small islands, many of them high and wooded. They were for the most part uninhabited but had many bays and harbors where the water glowed like panels of stained glass. With Daniel pointing the way, we visited hamlets where the natives had apparently never seen a white child before. Everywhere we walked, the native children reached out their hands to feel Jessie's golden tresses, and she in turn groped delightedly at their thick, wooly hair, all without any self-consciousness. When we asked some of the children aboard the boat, they were delighted by such simple wonders as our gas stove. How, they wanted to know, could it burn without visible fuel?

Until we neared Georgetown, I thought I had seen every possible shade of water that God could have devised, but Elizabeth Harbor was a light powder blue of such intensity that I kept blinking my eyes, thinking it was some sort of a fantasy that would go away. It was the time of the out island regatta, and the white sails of graceful, clipper-bowed native sloops crowded the horizon.

"Don't *dare* to write you were bored by the Bahamas!" Betty said.

Even if fundamentally I had discovered that natural beauty, however spectacular, isn't enough to sustain me for long unless I have some project to work on and dream about, I found surprising satisfaction in Georgetown. It was there I realized that it might conceivably be possible for an ingenious man to find opportunities which could make world travel more than an idle dream. Even at the time I think I realized that most schemes for starting a business in the islands were doomed to failure, but in Georgetown I managed to begin the effort to change myself from an idle dreamer to a man actively seeking practical ways to live the way he wished.

It was Jessie who led the way. Sitting in the courtyard of the Two-Turtle Inn in Georgetown, we saw a pleasant-appearing bald man with two little boys. Almost immediately, Jessie walked over to their table and sat down with them. When I asked the man if this was permissible, he invited Betty and me to join them. In this way, we met an advertising man currently engaged in making new maps of the Bahamas, the Lesser Antilles and other islands.

The moment he spoke, Betty spotted him as a Scotsman.

"How did you get into the map business way over here?" she asked.

"I like to travel. I'm the sort of guy who isn't happy settling down anywhere. The map business lets me visit the places I wanted to see all my life and get out before I get tired of them."

As it turned out, the map maker was having difficulty finding transportation back to his home base in Miami, for the airline was busy bringing tourists home from the regatta. Before the evening was over, we invited him and his children to join us aboard the *Pretty Betty*.

The weather was good on the voyage back to Nassau, and Daniel obviously didn't need any supervision as he threaded his way through the intricate channels on the western side of the islands. Seated in the cockpit at the stern, our new friend told me how he hired technicians to make maps of islands which hadn't been charted in decades and printed them in pamphlets to which he sold advertising.

"If I could find a writer to do a description of all these islands to go with my maps, I could put out some good guidebooks," he said. "There might be a surprising amount of money in it if we published them ourselves and sold advertising."

"What territories would your guidebooks cover?" Betty asked casually.

"I'd like to do all the West Indies, as well as the Bahamas. My wife comes from Brazil, and we could do several fine books on South America."

"Did you ever think of going back and doing one of Scotland?" Betty asked.

"That's always been in the back of my mind. Surprisingly enough, I think there's a real need for guidebooks of Ireland, Scotland and Wales. There might be a mint of money in them if I could find the right writer."

"I wonder who that might turn out to be?" Betty asked with apparent innocence, a trace of her Irish accent returning.

# 28

⚓

It was curious how, once I got hungry for a business, more and more opportunities, or at least the illusion of opportunities, seemed to show up. On the way back to Florida we stopped at Cat Cay, which was described in my pilot book as a millionaire's club. To our astonishment we found it a ghost island, almost entirely deserted since the death of its owner. The latest hurricane had wrecked its piers. As we came alongside a wharf which had been twisted into the shape of a small roller coaster, a bearded man dressed only in dungarees climbed from a small sloop to greet us. Anxious to discover what had happened to the once luxurious club, we asked him aboard. He proved to be an actor who had discovered Cat Cay while cruising the islands.

"This would be the greatest set you can imagine for a movie," he began as soon as we gave him a drink. "Crumbling mansions, a gambling casino with the tables all covered with dust, an overgrown golf course with tattered flags flying at the holes—my God, what a place for a movie about the end of the world! I know people who are dying to shoot a film out here because of the tax advantages. All we need is a script. . . ."

By midnight we had agreed to write our agents and try to put together the pieces of a movie company.

In Bimini, our last port before returning to the States, we

moored alongside a ragged workboat whose skipper tried to sell
me a partnership in the island freight business.

"The planes are running light cargo all through the Bahamas
and the Antilles now, and big ships handle the heavy stuff on
regular schedules," he said, "but there's still room for small
vessels with refrigerated holds. We could make a fortune ped-
dling milk and meat alone. . . ."

"This is crazy," Betty said as I sat up late studying a new
Dutch refrigerator ship design my friend had given me.

"Don't forget that during the war I spent three years running
freight."

"I know, but now we're going to publish guidebooks, make a
movie and set up some kind of a floating supermarket. If you
want to make money, why don't you just stick to your last and
try writing books?"

"It doesn't hurt to have other irons in the fire. . . ."

"Unless you get so busy fussing with them that you don't do
any real work. What are we going to do now, fly to Hollywood
or Holland?"

"We'll tie up in Miami until we know what we're going to
do," I replied.

"Why Miami?"

"Our map maker friend thinks we ought to test the guidebook business by trying a pamphlet on the Florida Keys. Anyway, Miami is the logical headquarters for anyone trying to do
any business down here. Sometimes I get awfully mad at my
country, but I think it's the only place in the world where I can
really work. Even if we make a movie in the islands or go into
the freight business, all the arrangements will have to be made
at home."

So it happened that our initial voyage of exploration ended
in, of all places, Miami. This was especially odd because that
was one of the last cities in the world we, who generally dislike
resorts, had ever thought of making even a temporary headquarters, but we soon found that, like most large cities, Miami

is many communities. In Coconut Grove, several miles from the gaudy hotels of Miami Beach, we found a surprisingly quiet marina owned by the city which in some ways was more like my dreams of the Bahamas than the Bahamas had turned out to be. In the first place it was cheap, an important consideration if we were to save for a larger boat. A dock, protected from most storms, cost only $130 a month in the winter and half that in the summer. A small island which the dredges had cast up in Biscayne Bay only a few hundred yards away offered soft beaches and swimming for Jessie and a shopping center with several good laundries and many physicians was within walking distance. It was obviously a good place to settle down for a stint of hard work.

During the first six months we stayed in Coconut Grove I was so busy with all my projects that I never stopped to wonder whether I liked this new almost stationary life aboard a boat. Except for short cruises to gather information about the nearby keys, we never budged from our slip. Instead of pouring over charts of the Bahamas, as I had for so long in New York, I contracted to write two new books for a New York publisher and worked on the pilot project on the keys. Even before that was finished, we began planning the second of our series of guidebooks, which took us to the West Indies. Most of the time I traveled by airplane, because like any harried businessman, I didn't have time to monkey around with a boat.

Even when I wasn't pounding the typewriter in our after cabin or flying over to the Antilles, I never found time hanging heavy on my hands at the marina in Coconut Grove. For one thing, there was the problem of keeping up the paintwork of the boat. The *Pretty Betty* was in bad shape after a year of steady cruising in the tropics. Although I liked the idea of doing the painting and varnishing myself, I rarely found time for it in practice, and when I did set a few days aside for refinishing the rails, I found that, as usual, I hated getting right down to manual work and hurried so much that I did a sloppy job. My ineptitude was increased by the problem of living aboard a boat

with a child in the midst of wet varnish. Finding small hand-
marks in the middle of a hatch I had just refinished, I gave up
and put the boat in a yard to be completely refurbished while
we accepted an invitation to go north and pay a long visit to my
mother.

Although we hoped to get a bigger boat eventually, we still
loved the *Pretty Betty,* and I told the superintendent of the
yard to do anything necessary to put her back in mint condition. Everything, both above and below decks, needed to be
refinished, and it seemed wiser to do the job all at once when we
were away. While they were at it, I told the workmen to con-
trive a big double bunk that could slide out from the bulkhead
in the forward stateroom.

"It's hard to give an estimate," the superintendent said when
I asked him what all this work would cost. "These things go on
time, and I can't even guess what the bottom needs before we
haul her."

The yard was a reputable one, and I decided to trust it.
Probably the entire job would cost about $2,500, I thought, and
I had a couple of magazine articles in the works that would pay
for it.

This proved a disastrous miscalculation. When we returned
to Miami, we found the *Pretty Betty* looking like a new boat,
but the bill came to almost $8,000.

"Don't pay it," a friend who owned a similar boat advised me.
"These yards often pad their bills if you're not there to watch
them every minute."

"If I refuse to pay, they'll put a lien on the boat, won't they?"

"Get a lawyer to put up bond. That will free the boat while
the thing drags through the courts for a year or two. Faced with
a delay like that, the yard will probably settle for much less
anyway."

This might have worked but I didn't feel on firm moral
ground, for a great deal of labor obviously had gone into
scraping most of the brightwork down to the wood and painting every inch of a 54-foot boat. The yard had done a beautiful

job, and the professional captains of immaculately kept yachts did not seem in the least surprised when I told them what it had cost. My main mistake had been in going to a kind of Tiffany of boatworks and giving them carte blanche.

In something like panic, I telephoned Mort Leavy and asked him if we could raise enough money to pay the bill.

"For the short run you're in luck," he said. "They showed one of your old movies on television, and you've got some money coming in. But what are you going to do if you run up this kind of bill on the boat every year?"

I was too relieved at being able to solve the immediate problem to take on that worry right away. The writing profession has the drawback of offering no steady, predictable income, but it has the God-given asset of offering occasional windfalls after one has been in it a long while. Grateful that my own special star seemed to be continuing to take care of me, I paid the bill and sailed our sparkling boat back to the marina in Coconut Grove.

It didn't take long, however, for the euphoria of surviving that crisis to wear off. That very night I found I couldn't sleep because of worrying about the problem of maintenance. If it was going to cost me so much to keep the *Pretty Betty* in shape how did I even dare to dream about acquiring a still bigger boat?

The answer lay partly in listening to the many new friends I acquired who had maintained large boats on relatively low budgets in Coconut Grove for years. In the first place, they had more sense than to cruise for a year without doing any serious varnishing—it takes much more work to put a boat back in shape than to keep it in good condition by doing a little sanding and varnishing every month. In the second place, they rarely had yards do any painting above the waterline. If they didn't like to do the work themselves, they hired skilled craftsmen for the wages the yards paid—usually about $2.50 an hour—instead of letting the yard act as a middleman and charge $6 or more an hour for the same kind of labor. One advantage of staying in port for a long period of time was that it became possible to find individual craftsmen willing to work on boats, a process which was difficult because they rarely advertised and there weren't enough to be hired without considerable planning. In addition, the thrifty yachtsmen never went to the big, much-advertised yards to be hauled out. Instead, they sought little out-of-the-way marine railways which were looking for business and did the job of day-to-day supervision themselves.

It took a few weeks to find individuals who were able to fit the maintenance of the *Pretty Betty* into their schedules, but when that was accomplished, I felt that I could realistically look forward to keeping the boat in fine shape for about $2,500 a year. This made it a lot easier for me to sleep and even to dream of getting a 70-footer capable of going to Ireland and the Greek isles, if I kept working on all my projects.

Perhaps inevitably, the map maker and I soon found that it is hard to pile up profits in the guidebook business. When he tried to hire a staff of advertising salesmen, he got in all sorts of trouble. The kind of salesman you can hire for short-term projects by advertising in the newspapers has a strange penchant for getting into trouble. During one dark week, two of his representatives wound up in jail for drunken driving and a third butchered all the business we had built up on one West Indian island by insulting a taxi driver who proved to be related to every advertiser in the place.

The island freight business also didn't exactly guarantee any immediate pot of gold, I discovered as I studied the facts and figures my friend in Bimini mailed me. Although there continued to be some prospect of finding people who wanted to make a movie on Cat Cay, I found it increasingly difficult to work up much enthusiasm for writing a script about the end of the world. The only progress I made was in the thickening manuscripts I had contracted to finish for the publisher in New York, and certainly they offered no promise of profits spectacular enough for the purchase of a vessel capable of cruising to Europe. There were times when it occurred to me that the idea of buying a 50,000-dollar yacht while I was sending children through college might possibly prove overambitious, if not grandiose to the point of insanity.

There are some realities it is better not to confront too directly, and for the better part of a year I simply tried not to think about money. It was enough to prepare for our voyage across the Atlantic as best I could, typing as much as possible and brushing up on my celestial navigation during the evenings. From a passing merchantman I bought a good sextant and found I could take fairly accurate star sights right at the wharf.

Despite a rather frantic schedule of work, Betty and I found the marina in Coconut Grove pleasant enough as a temporary home. For one thing, Jessica was getting older and was adapting marvelously to life on the waterfront. We began giving her intensive swimming lessons, both on the little island nearby and in the pool of a motel across the street. Although she was too young for the Australian crawl which Betty kept demonstrating for her, it wasn't long before she learned to keep her chin above water long enough to cry out if she fell overboard at the wharf, and to dog-paddle her way to something she could hang on to. This took care of the worst nightmare connected with raising a child on a boat.

Jessie also removed another problem which had concerned us by finding a surprising number of children her own age living on boats nearby. In some ways the marina turned out to be like any suburb. Children visited back and forth, and mothers took turns driving them to nursery school or entertaining groups of them aboard.

"It really is a marvelous life for a child," Betty said one afternoon as we sat on the sunny afterdeck watching Jessie and one of her tanned friends swinging from the stanchions of the awnings. "They're turning this whole boat into a kind of giant jungle gym."

Silently we watched the children as they tired of their acrobatics and began to show each other what they had learned about how to help run a boat. Jessie knew how to coil a line, and the other little girl proudly demonstrated her ability to hold a fender over the side in preparation for mooring.

Many people had warned us of the folly of trying to raise a child on a boat, and secretly both Betty and I had felt a little guilty about the attempt. For that reason there was special joy in the realization that Jessie was not turning out to be miserable.

It wasn't only the great outdoors which made it such a pleasure for me to see Jessie grow up. Never before had I been so relaxed with a child. Perhaps that is one of the advantages of becoming a father again when one is in his forties. There was no doubt about the fact that I was far less tense than I had been in my twenties, when the slightest cough from a child was enough to set me thumbing frantically through the pages of Dr. Spock. Jessie was being raised without rules and without much worry on the part of her parents. Now that we had a double bed, she rarely stayed in her bunk in the forecastle for more than a few hours. Often her mother and I awoke in the morning to find her snuggled between us, usually with the dachshund puppy we had recently given her.

Although it was easy to find sitters from other boats in Coconut Grove who didn't mind taking care of a child afloat, we had fallen into the habit of taking Jessie everywhere with us, even to the movies, where she slept contentedly in Betty's arms when she got tired of the show.

Jessie was with us so much that she sometimes gave signs of an increasing precocity that was a little alarming. I've always disliked small children who call their parents by their first names, and I was surprised when Jessica started referring to her mother occasionally as Betty.

"It's natural," Betty said to me when I mentioned it one night. "She hears everyone else call me that. Have you noticed how selective she is with the name?"

"What do you mean?"

"When she wants comfort or for me to do something for her,

I'm Mommy. When she just wants to make some companionable observation, I'm Betty."

This was true, and it seemed wrong to object to it, even though I never in my life had even thought of my mother as Ruth.

"Why doesn't Jessie ever call me by my first name?" I asked Betty, perhaps with a tinge of hurt feelings.

"I don't know. Sometimes she refers to you as Sone to me. Usually it's when you've done something especially nice."

Because we so rarely moved from our slip in the marina for an entire winter, it occurred to me that we were perhaps foolish to put up with the cramped quarters and the expense of living aboard a boat. Why not sell the *Pretty Betty* and rent a small house in Coconut Grove while I worked and saved to buy a vessel capable of voyaging to Ireland and the Greek isles?

Practical as this idea sounded, I hated it and on reflection was glad to find that there were reasons why I enjoyed the docks more than any neighborhood I could remember. In the first place, people seemed to be friendlier on the water than they were ashore, perhaps because less risk was involved—if enmities of some sort developed from a close relationship, it was easy for one family to invent some pretext for moving to a different pier, a different marina or even a different town. This shuffling around to find congenial surroundings resulted in each wharf's acquiring different characteristics.

This was illustrated by a curious development. Shortly after giving up constant cruising to go on a hard work schedule, something seemed to click deep in my being, and I felt it suddenly necessary and possible to stop worrying about limiting the amount of my drinking and to give up booze entirely. As the months went by without liquor, I found that I didn't need any of the business about pretending to myself that I was going to abstain just for another 24 hours—it was clear to me that I had outgrown a crutch and that with reasonable effort I could walk without it for the rest of my life. The only times I had to exert much willpower to stay dry was when everyone around me was drinking. Fortunately, Betty rarely drank and didn't seem to mind when I coddled myself by refusing to go to cocktail parties or serve liquor aboard. That was a small price to pay, she said, for a sober husband, and for one who was miraculously beginning to lose weight.

By some natural process of selection, I discovered to my astonishment, our pier soon became known as the marina's "dry dock." People who wanted to exchange cocktail parties soon moved to be near more convivial neighbors. For a time transients went in and out of their slips, and many of those who chose to stay for the season were people who, for one reason or another, didn't drink. Within a few months we could easily get up a party of twenty people of all ages who sipped nothing but tea, coffee and soda pop.

Not everyone at our wharf, of course, was an abstainer. Some stayed because there were others near with small children, and there seemed to be an unusually large percentage of middle-aged men with young wives. Most of us at that dock were working hard, either at shore jobs or in waterborne offices. The old retired people and the playboy set had piers of their own. Another common denominator at our dock appeared to be a high degree of marital contentment. Restless husbands and wives who enjoyed flirtations or bed-hopping soon became bored and moved to places which better justified the raffish reputation of the waterfront.

Yet I didn't find our dock stuffy. One of the really serene couples confided that they weren't married at all—they were afraid that if they went before a preacher they would start acting like most married people. Another pair had just taken up some Eastern religion which seemed successful in keeping them at a high pitch of elation most of the time.

Although the people at our dock were drawn together by views they held in common, their income and background varied far more than is usual in most suburban or city blocks. Two of our new friends had yachts close to 100 feet long and supported themselves largely by playing the stock market. Several others lived on tiny craft they had built themselves and made a living as marine carpenters or painters. In a moment of euphoria I reported to Betty that at a brief ginger-ale-sipping party on our pier, one friend gave me a tip on the stock market which made me several hundred dollars and another had agreed to make us new awnings for a similar amount.

Yet the monthly statements Mort Leavy sent me still did not show much progress toward the goal of buying a big trawler to go to Europe, and sometimes I felt silly as I stood at the end of our pier taking star sights just to be sure I had the skill. The only way to beat my sense of frustration was to work harder, and when I was too tired for that, to row Jessie over to her little island, where she could dig in the sand and swim.

At Christmas that year Peter and Lisa came down to make a formal announcement of their engagement aboard our boat. Peter had received a fellowship in a good graduate school, and Lisa had a new job. They were planning to get married and go for a honeymoon in Ireland in the spring. To celebrate we cruised to Key West and Peter took 16-mm. movies professional enough for me to use on a lecture tour if I were ever moved to go on one.

When we returned to Coconut Grove, they went back to Philadelphia and I resumed my schedule of typing in the after cabin of the *Pretty Betty*. The docks were quiet, and a cool breeze blew through the open ports above my improvised desk. The marina turned out to be a surprisingly good place for sustained work.

For diversion and to keep our dreams alive, we began to spend our weekends roving the Florida coast looking for a vessel stout enough to take us to Ireland and the Greek isles, hopefully the next year or the year after that. All the suitable craft we saw were much too expensive, but we had already discovered that a man has to keep looking for a long while if he hopes to find the embodiment of a dream.

We had been in Coconut Grove almost a year before I made a curious discovery: I was happy, that is to say, relatively content with the present and the recent past as well as excited about dreams of the future. This had never happened to me before, and I regarded the revelation with some suspicion as a transitory phenomenon bound to fade. But a few weeks went by and I found I was still satisfied with our situation in Coconut Grove, not blissful enough to give up plans for further travels, for they were obviously an important part of my ability to enjoy my immediate surroundings, but happy enough not to be impatient and not to regard every business disappointment as the end of the world.

"It's funny," I said to Betty one night. "I keep liking it here."

"You do?" she replied with astonishment. "You mean you're not really itching to cast off the lines at dawn?"

"No, I don't mind it here, even if it takes years to get a bigger boat. Are you having a good time?"

"Yes. I was sort of afraid to tell you."

"Are you beginning to hope we'll never get a boat for Ireland and Greece and all that?"

"I haven't thought about it much lately. There are still plenty of places we can go in this boat if we get restless, aren't there?"

"It might be fun to go up the Mississippi and through the Great Lakes to Canada some summer. We could continue right down the Hudson to New York."

She hesitated before she spoke.

"Of course, if it's ever possible, I'd still like a bigger galley, and I'd love a boat that could steam right up the River Liffey to spend a year in Dublin with Dad."

A longer pause followed, during which I noticed that she was stroking the newly varnished rail of the *Pretty Betty.*

"If we ever do sell this boat, though, I'm going to feel terrible," she continued. "Whoever could have believed that a funny old yacht would have given us so much?"

"If we get a bigger boat, you'll love that one too."

"Maybe. The *Pretty Betty* has taught me a lot. But I want you to promise me something."

"What?"

"Before there is the slightest chance of our selling this boat, I want to have a really good model of her. So much that we love disappears without a trace."

The next day I bought an elaborate kit for making models and found a ship's carpenter nearby who helped me to build a tiny replica of the *Pretty Betty* based on the original blueprints. Even when scaled down to a foot in length, the graceful hull still seemed to me to be full of mysterious excitement. When I gave it to Betty, she sent it to her father, partly as a gift, partly for safekeeping. She says that it makes her feel good to know that if we ever do get to Dublin aboard a bigger boat, this small talisman of the past will be waiting to guide our future.